# MARXISM GOES TO THE MOVIES

Introducing the key concepts and thinkers within the Marxist tradition, *Marxism Goes to the Movies* demonstrates their relevance to film theory and practice past and present.

Author Mike Wayne argues that Marxist filmmaking has engaged with and transformed this popular medium, developing its potential for stimulating revolutionary consciousness. As the crisis of capitalism deepens, this history and these resources are vital for a better future. Marxism is one of the few approaches that can bring together political, economic, formal and cultural analysis into a unified approach of studying film, and how films in turn can help us understand and even critically interrogate these forces. The book examines how filmmakers, who have been influenced by Marxism, have made some of the most significant contributions to film culture globally, and provides historical perspective on the development of Marxism and film. Each chapter covers a broad theme that is broken down into sections that are cross-referenced throughout, providing helpful navigation of the material.

Clear and concise in its arguments, this is an ideal introduction for students of Marxism and film, inviting readers to deepen their knowledge and understanding of the subject.

**Mike Wayne** is Professor of Screen Media at Brunel University, London.

# MARXISM GOES TO THE MOVIES

*Mike Wayne*

Routledge
Taylor & Francis Group

LONDON AND NEW YORK

First published 2020
by Routledge
2 Park Square, Milton Park, Abingdon, Oxon OX14 4RN

and by Routledge
52 Vanderbilt Avenue, New York, NY 10017

*Routledge is an imprint of the Taylor & Francis Group, an informa business*

*British Library Cataloguing in Publication Data*
A catalogue record for this book is available from the British Library

*Library of Congress Cataloging-in-Publication Data*
Names: Wayne, Mike, author.
Title: Marxism goes to the movies / Mike Wayne.
Description: London ; New York : Routledge, 2020. | Includes bibliographical
references and index.
Identifiers: LCCN 2019033660 (print) | LCCN 2019033661 (ebook) |
ISBN 9781138677869 (hardback) | ISBN 9781138677876 (paperback) |
ISBN 9781315559308 (ebook)
Subjects: LCSH: Motion pictures--Political aspects. |
Motion pictures--Social aspects. | Communism and motion pictures.
Classification: LCC PN1995.9.P6 W39 2020 (print) |
LCC PN1995.9.P6 (ebook) | DDC 791.43/6581--dc23
LC record available at https://lccn.loc.gov/2019033660
LC ebook record available at https://lccn.loc.gov/2019033661

ISBN: 978-1-138-67786-9 (hbk)
ISBN: 978-1-138-67787-6 (pbk)
ISBN: 978-1-315-55930-8 (ebk)

Typeset in Bembo
by Taylor & Francis Books

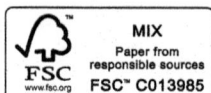

MIX
Paper from
responsible sources
FSC
www.fsc.org   FSC™ C013985

Printed in the United Kingdom
by Henry Ling Limited

For Dee and Jake and all that going to the movies

# CONTENTS

# FIGURES

# 1

# MARXISM

## 1.1 Marxism and Marx

Marxism is the name for the body of work associated with the German revolutionary thinker and political activist, Karl Marx. Born in Germany in 1818, he died in London in 1883 and was buried in Highgate Cemetery in the north of the capital. He had lived most of his adult life in London as a political exile from the German authorities. Britain was the first country to undergo an industrial (especially textile-based) revolution. Before that, it had been developing capitalist agriculture for around two centuries and it had an expanding empire to boot. So, the British authorities probably calculated that Herr Marx was unlikely to be much of a threat to them. Possibly they even thought that the free market system so well entrenched already in Britain would deal with Marx more effectively than the police spies, either by driving him to gainful employment that would keep him otherwise occupied or by driving him to starvation. Marx called this the 'dull compulsion of economics'.[1] Marx came close to starvation and it was only because of his lifelong friend and sometime co-author, Friedrich Engels (whose family owned a cotton mill in Manchester) that he was able to both survive and write, and leave the world with an explosive body of work. The world historical importance of that work is that, without Marx and Marxism, we would not have a coherent theoretical framework with which to understand the most powerful, paradoxical and dangerous type of social arrangements ever to exist: capitalism. This 'framework' though is not a finished body of work. It comes down to us with many different strands, arguments, disputes and controversies within it. It is a living, exciting, dynamic and historically developing body of work that has been made in response to the continuities and changes in the capitalist system it critiques. Marxism's impact on modern culture – although often denied – is hard to over-estimate. Its considerable influence in and through film and its major contribution to understanding film and the significant cultural impact film has had and continues to have, despite our new multi-media environment, are the subject of this book.

## 1.2 Commodity fetishism

Marx wrote some of the most explosive works ever. His 1848 *The Communist Manifesto* has only been outsold by the Bible. His mature magnum opus *Capital*, the first volume of which was published in 1867, sets out his analysis of the systematic tendencies of capitalism. It opens with these words: 'The wealth of those societies in which the capitalist mode of production prevails, presents itself as "an immense accumulation of commodities", its unit being a single commodity. Our investigation must therefore begin with the analysis of a commodity.'[2]

The subtitle of *Capital* is *A Critique of Political Economy*. Political economy was the science of capitalist economics, as elaborated by Marx's predecessors, such as Adam Smith who famously wrote *The Wealth of Nations*. Marx's *Capital* begins with the statement that how 'wealth' presents itself under capitalism is very particular. It presents itself as 'an immense accumulation of commodities' and Marx here quotes from one of his own earlier works, suggesting that this line of thought has remained important to him, nagging away in his mind. Actually, the original German word, *erscheint* is closer in meaning to 'appears' than presents. The term *appearance* has a double sense in the German philosophical tradition that Marx inherited from his immediate philosophical predecessor, G.W.F. Hegel (1770–1831). What appears is both a *real* phenomenon (commodities really do exist, of course) but also this appearance or manifestation is not quite the full story. The 'immense accumulation of commodities' appears spontaneously to us as a 'level' of reality that rests on deeper structures and relations that do *not* register immediately in the appearance. What perhaps had been nagging away at Marx was the idea that these deeper structures worked according to principles that were very different from *the appearance*.

Immensity itself is a category of quantity, and one theme in Marx's analysis of capitalism is that it is a system where the quantitative is out of control. A logic of quantification, of 'immensity' is a brute, crude measure of the social and within a logic of quantification, more fine-grained judgements (such as needs) are obliterated. For example, an immense accumulation of commodities will conceal (as did the science of political economy before Marx) the social and economic power relations on which a society of commodities relies. Since Marx's day, advertising has expanded into a gargantuan industry commanding a global budget of several hundred billion dollars devoted to promoting commodities. And cultural industries have in turn also expanded to produce an immense accumulation of images associated with commodities (films, comics, film-related merchandise, etc.), whose appearance is in contradiction to the real power relations that produce those images and commodities. As Guy Debord famously put it, we live in a society of bewitching spectacles.[3]

In a very famous section of *Capital* called 'The Fetishism of Commodities', Marx returned to the intuition he had that the way the capitalist system appears to us, the way it strikes us in everyday life and activity, the way we interact with the capitalist system, all raise profound obstacles to our understanding and knowledge of that system. The commodity was, Marx insisted 'a mysterious thing' in which the social relations which produce it disappear and leave the commodity to appear as if it had a life of its own, independent of the social relationships that produce it.[4] Marx gives a satirical metaphor in the form of a wooden table, which, once it becomes a commodity, 'evolves out of its wooden brain grotesque ideas' of its own power and autonomy and starts dancing.[5] The commodity that 'comes to life' is indeed a trope of contemporary advertising. Contemporary dominant political discourse is full of discussions of 'the market', as if it were a force of nature with a life of its own and not a social institution produced by social relationships. Within the world of commodity fetishism, the independence of 'the market' from our control as a whole is counter-balanced by the inflated hopes we have of agency within the market at an individual level. As we dip our hands into our pockets to access a portion of all that wealth dancing before us as an immense accumulation of commodities, we take another commodity (money) out of our pocket and exchange it for the commodity we can actually do something with and use. We feel, says Marx elsewhere, empowered by this exchange:

> Out of the act of exchange itself, the individual ... is reflected in himself as its exclusive and dominant (determinant) subject. With that, then, the complete freedom of the individual is posited: voluntary transaction; no force on either side, positing the self ... as dominant and primary.[6]

In pre-capitalist societies, the fetish was a thing invested with magical super-human powers. Capitalism has reinvented the fetish in the form of the market, money and the commodity world, a world of things independent of democratic collective human control but not human and social origins. Necessarily, then, this is a world of things that resists *social explanation* as a result of resisting social control. This is a commodity world that conceals the processes that produce it. It conceals the struggle that goes on inside the system. The blood, sweat and tears. In the subterranean currents of our psychology and culture we feel not empowered but subordinated to this world of things, this system of things. And this is compensated for by unrealistic fantasy projections of individual agency. Marx's 'big idea' about what is concealed, his main contention concerning those power relations atomised by the immense accumulation of things, has to do with *classes* and *class struggle*.

## 1.3 Classes

'The History of all hitherto existing society is the history of class struggles.'[7] This was the ringing opening line to *The Communist Manifesto*. Society is fissured by different class interests. This emphasis on class struggle can be a painful and difficult reality for non-Marxist outlooks to admit and is often in various ways repressed (completely denied) or disavowed. This latter term (borrowed from Freud) refers to a more ambiguous social-psychological response along the lines of 'yes, I see what you are saying ... however, I believe ...' with the 'belief' in some way downplaying, softening or in some other way explaining away the centrality of unpleasant things like class conflict. The history of class struggle tends to elude full and frank representation (in capitalist political economy *and* cultural images) because its implications for cultural myths, visions of national or community identity and self-identities are so profoundly destabilising and unsettling.

Marx defined classes as social groups that share a relationship to the economic means of production, and this differentiates them from other groups of people who have different relationships to the means of production. One of the key relationships in question here concerns *ownership* and *non-ownership* of the means to produce the 'immense accumulation of commodities'. In a class-divided society, different groups have different positions and roles in that activity of production. The *means* or *forces of production* refer to all the things that are required to produce, such as land, tools/machinery, techniques, raw materials, but also labour power and buying capacity. Capitalists are defined by their *ownership* of the means of production. Labour, the workers or the working class *works* the means of production (and is a means of production) on behalf of the capitalists. This ownership/non-ownership relation to the means of production is prioritised by Marxism because they are the means of social life itself. Economically, socially and philosophically, *production* is a crucial concept within Marxism.

Marx defined the working class as 'propertyless' (the meaning of the term 'proletariat') in the sense that they do not own any means of production themselves. They could and have gone on to own means of consumption (televisions, cars, phones, all the 'goodies' of mass consumer society) but that is something quite different. Not owning the means of production ensures that the working class must sell their ability to labour (their labour power) to the capitalists in order to survive. This means that while labour is formally free to sell their labour to any capitalist, there is a huge economic compulsion on them to do so (in order to survive) and to accept the terms and conditions which the capitalist tries to impose on the worker and which in turn shape their access to consumer goods and all the necessities of life. Marx's basic point about this relationship is that it is inherently exploitative, with the capitalist always getting more value (what Marx called 'surplus value') from the worker (in terms of the value of the outputs they contribute to producing) than the worker receives in the wage they get for working. Marx argues that the exploitation relationship was the core relationship of the modern capitalist era.

If we probe the category of 'capitalists' a bit more, we see that there are different types, distributed according to a *social division of labour*, which is an important second feature of the Marxist definition of classes, as the Russian revolutionary, V. I. Lenin noted.[8] For example, there are the landowners who cream off revenue from capitalists simply by renting out their land or owning the land on which property is built and/or agriculture is cultivated. There are bankers and shareholders who cream off revenue from other capitalists by loaning interest-bearing capital to them so they can expand. Then there are the small capitalists (sometimes called the petit-bourgeoisie) who employ a small number of people, but who typically work alongside their employees. Then there are the industrial capitalists whom Marx thought were the core class of capitalism, because it was their relationship to the working class that really lay at the heart of the dynamics of the modern social system and its system of exploitative wealth creation. Film, we should remember, is a form of industrial manufacture. It also has elements associated with the petit-bourgeois control over the creative inputs by some of those occupying the highest echelons in the technical division of labour (directors, stars, scriptwriters, set designers, even though they are paid a wage). It is also, in its dominant commercial form, closely interlocked with the banking and shareholder systems of capitalism.

The social division of labour refers to all the different branches of activity which a social order needs to produce and meet its needs. So, we can break a social division of labour down much more minutely than just in relation to land, industry and finance. Cultural and media production would constitute an increasingly significant branch of activity within the social division of labour, meeting communication, entertainment, information and leisure needs. One consequence of a complex social division of labour is that workers may not have the opportunity to develop and co-ordinate their common interests practically across the many branches.

Film workers may form bonds of shared interests with other film workers and express this through trade union organisations. But for film workers to perceive a shared set of interests with transport workers, for example, requires a politics that can bridge the gaps between their immediate situation. But film workers, like all workers are also internally divided by the *technical division of labour*, which refers to the complex ensemble of tasks that have to be combined within the labour process of a given occupation. The plan of the Lasky Studio in Hollywood from 1918 (see Figure 1.1) shows how this technical division of labour is built into the layout and design of the building complex. The technical division of labour is linked to class formation because the people who are in the controlling positions within the technical division of labour tend to share certain social characteristics (background, attitudes, resources). Notice in Figure 1.1, in the layout of the Lasky Studio, how directors, executives and stars are clustered together while the areas for the more manual labour of painting, carpentry, set construction, the blacksmith for the horses in the western pictures, etc. are on the opposite side of the lot and how the perspective of the sketch and the numbering suggest a certain social perspective as to who is important. The social division of labour is linked to class formation because across the various branches of productive activity designed to meet variable social needs, the same social types in control of those branches have more in common with each other than they do with their immediate workers, who have the least control, least power and lowest remuneration in the production process. Vice versa, those who are doing 'manual' jobs, for example, across the division of social labour (or the same kind of job, such as carpentry across different industries)

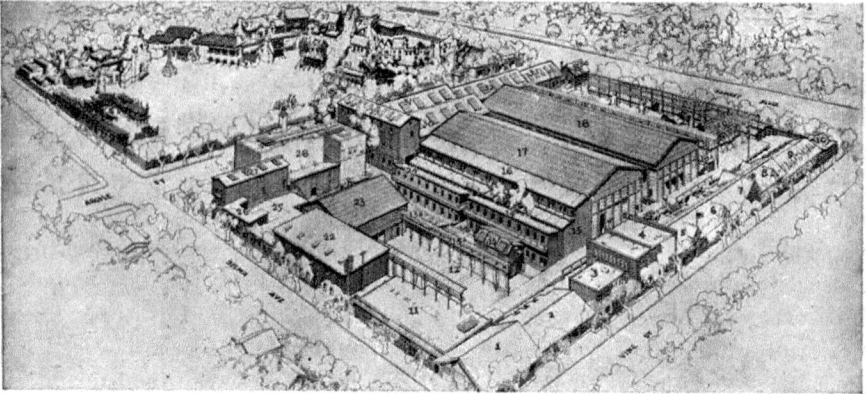

Here we have the Lasky Studio in Hollywood, California, where
the Western productions of Paramount and Artcraft are made

1. Property room.
2. Outgoing property room.
3. Star dressing room building.
4. Wardrobe building.
5. Engaging department.
6. Executive offices.
7. Cecil B. deMille's office.
8. Directors' offices.
9. Scenario department.
10. Mary Pickford's dressing room.
11. Incoming property room.
12. Stage No. 1.
13. Wilfred Buckland's office over dressing room used by Geraldine Farrar.
13a. Title department, and printing plant, and electrical department.

13b. Projection room No. 2.
14. Extra dressing room.
15. Scene docks.
16. Principal dressing rooms.
17. Stage No. 2.
18. Stage No. 3.
18a. Company dressing rooms, entire length of stage.
19. Stage No. 4.
20. Scene docks, entire length of Stage No. 4.
21. Sail boat in tank.
22. Dark stage.
23. Small glass stage.
24. Extra dressing rooms—and hospital.
25. Stock room.

26. Purchasing department. Press photographer's rooms.
27. Old paint frame now upholstering and wall papering department.
28. Laboratory. Frame building under number now removed and addition to laboratory erected.
29. Paint frame.
30. Fitting room.
31. Carpenter shops
32. Planing mills.
33. Property construction department.
34. Plaster shops and blacksmith shop.
35. Garages.
36. Douglas Fairbanks' offices and dressing rooms.
37. Exterior sets built for productions.

**FIGURE 1.1** Layout of the Lasky Studio in Hollywood, 1918
Source: *Theatre Magazine*, June 1918.

have more in common (according to Marxism) with each other than with those who occupy the higher echelons of ownership and control in the technical division of labour within their own productive sector.

In relation to such divisions, Marx made an important distinction between a class existing *in itself* and a class existing *for itself*.[9] The working classes exist as objective features of any capitalist economy, since their labour is the basis of the profits which drive the system. Hence the working class exists in itself. But if it does not exist *for itself*, it lacks extensive independent self-awareness of its interests and needs as a class; it lacks the political culture and organisations which it needs to act across the internal technical division of labour within occupations and even more crucially, across the social division of labour that would unite workers in different branches of labour. Political cultures are a crucial issue then for *class consciousness*. The role of the mass media and mass culture in encouraging forms of identity and identification and consciousness that steer workers away from class solidarity and towards institutions embedded in the power structure of capitalist society has been a significant part of the Marxist literature on culture and politics.

The role of the middle class who occupy a very significant position within the technical and social division of labour has also complicated the class map. Their 'interests' are often sufficiently different, thanks to their different position in the technical division of labour, to make it difficult to integrate them into a working-class identity or programme of action. Their 'middle' position means that significant numbers of people have a rather more complex relationship to capital, for example, that involves certain 'privileges'. This middle class is distinct from the old middle class or petit-bourgeoisie insofar as they do not (necessarily) own small capital and do, like the working class, sell their labour to an employer. However, the nature of their work means acquiring sophisticated skills which are restricted by education and professional qualifications. In a society in which the price of commodities is determined in part by supply and demand, this restricted supply of skills means the middle class can get preferential terms for their labour power (although the attraction of work in the culture industries is also under-mining the price this kind of labour commodity can command with huge reservoirs of spare labour capacity building up through the explosion of, for example, film, television and media studies courses with increasingly vocational/training content and aims).

These preferential terms include not only earning more than the average member of the working class, but also enjoying greater autonomy over their immediate work process, a highly valued prize. Economically, therefore, and culturally, this group seems different from the working class. Their 'middle' position between capital and the workers means that often their work involves them in regulating, monitoring, co-ordinating, supervising and assessing the working class for both business and state bureaucracies. This is why Ehrenreich and Ehrenreich called them the professional-*managerial* class.[10] In the technical division of labour within film production, such roles would be allotted to producers and production managers and maybe also directors. The middle class also have a significant role in product innovation,[11] something which is also very central to the cultural industries and key roles in the film industry, as we shall see. The middle-class strata also play a key role as knowledge producers, educa-tors, symbol-makers, opinion leaders, public relations professionals, taste-makers, and so forth. Again, this is clearly pertinent to a culturally influential medium such as film.

The father of modern sociology, Max Weber described the middle class as the propertyless intelligentsia and it included specialists of various kinds (lawyers, engi-neers, architects, civil servants, teachers) and the upper echelons of white-collar workers. It would also include creative workers in the mass media. Weber also noted that in addition to ownership of the means of production, another form of power within capitalist societies was 'status', which he defined as a form of esteem. Weber suggested that classes were defined by their relations to the production of goods (following Marx) but that 'status groups are stratified according to the prin-ciples of their *consumption* of goods as represented by special styles of life'.[12] This shifts attention to how a condition of life changes with the differential access to social wealth opened up by income, other sources of economic revenue (shares, rent, fixed assets, etc.) and other forms of assets beyond the economic.

The radical sociologist Pierre Bourdieu developed this idea of status, esteem, lifestyle and consumption further by analysing the different kinds of assets that people could use to enhance their position in the marketplace, such as cultural knowledge or educational training or networks of people who could help open doors for them in the labour market (something that is very prevalent in the cultural industries). Although Bourdieu called these assets different types of 'capital', such as cultural capital, educational capital or social capital respectively, this is unhelpful. They are assets that have value but these are not forms of capital as Marxism understands the term (see Section 1.4) and to speak of people in general having 'capital' is deeply misleading. Only capitalists have capital. However, the general point that there is a much more complex differentiation among people who are not capitalists (large or small) than ownership/non-ownership of the means of production, ought to be well taken.

As well as economic relationships to the means of production, the social and technical divisions of labour produce a great deal of income diversity which has knock-on implications for access to other resources. Some of those resources include social resources (networks of friends, family and acquaintances), cultural resources (taste, judgement, cultural knowledge) and educational qualifications (credentialised knowledge). For Bourdieu, the assets which he analysed were used by the middle class to create various kinds of 'distinctions' (markers of preferred difference) both within the middle class (class fractions) and between the middle class and the working class (and indeed between the middle class and the 'philistine' capitalist class). Cultural consumption was a key battleground in these markers of difference (or esteem).[13] This is readily observable in a comparison between different sites of consumption, for example, between a multiplex cinema and an art house cinema. In these different venues, the composition of the audience, the style of the décor, the kind of films available to watch, the types of food and drinks sold and the behaviour expected within these respective spaces, seem to be strongly marked in class terms.

Mainstream sociology has tended to focus on how income differentials and other assets, especially educational qualifications and cultural knowledge and value systems, produce a class system that is more multi-layered and highly segmented than Marx's vision of two classes clashing in *Capital*. Sociology will typically classify people into five or more main classes, with the upper classes at the top, including executives, senior managers and top professionals, through to white-collar workers, then skilled manual workers, then unskilled, and so on. Bridging sociology and Marxism, Erik Olin Wright introduced the idea of 'contradictory class locations' to try and account for the middle-class strata. This stratum is very heterogeneous and there are groups within it that are more or less on the boundaries of either the capitalist class (such as senior executives with shares) or the working class (routine white-collar workers). In the middle of the middle class are groups which have only partial, minimal or no control over the allocation of capital resources, the means of production and the labour power of others. They do, however, typically have some workplace autonomy. However, such privileges are likely to be subject to the various pressures which capital exerts on the workforce.[14] The 'proletarianisation' of the middle class (i.e. loss of jobs, decline of wages, opportunities, autonomy and status) is an increasingly remarked-upon phenomenon within the mainstream news media.[15] Thus, the Marxist stress on the relationship to the means of production remains relevant even for the middle class and points to social imperatives that I discuss in more detail below.

Clearly the middle class are important for any Marxist film analysis for at least three reasons which we can here briefly specify:

1.  *Production*: Typically creative workers, directors, screenwriters, cinematographers come from the middle class and have leveraged their initial advantageous starting point to accumulate the levels of educational, cultural and social capital for success. There is then a question of class-stratified access to creative opportunity. Structurally, we may note that creative workers are situated between the capitalists and the working class and this contradictory class location may be expected to impact on their work. The feature of autonomy, which sociologists have identified as typical of middle-class work, is also particularly evident and perhaps heightened, when it comes to creative labour. Yet autonomy is also relative and hemmed in by the ownership and control questions – so conflicts between autonomy and the assertion of capital imperatives are frequent. Furthermore, when cultural workers *organise* themselves as workers, this typically means trade union activity to defend pay and conditions. For example, the Writers Guild of America went on strike at the end of 2007 and the beginning of 2008 to get an increase in royalties for their members (scriptwriters) on DVD sales. Here the *identity* of cultural workers *as workers* is fostered and that has potentially at least *political* implications and possibilities. In London, workers at the Picture House cinema chain (owned by Cineworld) have been striking sporadically since 2016, demanding a living wage.

2.  *Consumption*: Clearly audiences are classed and so what they go and see and/or how they watch the same film material might be differentiated according to some of the assets that Bourdieu identifies. These assets give social classes different types of competences in, for example, cultural knowledge and consumption, which is to say the ability to engage in a range of different kinds of cultural experiences (such as an art film, a foreign language film, a 'slow' film, a film with a different type of narrative structure from the norm, etc.). Cultural knowledge and expertise also come to shape the dispositions which people have to seek out and engage in certain kinds of cultural experiences in class-defined ways and even just feel comfortable in certain types of cultural venues. More generally, of course, we may say that the social and cultural experiences different classes bring to their encounter with films shapes that encounter.

3.  *Representation*: The middle class have been hugely important to capitalism because they have typically been portrayed in the mass media, as well as within political discourses, as the *norm* to which people can and should aspire to. This may seem more plausible than an appeal to join the capitalist class – which is necessarily very small – and so the middle-class lifestyle may function as a more 'universal' image that everyone could/should identify with. This is problematic, however, because of the following:

    a   In a capitalist society, class divisions cannot by definition be abolished by everyone joining the 'middle class'. Middle-class privileges are built on *restricting* the skills which they sell in the labour market. Increasing access to those skills will depress the economic value of middle-class labour as supply outstrips demand, thus simultaneously devaluing middle-class assets.

b    Celebrating middle-class norms often involves tacitly or explicitly denigrating working-class cultures (since there is a hierarchy of legitimacy) while turning a blind eye to the many aspects of middle-class culture that are questionable. Interestingly, film is one place where there is, relatively speaking, a licence to depict middle-class hypocrisy, snobbery, careerism, superficiality, selfishness and individualism in scathing terms. Much of French art cinema seems to delight in excoriating critiques of its French middle-class audience.

c    The middle-class status of the creative labour behind filmic representation can be detected more generally as the perspective through which the anxieties generated by class difference and capital dynamics are narrated.[16]

## 1.4 Capital's dynamics

While the sociological attention to empirical differences of income and other social and cultural assets is necessary to correct the abstract model of two classes confronting each other, it is also very problematic. The sociological model typically ranges up to the chief executive level but rarely acknowledges capital itself as a socio-economic force, relation or a set of *social imperatives*. Yet capital is a hugely powerful and transformative force and its absence from the standard sociological mapping of class tends to lead to rather static accounts of class. It is at this point that the very macro-historical level at which Marx's analysis take place comes into its own, providing a lens through which to understand vast historical forces and dynamics.

What distinguishes capitalism from previous modes of production, such as feudalism, is not only that labour is bought and sold in the marketplace, but that capital is relentlessly profit-orientated. 'Accumulate, accumulate! This is Moses and the Prophets!' wrote Marx of capitalism.[17] This accumulation imperative is one which unfolds with many capitals in competition with each other, each driving the other to bear down on labour costs (i.e. heighten the exploitation of labour). This dynamic of competitive accumulation makes capitalism a force of massive cultural and technological change as Marx wrote so evocatively in *The Communist Manifesto*. Here Marx vividly sketched how the drive to accumulate capital expanded markets internationally, which in turn capital conquered. Expanding markets requires developing new means of communication and transport, as well as revolutionising production through steam power and machinery.

The bourgeoisie cannot exist without constantly revolutionizing the instruments of production, and thereby the relations of production, and with them the whole relations of society. Conservation of the old modes of production in

unaltered form, was, on the contrary, the first condition of existence for all
earlier ... classes. Constant revolutionizing of production, everlasting uncertainty and agitation distinguish the bourgeois epoch from all earlier ones. All
fixed, fast-frozen relations, with their train of ancient and venerable prejudices
and opinions are swept away, all new-formed ones become antiquated before
they can ossify. All that is solid melts into air ...[18]

For Marx, the dynamics of capital make it intrinsically 'revolutionary' in the sense
that it constantly transforms production and therefore all the relations of society,
including cultural habits and sentiments. It is this dynamicism which mainstream
sociology has a poor grasp of compared to Marx's sweeping historical vision of
capital as class power and social imperatives and the centrality of production as a
concept in his analysis. Note also the ambivalence or contradictory quality of this
change. On the one hand, it clearly appeals to Marx as it overturns 'ancient and
venerable prejudices', liberating humanity with new forms of knowledge and new
modes of connections, just as the internet has done today. On the other hand, it is a
process of 'uncertainty and agitation'. This is because the process which capitalist
revolution unleashes is literally beyond the control of individuals or, even in some
respects, the capitalist class itself. The capitalist class can only steer the process
according to the imperatives of competitive accumulation. They can only internalise
this law of capital; they cannot change it. This is why Marx writes of capitalists as
personifications of capital. Should they try to be kind and generous to their workers
(as in some Hollywood movies!), they would soon enough be put out of business by
other capitalists obeying the logic of the situation.

Not only is the process of capital's perpetual revolution beyond the control of
capitalists, it is conducted with the sole aim of making a profit: the economic value
of a product ultimately means more to the capitalist than what Marx called its 'use-
value' (literally its usefulness to meet certain human needs). This means that a
broad stream of ambivalence runs through modern capitalist culture, as change and
technological innovation are constantly motivated by, tied to and seen as a means
of, accumulating capital or turning a profit. The powers of humanity that have
been unleashed, the soaring ambitions which have been realised or become realistic
propositions, the potentialities which science, technology and culture have revealed
lead Marx to ask: 'what earlier century had even a presentiment that such productive forces slumber in the lap of social labour?'[19] And yet it is all for capital
accumulation, which as Marx shows, constantly distorts, limits, blocks and makes
selectively available the possibilities to meet and extend human needs. Consider
how technology works to displace people from employment instead of benefitting
workers. Consider how technology is used to increase surveillance, monitoring and
manipulation of populations by corporations and states instead of increasing transparency and accountability of systems and democratic participation in the economy
and society. The ambivalence over technology is deeply rooted in the stories
we tell ourselves through film and the media generally (especially in the science
fiction genre). The link between accumulating capital and controlling people is

a lived experience for most people who have any experience of the labour market and so it is not surprising that this is a condition that films meditate on continuously. It is important to note that while capitalists must obey the logic of capital, workers do not, and can resist. For Marx, only the working class – strategically placed at the nexus of exploitation and whose objective interests are opposed to capital – can break with capital. But for that to happen objective interests must coincide with a subjective apprehension of those interests – hence the importance of culture and the media where a sense of class *may be forged or blocked*.

Marx also noted that if the dynamic of capital is to seek its ever-growing enlargement, then capitalist industry would be characterised by what he called the concentration and centralisation of capital. Concentration refers to the fact that capital becomes ever larger, ever more powerful, commanding ever more territories, companies, markets and workers. Centralisation refers to the process whereby through the struggle for competitive accumulation, ownership of capital is drawn into ever *fewer* units of capital. 'Capital grows in one place to a huge mass in a single hand, because it has in another place been lost by many.'[20] This is the tendency towards monopoly. As we shall see in Chapter 4, this is indisputably the case for the film industry and the media and cultural industries in which film is embedded.

## 1.5 Marx's method

Marx's method stresses that it is the social production of life that shapes needs, wants, desires, consciousness, culture and interests. At the same time we have seen that, for Marx, consciousness of one's position in a set of class relations is crucial for an exploited class to be able to try and change that position. So consciousness, desire and culture also shape the production of social being. Trying to integrate these two insights into a single philosophical framework is surprisingly difficult. As we might expect, this difficulty is itself socially and historically grounded. Capitalism's dysfunctional and divisive dynamics is constantly separating our ability to link thought and practice. Even Marx himself did not always manage to integrate being and consciousness in successful formulations. In *The German Ideology*, Marx and Engels write:

> [W]e do not set out from what men say, imagine, conceive, nor from men as narrated, thought of, imagined, conceived, in order to arrive at men in the flesh. We set out from real, active men … men, developing their material production and their material intercourse, alter, along with this their real existence, their thinking and the products of their thinking. Life is not determined by consciousness, but consciousness by life.[21]

Now this is a radically unsatisfactory formulation, especially the first part, and not only from the perspective of cultural theorists who are typically very interested in acts of narration, but also from a broader philosophical view. As the Marxist literary theorist Raymond Williams argued, this formulation relegates culture ('men as narrated, thought of, imagined, conceived ...') to a less than secondary importance and implies an 'objectivist fantasy'.[22] For we cannot know 'material production and material intercourse' without the tools of consciousness that involve narration, conception, imagination, etc. The final sentence about life determining consciousness and not vice versa offers clarity in terms of methodological orientation, but as Williams argues, the temptation is to then abstract consciousness *out* of material life and/or imply a temporal sequence (*first* material life, *then* consciousness).

Marx compiled a better-known and better formulation elsewhere, although one that still raises a host of complex questions. Discussing the development of his method, Marx noted that his study of law and philosophy had convinced him that their real development could not be properly understood as purely shaped by law or philosophy itself, independent of the wider context. Marx argued that the decisive wider context had to be understood as the economic class relations that shaped a society's mode of production. This methodological re-orientation was an important advance in the modern understanding of social processes and is particularly important, given how routinely culture is discussed as if it could be insulated from both capital's social imperatives and class stratification. Here Marx sketches out his basic starting point for research:

> The general result at which I arrived and which, once won, served as a guiding thread for my studies, can be briefly formulated as follows: In the social production of their life, men enter into definite relations that are indispensable and independent of their will, relations of production which correspond to a definite stage of development of their material productive forces. The sum total of these relations of production constitutes the economic structure of society, the real foundation, on which rises a legal and political superstructure and to which correspond definite forms of social consciousness. The mode of production of material life conditions the social, political and intellectual life process in general.[23]

Marx stresses the fact that because we are social creatures, we are dependent on the social relationships that are already set up and operating before we enter the world. In this sense they are 'independent' of our will and 'indispensable' to our survival. These relations 'correspond' to the general development of our material resources or forces of production (technology, skills, science, and so forth). Feudalism and its peasant economies could not, for example, have produced the film camera, the steam train or the internet. Together, the social and material relations constitute the 'real foundation' of the social order and the basis on which various institutions such as law and politics, but also religion, philosophy and the 'intellectual life process in general' (e.g. the arts) develop. Marx labels such institutions, in comparison to the 'economic structure of society' (the real foundation), the 'superstructure'. And this superstructure is conditioned by the mode of production. This model is classically depicted using a rectangle for the 'base' and triangle for the 'superstructure' as in Figure 1.2. This is a fairly complex version of what is still a schematic abstraction, and one which the reader could usefully return to in the course of reading this book.

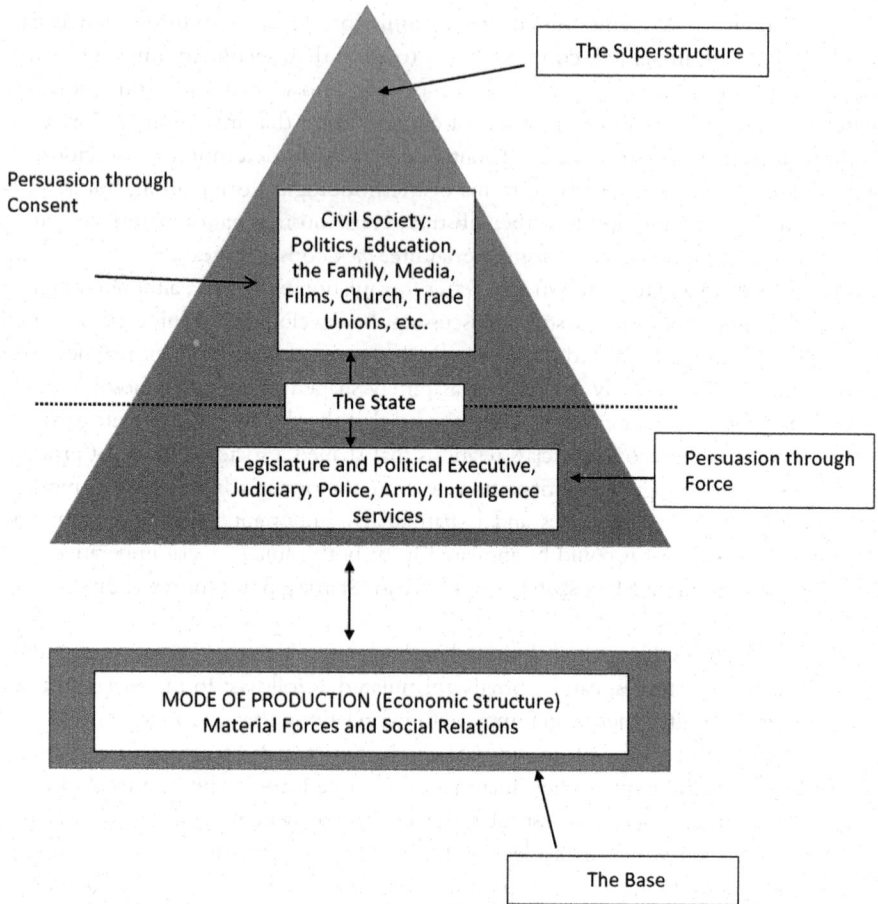

**FIGURE 1.2** The base–superstructure model

But it is crucial to understand that this schematic abstraction is really a 'guiding thread' (Marx), an initial orientation and pointer for a programme of research: for exactly *how* this conditioning takes place has to be ascertained by concrete analysis. The distinction between the economic structure of society and the superstructure is for analytical purposes only. No society is really divided into a separate 'base' and a 'superstructure' any more than we can really divide material life from consciousness. We must also remember that the 'economic structure' is always a socio-economic structure, to stop us from the temptation of thinking about the economy as something that works without any social forces at play pressing it in this or that direction. Furthermore, there can be no one-off universal answer to how the conditioning between the socio-economic structure and superstructure works, as this will be historically and socially variable.

The advance which Marx's methodology represented – the advance of grounding culture in material, social practices – also contains the danger of interpreting such institutions and practices as politics, law and culture as the mere reflection or reflex of the mode of production (the economy) and its class struggles. Raymond Williams summed up how this looked to those outside Marxism:

> According to its opponents, Marxism is a necessarily reductive and determinist kind of theory: no cultural activity is allowed to be real and significant in itself, but is always reduced to a direct or indirect expression of some preceding and controlling economic content, or of a political content determined by an economic position or situation.[24]

In the years after Marx's death, Engels, Marx's lifelong friend and sometime co-author, tried to clarify in a series of letters with friends and comrades, Marx's method. He was highly critical of some German scholars who reduced it to a formula or 'neat system' and refused to study history afresh. For Engels, as for Marx, the method was a 'guide to study', not a substitute for it, not an *a priori* construct, not a finished picture of any actually existing society.[25] Engels partly blamed Marx and himself for over-stressing the 'economic side' against their intellectual and political adversaries, 'who denied it'.[26] Engels was at pains to insist that as a general principle, political, legal and religious institutions and principles, as well as philosophy, could 'also exercise their influence upon the course of the historical struggles and in many cases preponderate in determining their *form*'.[27] That is to say that the study of such institutions and practices is precisely what constitutes what is historically specific about this or that form of capitalism at a national level, for example. The political sphere in particular is crucially important in shaping the course of the class struggle in 'the base' as it is in setting the context within which other practices, such as filmmaking, take place and respond. Legal and juridical relations – which are closely linked to the outcome of political battles – likewise open up or close down certain possibilities or shape the outcome of particular battles. For example, legislation can encourage the concentration and centralisation of capital into larger and larger oligopolies, or it can, to some extent at least, check that in-built tendency and even break up monopolistic practices. Or to take another example, legislation can provide protection for national film markets against Hollywood's global dominance, or alternatively open up those markets further to Hollywood.

In his discussion of Marx's method, Raymond Williams asked us to think of the mode of production or economic 'base' (a particularly unhelpful metaphor, in fact) not as a static, inert 'block' but rather as *process and activity*, which because it is conflictual and filled with tensions, is precisely, *relatively* open-ended (as different political outcomes suggest). This is how Williams puts it:

> We have to revalue 'determination' towards the setting of limits and the exertion of pressure, and away from a predicted, prefigured and controlled content. We have to revalue 'superstructure' towards a related range of cultural practices, and away from a reflected, reproduced or specifically dependent content. And crucially, we have to revalue 'the base' away from

the notion of a fixed economic or technological abstraction, and towards the specific activities of men in real social and economic relationships, containing fundamental contradictions and variations and therefore always in a state of dynamic process.[28]

Williams gives us some useful conceptual refinements on the question of determination, now revalued towards setting limits and exerting pressures. The superstructure includes practices and activities that must be studied in their own right and not seen as pale reflections of something happening elsewhere, while the mode of production refers to social and economic relationships that are dynamic, variable and conflictual. For cultural theorists, the task is to ask how the socio-economic relations typical of capitalism impinge concretely on the specific cultural practice. This is particularly helpful for thinking about film and media production which is simultaneously an economic practice shaped by class relations and a cultural practice that involves the production of culture and meanings. Film is both 'base' and 'superstructure' in that sense and as the cultural industries have grown in importance, both their economic power and cultural reach have fused together.

Williams' idea of determination as 'setting limits' and 'exerting pressures' needs to be supplemented with two other concepts. First, there is the concept of *mediation*. The American literary and cultural theorist Fredric Jameson argues that the concept of mediation allows us to think about 'the possibility of adapting analyses and findings from one level to another.'[29] If we know that capitalism has certain socio-economic dynamics in general, how does that translate to a specific practice such as filmmaking? If research can show that the political realm shapes the economic level through policy making, how does that impact on film? If certain social and/or cultural trends help make sense of a given text, how does that text produce its own *unique* response to a common dynamic? Mediation is a form of establishing connections while preserving the specificity of a practice, such as filmmaking. Cultural industries are industries but making a cultural product is *not* the same as making material goods such as toasters or cars as we shall see.

The second concept which needs to be added to Williams' clarification of determination is something like the idea that practices are *emergent*, a term I draw from the Critical Realist philosophy of thinkers such as Roy Bhaskar, Margaret Archer and Andrew Collier. This term means that conditions that make a practice possible (such as the social relations and forces of capitalist production) do not *pre-determine* the outcome of the practices which emerge out of those conditions. Filmmaking, like any other practice, has conditions, but any given film is also a relatively open-ended emergent practice or *production* whose outcomes cannot be controlled or predicted or reduced to its conditions (e.g. capitalist Hollywood automatically produces films that support capitalism). Emergence 'acknowledges irreducible real novelty' argues the critical realist philosopher Roy Bhaskar.[30]

## 1.6 Ideology

While the value-systems characteristic of capitalist societies are plural and have grown increasingly so, the value-systems closely associated with capital's dynamics and imperatives, are massively present. The workplace dominates social life, and the values of competition, accumulation, the language of selling, buying, the market, the norms of obedience, conformity, status acquisition, individualism, making money, career hopes (for the middle class) and so forth are part of the fabric of everyday life. While values may come into contradiction with capitalism, plenty of them do not, and here we need a concept that identifies those system-supporting values, beliefs, habits and perceptions and explores their relationship to capitalism.

With such questions, we get into the whole complex debate around 'ideology' and ideology critique. 'Critique' because ideology has typically – although not exclusively – been associated with ideas, values, norms, conceptions, representations and cultures that are in some way deserving of criticism because they work in some way to legitimise the capitalist social order. Thus, culture and ideology are related – the former is the medium in which the latter works - but it is best, in my view, to maintain a distinction between the two terms.

Marx and Engels famously deployed and defined the term 'ideology' in *The German Ideology*, an early work designed to formally announce their political and methodological break with the Hegelian philosophy that dominated German thought and which they themselves had had to pass through as part of their intellectual formation. For Marx and Engels, Hegelianism and philosophy in general were ideological to the extent that they did not *ground* their own emergence socially and historically. 'Ideology is then "separated theory"', remarked Raymond Williams, 'and its analysis must involve restoration of its "real" connections.'[31] This *re-grounding* of ideas, theory, values, beliefs, culture, art and so forth is central to Marxism as a political and research project and is one of its major contributions to intellectual life in the modern period. Indeed, I would go so far as to say that, given the powerful trends at work encouraging 'separation', Marxism remains one of the crucial intellectual and political resources we have available to us to resist such pressure and defend critical reason.

In *The German Ideology*, Marx and Engels also made their very well-known formulation about ideology and class when they stated that:

> The ideas of the ruling class are in every epoch the ruling ideas, i.e. the class which is the ruling *material* force of society, is at the same time its ruling *intellectual* force. The class which has the means of material production at its disposal, has control at the same time over the means of mental production, so that thereby, generally speaking, the ideas of those who lack the means of mental production are subject to it.[32]

As a broad initial orientation this formulation would certainly make sense of much of our intellectual and cultural life today. It can hardly be denied, for example, that compulsory education, in terms of what is taught and how and with what aims, is very profoundly shaped by the needs and interests of the employers who dominate the economy, nor how stratified in class terms our education systems (in the UK especially) are. Meanwhile the mainstream media does not spend much or any of its time fundamentally attacking the capitalist system of production, always preferring to discuss problems without tracking them back to a deeper causal nexus (i.e. adequate mediation). The extent to which, generally speaking, the ideas of those who 'lack the means of mental production are subject to' those who own the means of production, is a historical and socially variable question for sure. We also will certainly want to nuance the formulation a little bit more. It may be, for example, that there are ideas and value systems that predominate across public opinion but because they are inconvenient or incongruous with the dominant class view of the world, go unacknowledged within the dominant ideology, at least officially.

This is where film may articulate feelings and perspectives and values that the dominant culture and ideology, especially in its news and information output, cannot easily acknowledge. We may also want to think that the 'dominant ideas' are actually more composite than simply being the ideas of the ruling class. The ruling ideas may instead be the outcome of a series of concessions and compromises which the ruling classes have had to cede in order to stabilise their rule. This is an idea associated with the work of the Italian Marxist, Antonio Gramsci. In addition to idea complexes being hybrid, they are also, in principle at least and often in practice, open to contestation and debate, rather than being monologically settled within the terms favoured by the dominant classes. Culture is intrinsically dialogic, argued one of the most creative Soviet theorists, Mikhail Bakhtin:

> Any concrete discourse (utterance) finds the object at which it was directed, charged with value ... The word, directed toward its object, enters a dialogically agitated and tension-filled environment of alien words, value judgement and accents, weaves in and out of complex interrelationships, merges with some, recoils from others ... The living utterance ... cannot fail to brush up against thousands of living dialogic threads, woven by socio-ideological consciousness around the given object of an utterance.[33]

The representation of social types, for example, in filmic representation, always involves this kind of dialogically agitated brushing up against existing and surrounding representations and discourses. The representation of a black women in a French film or a black man in an American film, instantly bristles with the respective histories of colonialism and slavery, contemporary racism and continuing subordinate positions within a culture and society that people of colour have to endure within western capitalist states. This dialogic quality to cultural production and consumption is enhanced by the plurality of media available and the fact that film consumption is only one small part of anyone's menu of media consumption that will typically also include, press, magazines, television, radio, music, etc. Unless we have a view of this range of mass media as an overly seamless integrated unity, it seems likely that a degree of pluralism, nationally and historically variable of course, must be acknowledged.

Marx himself was an adept practitioner of *ideological critique*. In his masterpiece work, *Capital*, he meticulously dismantled the conceptual system of the economic theorists who had preceded him and who had internalised within their concepts and definitions, assumptions that shielded capitalism from critique. The *Grundrisse* was composed of Marx's notebooks that he collated in preparation for writing *Capital*. The *Grundrisse* opens with a critique of the founding ideological assumptions of economists like Adam Smith and David Ricardo. The critique is especially interesting to us because it takes the form of identifying a certain *image* of economic life which Marx calls 'Robinsonades'. The name here refers to Daniel Defoe's famous novel *Robinson Crusoe* (1719) about the sailor shipwrecked on an uninhabited island. What is interesting is that this image of the 'individual and isolated hunter and fisherman'[34] which the novel crystallised and popularised is also to be found in the works of the economic theorists, a good example of culture shaping economic science. Marx suggests that these Robinsonades 'in no way express merely a reaction against over-sophistication and a return to a misunderstood natural life, as cultural historians imagine'.[35] Rather than seeing the Robinson model as mere nostalgia, it is instead

> the anticipation of 'civil society' [the market], in preparation since the sixteenth century and making giant strides towards maturity in the eighteenth. In this society of free competition, the individual appears detached from the natural bonds etc. which in earlier historical periods make him the accessory of a definite and limited human conglomerate.[36]

In the earlier feudal period, then, the individual was solidly embedded in a limited local community, while under capitalism, the individual is prised out of their community and becomes increasingly a free agent within a market economy; their connections to their fellow human being are increasingly tenuous and merely contractual rather than based on custom or appreciations of the common good. The individual 'appears detached' says Marx, because although capitalism is indeed a more individualistic mode of production, this individualism still rests on social relationships and interdependencies. When economists imagine economic activity and begin with the image of the isolated individual who trucks and barters with another isolated individual, this is an *ideological* image because it denies such social relationships as wage-labour, the market and capital as the necessary condition for this individualism. One of the things that make the Robinsonade a powerful and compelling ideological image is the way this very modern notion of the isolated individual is grafted onto a pre-modern scenario apparently 'closer' to nature. Here we see a very common technique of ideology, the attempt to shield itself from scrutiny by giving itself a veil of *naturalness*. Crusoe establishes a private dominion over *his* island and is a moral example of what can be achieved by individual hard work, self-reliance and self-discipline – the very model of capitalist subjectivity.

The tendency to de-contextualise the individual from the social nature of production is evident in contemporary survival stories of man (it is usually men) battling against and yet also immersed in nature in such films as *The Martian* (2015) and *The Revenant* (2015). The enduring appeal of such films makes sense in a society that embraces the struggle of the individual, on their own, heroically triumphing against the odds, sheer individual will-power as the key to 'making it', and so forth. Recognising this 'making sense' dimension of ideology is important because it reminds us that its efficacy and power and plausibility come from the fact that society really is like that, at least at certain 'levels' of reality, capitalism makes it so. The power of ideology is that it makes sense because it corresponds to real features of the social relations we live by, those forms of appearance (or sometimes called phenomenal forms) that are generated 'up' as it were from the base of society as commodity fetishism. It is a form of *practical consciousness*, the means by which people navigate their way around the market, buying and selling, for example, and competing with each other.[37] As Stuart Hall argues, phenomenal forms generated up by commodity fetishism, are:

> what is on the surface, what constantly appears … what we are always seeing, what we encounter daily, what we come to take for granted as the obvious and manifest form of the process. It is not surprising, then, that we come spontaneously to *think* of the capitalist system in terms of the bits of it which constantly engage us, and which so manifestly announce their presence. What chance does the extraction of 'surplus labour' have, as a concept, as against the hard fact of wages in the pocket, savings in the bank, pennies in the slot, money in the till … In a world saturated by money exchange, and everywhere mediated by money, the 'market' experience is *the* most immediate, daily and universal experience of the economic system for everyone. It is therefore not surprising that we take the market for granted, do not question what makes it possible, what it is founded or premised on. It should not surprise us if the mass of working people don't possess the concepts with which to cut into the process at another point, frame another set of questions, and bring to the surface or reveal what the overwhelming facticity of the market constantly renders invisible.[38]

This practical consciousness is *not* illusion or mere 'error'. It is *not* 'false consciousness', a term that is often associated with Marx, but which he never used. Ideology may be thought of as the socially, culturally and historically specific productions deriving from the superstructure that reinforce the spontaneous ideology of commodity fetishism coming from the socio-economic base of capitalism. The Robinsonade of the seventeenth century, for example, as an ideological image emerges out of a number of disparate superstructural sources. These include: literary predecessors such as literary forms that imagine faraway or magical lands, from Thomas More's *Utopia* to Shakespeare's *The Tempest*; the diary form which *Robinson Crusoe* uses had become, along with the personal letter, increasingly popular among the middle class, helping them to expand and enrich their subjectivity with reflective thought;[39] it also includes popular responses to the emerging colonial experience for an expanding West (including the slave trade) and philosophical ideas about 'natural rights' (the inalienable equality of men as championed by Rousseau, for example, against the artificial inequalities of the feudal period). Once forged out of a specific historical constellation, the image of the Robinsonade not only circulates into political economy but becomes a potential cultural resource for future generations, cultures and media, adapted and reconfigured no doubt in new contexts but often with plenty of continuities in old social relationships (capitalism) to continue to convey comparable ideological messages now as it did in the seventeenth century.

Ideology reinforces commodity fetishism in historically specific ways then. Ideology is ideology because it accepts the world, it evaluates it as necessary, or just, or inevitable, or empowering, or better than something else imaginable or whatever. Ideology is ideology because it blocks us off from the full range of options and the full range of knowing the determining forces at play in our environment. It does so in a relatively systematic way and is relatively insulated against argument and evidence because it is linked to social interests invested in the status quo. And in this sense ideology is inadequate, partial, one-sided. It is a form of cognitive and/or empathetic restriction bracketing off the deep contradictions of the system, its irrationality and the emergence of forces that could, if they were to be cultivated (such as workers' solidarity) provide the basis of a real alternative to it. But as we have seen, ideology is never seamless, unified or uncontested.

## 1.7 Philosophical concepts

As well as drawing on and reconstructing economic and political theories, Marx also drew on and refashioned concepts drawn from the German philosophical heritage (especially Hegel, but also, in a more disguised form, Kant). One such concept was the dialectic. It is an old term that can be traced back to ancient Greek philosophy where it refers to a way of thinking through problems and issues by dialogue, debate and, importantly, disagreement. Marxism, very characteristically, grounded the concept and suggested that it is social reality itself that changes (rather than just philosophical debates) according to 'disagreement', i.e. conflicting class interests. Yet the older sense of a dialectic of discursive positions (albeit associated within and between social interests) continues on in textual analysis, as we have already seen, in, for example, Bakhtin's concept of the dialogic nature of representation.

Capitalism's inflation of the individual into an ideology of individualism is part of capitalist culture's general tendency towards atomistic conceptions and perceptions (the immense accumulation of commodities). The dialectic strikes a blow against this de-contextualisation bias because the dialectic stresses the contradictory interrelated dimensions of our existence as social beings. Intrinsic to the concept of change and movement which the dialectic brings to our thinking is the idea that everything is related, everything exists in a relationship to something else and comprehension of the world is impossible without situating people, events, processes, objects, actions, in a context of relations.

It is precisely this insight which made Marx the original interdisciplinary thinker, forging new insights by bringing the formerly *separate* traditions of philosophy, economics and politics into a new synthesis. Capitalism has hardened the division of labour at the intellectual level into very rigid compartments. So that sociology, for example, in its mainstream versions, has only very weak senses of political and economic relations precisely because these are thought of as dynamics best studied by politics or economics respectively. What happens to our intellectual understanding of society when the social field is broken up into rigid compartments is that the social comes, typically, to be conceived either in terms of self-sufficient systems (without agency) or collapsed into more individualistic and psychologising models (bracketing off social relationships). As a society that occludes collective democratic control, capitalism tends to view the 'social' as an autonomous system. As a society based on private ownership, it tends to counter this vision and practice with various models based on the private, individual, personal and psychological accounts of agency and action. Dialectics is a way of thinking through this impasse or dualism in thought and deed.[40]

Dialectical thinking is best understood as a style of thought, another part of the Marxist armoury in the guide for study. Like the base-superstructure metaphor, it should *not* be turned into an overly schematic formula (that is a 'dialectical system') and applied independent of *actual* social and historical analysis. Instead it should be used to attune research to a loose cluster of patterns characteristic of life under capitalism. The concept of the dialectic can help us overcome the tendency of concepts to harden into rigid binary oppositions and dualisms, such as we found earlier with the distinctions between material life and consciousness or base and superstructure. Raymond Williams was constantly warning us not to take analytic distinctions as real substantive divisions.[41] Marxism tries to combat this tendency in capitalist society and thought. The 'social' and the 'individual', 'form' and 'content', 'production' and 'consumption', for example, are all important analytic distinctions that help us understand this or that aspect of interdependent phenomena, except when we begin (as we seem continually tempted to be) to think that the phenomena's parts are as contained and as separate as the words we use to identify those parts. The dialectic keeps the boundaries of words porous.

Marxists have also argued for the importance of thinking the *totality* of social relations. Like dialectics, this concept comes to Marxism via Hegel's philosophy. It may be understood as 'a methodological insistence that adequate understanding of complex phenomena can follow only from an appreciation of their relational integrity'.[42] The concept of totality is not to be thought of as an attempt to 'know everything'. Quite the contrary, it is a way of reframing that relativises everything, including Marxism, and by reframing within a larger perspective, it encourages us to ask 'what is missing' or assumed.

How does enlarging the frame change what we thought we knew about something? Take, for example, the image of the 'terrorist' in dominant political, media and filmic discourse: it tends to reduce them to an essence (mindless, evil, hateful, etc.) and associates terrorism with small groups who, because they are not states, can have no legitimate claim to use violence. The complicity of the dominant order in producing terrorist violence through its *own* violence (military, economic, etc.), and its *own* refusal to allow democratic solutions to problems, is denied. Thinking the totality in relation to film discourse also includes thinking of its relationship to news information systems and their uncritical acceptance of the way state actors frame the terrorism question and other modes of audio-visual entertainment culture, such as the games industry which Toby Miller notes, is deeply embedded with the military industrial complex.[43] Thinking the totality thus reframes and relativises dominant discourses and representation. It examines assumptions and strategic silences by enlarging the context in which we are thinking a problem. As Fredric Jameson has argued, the 'imperative to totalize' is less an exhaustive itemisation of everything we know than a methodological strategy to unmask the socially interested nature of what we are invited to assume *is known* about this or that phenomena.[44] A Hollywood film such as *Syriana* (2005), an art cinema film such as Claude Chabrol's *Nada* (1974) or a revolutionary film such as Arthur MacCaig's documentary on the IRA, *The Patriot Game* (1979) help expand our thinking about violence beyond the state-media ideological framing of terrorism.

Totality and dialectics are related to each other and the earlier mentioned concept of mediation. Mediation analyses how distinct phenomena influence each other 'internally', how their pressure and presence become manifest not just as an external check but as shaping how other phenomena work, albeit according to its own specific qualities. The last word in this chapter can go to Fredric Jameson whose defence of the concept of mediation sets up the political and methodological task we have before us in the rest of the book:

> But the concept of mediation has traditionally been the way in which dialectical philosophy and Marxism itself have formulated their vocation to break out of the specialized compartments of the (bourgeois) disciplines and to make connections among the seemingly disparate phenomena of social life generally … Mediations are thus a device of the analyst, whereby the fragmentation and autonomization, the compartmentalization and the specialization of the various regions of social life (the separation, in other words, of the ideological from the political, the religious from the economic, the gap between daily life and the practice of the academic disciplines) is at least locally overcome, on the occasion of a particular analysis. Such momentary reunification would remain purely symbolic, a mere methodological fiction, were it not understood that social life is in its fundamental reality one and indivisible, a seamless web, a single inconceivable and transindividual process, in which there is no need to invent ways of linking language events and social upheavals or economic contradictions because on that level they were never separate from one another. The realm of separation, of fragmentation, of the explosion of codes and the multiplicity of disciplines is merely the reality of the appearance.[45]

## Notes

1 Karl Marx, *Capital*, vol. I (London: Lawrence and Wishart, 1983), p. 689.
2 Ibid., p. 43.
3 Guy Debord, *The Society of the Spectacle* (London: Black and Red, 1977). See also for a more accessible introduction to the concept of spectacle, Douglas Kellner's *Media Spectacle* (London: Routledge, 2002).
4 Marx, *Capital*, vol. I, op. cit., p. 77.
5 Ibid., p. 76.
6 Karl Marx, *Grundrisse* (Harmondsworth: Penguin Books, 1993), p. 244.
7 Karl Marx and Friedrich Engels, *The Communist Manifesto* (Harmondsworth: Penguin Books, 1985), p. 79.
8 V.I. Lenin, 'Classes are large groups of people differing from each other by the place they occupy in a historically determined system of social production, by their relation, (in most cases fixed and formulated in law) to the means of production, by their role in the social organisation of labour, and, consequently, by the dimensions of the share of social wealth which they dispose and the mode of acquiring it.' ('A Great Beginning', in *Collected Works*, vol. 29, March–August 1919) (Moscow: Progress Publishers, 1974), p. 421.
9 Karl Marx, *The Eighteenth Brumaire of Louis Bonaparte* (London: Lawrence and Wishart, 1984), p. 109.
10 Barbara and John Ehrenreich, 'The Professional-Managerial Class', in Pat Walker (ed.) *Between Labor and Capital* (Boston: South End Press, 1979).
11 Jonathan Pratschke, 'Marxist Class Theory: Competition, Contingency and Intermediate Class Positions', in Deirdre O'Neill and Michael Wayne (eds), *Considering Class, Theory, Culture and the Media in the 21st Century* (Leiden: Brill, 2018), pp. 58–9.
12 Max Weber, cited in Anthony Giddens and David Held (eds), *Classes, Power and Conflict: Classical and Contemporary Debates* (Basingstoke: Macmillan, 1988), p. 67.
13 Pierre Bourdieu, *Distinction: A Social Critique of the Judgment of Taste* (London: Routledge, 1996).
14 Erik Olin Wright, *Class, Crisis and the State* (London: New Left Books, 1978).
15 Barbara and John Ehrenreich, 'Death of a Yuppie Dream', *Rosa Luxemburg Stiftung*, 2013. Available at: www.rosalux-nyc.org/wp-content/files_mf/ehrenreich_death_of_a_ yuppie_dream90.pdf
16 See Nick Heffernan's excellent book on middle-class anxieties and how they are mediated through literature and film, *Capital, Class and Technology in Contemporary American Culture: Projecting Post-Fordism* (London: Pluto Press, 2000).
17 Marx, *Capital*, vol. I, op. cit., p. 558.
18 Marx and Engels, *The Communist Manifesto*, op. cit., p. 83.
19 Ibid., p. 85,
20 Marx, *Capital*, vol. I, op. cit., p. 586.
21 Marx and Engels, *The German Ideology*, op. cit., p. 47.
22 Raymond Williams, *Marxism and Literature* (Oxford: Oxford University Press, 1988), p. 60.
23 Karl Marx, 'Preface to a Contribution to the Critique of Political Economy', in Karl Marx and Friedrich Engels, *Selected Works*, vol. I (London: Lawrence and Wishart, 1977), p. 181.
24 Williams, *Marxism and Literature*, op. cit., p. 83.
25 Friedrich Engels, 'Letter to C. Schmidt in Berlin', in *Selected Works*, vol. I, op. cit., pp. 679–80.
26 Engels, 'Letter to J. Bloch in Konigsberg', in *Selected Works*, vol. I, op. cit., p. 683.
27 Ibid., p. 682.
28 Raymond Williams, 'Base and Superstructure in Marxist Cultural Theory', *New Left Review*, 82, Nov.–Dec. (1973): 6.
29 Fredric Jameson, *The Political Unconscious: Narrative as a Socially Symbolic Act* (London: Routledge 1981), p. 24.

30  Roy Bhaskar, 'Critical Realism and Dialectic', in Margaret Archer, Roy Bhaskar, Andrew Collier, Tony Lawson and Alan Norrie (eds), *Critical Realism: Essential Readings* (London: Routledge,1998), p. 599.

31  Williams, *Marxism and Literature*, op. cit., p. 66.

32  Marx and Engels, *The German Ideology*, op. cit., p. 64.

33  M.M. Bakhtin, *The Dialogic Imagination* (Austin, TX: University of Texas Press, 1992), p. 276.

34  Marx, *Grundrisse*, op. cit., p. 83.

35  Ibid.

36  Ibid.

37  Stuart Hall, 'The Problem of Ideology: Marxism without Guarantees', in Stuart Hall, *Critical Dialogues in Cultural Studies* (London: Routledge, 1996), p. 28.

38  Ibid., p. 38.

39  Jürgen Habermas, *The Structural Transformation of the Public Sphere* (Cambridge, MA: MIT Press, 1989), pp. 48–50.

40  The classic tracing out of this in western philosophy was done by Georg Lukács in *History and Class Consciousness*, especially the essay 'Reification and the Consciousness of the Proletariat' (London: Merlin Press, 1975).

41  Williams, *Marxism and Literature*, op. cit., p. 129.

42  Martin Jay, *Marxism and Totality: The Adventure of a Concept from Lukács to Habermas* (Berkeley, CA: University of California Press, 1984), pp. 23–4.

43  Toby Miller, 'Terrorism and Global Popular Culture', in Des Freedman and Daya Kishan Thussu (eds), *Media and Terrorism: Global Perspectives* (Thousand Oaks, CA: Sage, 2012).

44  Jameson, *The Political Unconscious*, op. cit., p. 38.

45  Ibid., p. 25.

# 2

# HISTORY

## 2.1 The primal scene

*Workers Leaving the Factory* (1895) was the first film ever to be shown to the public. The short film had been shot by the Lumière brothers and it was screened to a specially invited elite audience in Paris. As its title promised, the astonished audience watched workers (mostly women) leaving a factory. The factory in Lyon actually produced photographic plates for still cameras and it belonged to the Lumière brothers. The business had been set up by their father, who had been a portrait painter, but they saw that the future very much lay with the cultural power and financial possibilities of the new technology of the still camera. The Lumière brothers took the technological developments to the next stage with a camera that could shoot moving pictures, building on Thomas Edison's Kinetoscope, which had been unveiled in Paris in 1894.

Harun Farocki's essay film *Workers Leaving the Factory*, made 100 years later, is a meditation on the significance of this origin story. This is what psychoanalysts call the 'primal scene', when the child fantasises about their own conception. In this moment of conception, the first subject that film turns its gaze on is 'the workers'. Farocki's film assembles a non-chronological montage of scenes from the many films that repeat this scene of workers leaving the factory. His thesis is that the fiction film almost always stops at the factory gate, rarely penetrating into what Marx called the 'hidden abode' of production. Narratives tend to begin precisely after work has finished, the moment when the collective body of the workforce dissolves into the individual lives of characters whom the film can now follow. This bias against production, against the collective, is hardly unexpected within a capitalist mode of production in which the individual and the private life are exalted and the process of production is concealed because it is also the site of exploitation. In the Lumières' film the camera stands at the border of private property watching the workers flow out into the public street, going left and right, separating and breaking up into the altogether less threatening form of the private individual or a crowd of atoms with no common purpose. When, as with the documentary genre, cameras did routinely penetrate past the factory gates and look at the actual production going on inside, they did so on the terms agreed with the owners and often as part of an explicit contract to promote the firm as a component part of the modern nation-state. Despite its progressive contribution to democratising a national culture, the British documentary film movement of the 1930s and the 1940s found itself constrained by just such parameters. In the case of the Lumières' film, the owners are directly controlling the camera, the means of production, which the brothers invented, building on the technological breakthroughs and inventions that preceded them. In the decades that were to come, the struggle between classes over the means of production, over who gets represented and how, would become a good deal more intense than the brothers or the workers in front of their camera could possibly have imagined in 1895.

## 2.2 From early American cinema to Hollywood

The struggle for control over the cinematic means of production on the terrain of culture is part of and develops in relation to the broader struggle between the classes over the means of production as a whole (e.g. the factory system and technology). How that struggle is gathered together and fought out in the sphere of politics will in the ensuring decades take the form of street protests, revolutions, counter-revolutions and war. But in a mode of production that turns on economic competition between capital, intra-class struggles in the form of struggles to control the market are also extremely important for understanding the development of film history. Certainly, the early years of cinema are shaped by the twin forces of capital in competition with itself to control this new popular entertainment *and* the 'proletariat' as audience, as screen content and as historical agent.

Intra-capitalist competition for control of the new medium was evident from the very earliest years. Monsieur Lafont, the representative of the Lumière Company in America, had to leave the country by boat in a hurry in 1897 when it looked as if he might have violated a new law brought in by the American government that hit foreign imports of film equipment with heavy taxes. The import duties were designed to protect American film manufacturers such as the American Mutoscope and Biograph Company, from French competition. The company had close links with the then President of the United States, William McKinley. Here we see how economic interests interact with politics and state power in a way that has been enduring within and beyond the film industry.

In America, the dynamic between intra-capital competition and consolidation of the industry around large corporate concerns, first took the form of the Motion Picture Patents Company (MPPC). This cartel of film and camera manufacturers and producers included the roll film manufacturer George Eastman of the Eastman Kodak company, and a film importer George Klein, and was led by Thomas

Edison, inventor and film producer. The MPPC tried to control the market by making it illegal to use (without payment) any film stock or equipment (including cameras and projectors) that the cartel held patents on. It was set up in 1908 but within a year it was clear that this type of control over the industry, which required constant state support in the courts, was going to founder. Independents, for example, began to use non-patent infringing cameras and film stock and relocated production far away from the East Coast offices of the patent cartel, in a northern suburb of Los Angeles in California. It was from this base that 'Hollywood' would eventually emerge, a new form (for the film industry) of corporate control over the largest film market in the world. This economic control over the industry and over access to audiences was far more suited towards a mass medium using technology that was becoming widely disseminated, than relying on patents and unending battles in the law courts. And, in fact, the MPPC was itself subject to federal government anti-trust action in the courts. The MPPC was declared an illegal infringement on free trade by a Pennsylvania court in 1915.[1]

One of the many contradictions of the free market is that it generates its own opposite – not only the proletariat – but also the consolidation of the market around large units of capital (the tendency towards monopoly). Capitalist states in the West have typically oscillated between endorsing this concentration of capital in the name of the free market (letting capital do whatever its logic dictates) *and* checking and breaking up this concentration of capital, in the name of the free market (preserving the ideal of a diversity of players in which market share is divided). Which way the state leans at any particular point in time depends on the political context and field of political struggle. As we have already seen (in Section 1.5) capital sets certain parameters, exerts certain pressures, *within which* real political battles, struggles and choices have to be played out, won or lost, rather than be pre-determined by capital.

But even as intra-capital competition was being played out in the early years of the industry, the American working class was laying its own claim to this new means of cultural production in ways that dominant forms of historiography have repressed. The heterogeneity of capital interests clustered around the MPPC (producers, importers, manufacturers, inventors) indicated that the corporate form suited to monopoly domination of the industry had yet to be found. This heterogeneity was also to be found, therefore, across the industry. Who made films, what kind of venues they were watched in, what kind of films were made, how long people stayed in the venues and how they behaved, were much more diverse, fluid and uncontrolled than later, when film became stamped as a commodity product in the Hollywood studio system model. The development of the Nickleodeons from 1905 confirmed film as a cheap form of mass entertainment that was enthusiastically embraced by an overwhelmingly blue-collar and routine white-collar audience.[2] Film developed in the context of urbanisation, spreading industrialisation, mass communications and mass culture. The latter benefitted from the decades of labour struggles that had gradually driven down the length of the working day or week, thus expanding the scope for various cultural activities. At the same time, America at the turn of the twentieth century was wracked by intense class conflicts between employers and their workers. There was considerable establishment anxiety over the role the new mass medium might play in drawing an ethnically and religiously divided immigrant working class together around a common cultural form. Film could potentially speak to this audience as a class in a way that the more respectable cultural forms, such as theatre, where the dominance of middle-class values was assured, rarely did. Writing in *The Atlantic*, in a 1915 article significantly entitled 'Class Consciousness and the "Movies"', Walter Prichard Eaton suggested that:

> In the average American village of a few thousand souls, even today, you will not find class-consciousness developed. The proletariat is not aware of itself. The larger the town, the greater the degree of class-consciousness—and the sharper the line of cleavage between the audiences at the spoken drama and at the movies.[3]

Marx had argued that the movement from a class existing *in itself* (without self-consciousness of its distinct class interests) to a class *for itself* was absolutely crucial if it was to become a political agent capable of leading the fight for social change. The prospect that film might help the proletariat achieve such a degree of class-consciousness and self-awareness was not outlandish in pre-Hollywood American cinema. The medium had yet to become that powerful promoter of American national identity or mythology that it would later be. Instead the screen teemed with ordinary people facing tough times. This typically proletarian milieu often included extended critical commentary on the dominant institutions of established society that made life for ordinary Americans so hard. Bosses, the rich in general, policemen, politicians, the courts, landlords, government officials and such like, were frequently shown as greedy, petty, corrupt, vain and vindictive. If *The Mill Girl* (1907) displayed a paternalist concern for the vulnerable waif, typical of liberal reformism in which middle-class progressives will intervene on behalf of the working class, *The Girl Strike Leader* (1910), *The Long Strike* (1911), *The High Road* (1915) and *Her Bitter Cup* (1916) featured women labour leaders exemplifying working-class resistance to the bosses.[4] D.W. Griffith's early work at the Biograph Company included such films as *The Song of the Shirt* (1908) and *A Corner in Wheat* (1909), which began to show how editing could be used to contrast the lives of the rich and the poor, and make visible how the actions of the former could have such a negative impact on the latter, using the cinematic tool of cross-cutting. *A Corner in Wheat* is particularly sophisticated and ambitious in that it shows how distant and remote speculators (not even the immediate boss) could detrimentally impact on the working class by causing bread prices to rise. D.W. Griffith also included an example of savage class conflict in his later epic, *Intolerance* (1916), where striking workers are gunned down by the National Guard, which in content, if not in form, anticipated the incitements to revolutionary action found in the Soviet films just a few years later. Some films were made by or involved the participation of labour organisations or political parties. *From Dusk to Dawn* (1913) was not an exceptionally early Quentin Tarantino film about vampires, but a commercially successful feature-length film made with the participation of the Socialist Party in Los Angeles. It explicitly endorsed socialism as the political solution to an America torn apart by class conflict.[5] Although ordinary characters and location shooting featured heavily, the majority of films, Kay Sloan argues, 'tended to privatize public issues; romance or personal redemption, for instance, became major subplots in the films which allowed the larger problems to be contained in the domestic sphere'.[6] Yet Frederic Howe, then chairman of the National Board of Censorship, was sufficiently concerned to bemoan in 1914 a tendency in which films 'tend to excite class feeling or ... tend to bring discredit upon the agencies of government'.[7] It seems likely that at least part of the success of Charlie Chaplin's comic persona on screen, the Tramp, was precisely because it excited 'class feeling' and discredited various figures of authority. In the brilliant opening of *City Lights* (1931), dignitaries and their wives make speeches before the grand unveiling of a statue meant to be a monument to 'peace and prosperity'. The pomposity and self-importance of the elites and the gap between their view of America and its Depression-era reality are exposed when the tarpaulin covering the statue is lifted and there, asleep in the lap of the seated stone figure, is the Tramp.

However, in the main, the orientation of the early American film towards a working-class social portraiture was to change radically in the late teens as the forces of monopoly began to coalesce around a small number of powerful corporations such as Fox, Famous Players Lasky, Triangle and Paramount. By 1919, vertical integration, control of production, distribution and exhibition were emerging as the key to the new form of monopoly control. Famous Players Lasky controlled which films were shown in around 400 movie theatres through ownership or controlling interests.[8] As money started to flow in ever increasing quantities to fewer and fewer companies, so those companies acquired greater capital power. Through mergers and acquisitions, they grew still larger and integrated their finances with Wall Street banks. The concentration of capital in fewer hands in turn changed the content of films. More and more money began to be spent on lavish sets, costumes and stars. This in turn raised barriers to entry into the market as film became defined in the minds of consumers with escalating budgets. With Hollywood putting production values (budgets) up on the screen, the film industry became integrated into the newly expanding consumer goods industry. Films and film stars would be increasingly tied in with fashion retailers, for example, for mutual cross-promotion.[9] This is a concrete example of the development of commodity fetishism. The more a culture enlarges the commodity as its focal point, the more consciousness of the exploitative social relationships underpinning the production and consumption of commodities (as revealed by Chaplin's Tramp) contracts. The whole social milieu of the film world shifted away from ordinary people at this time, stripping out a materialist, realist layer to early film. Instead the film world was increasingly populated with the rich and the middle class whose lives and luxury the audience were encouraged to aspire to rather than criticise. Nevertheless, the proletarian image could not be entirely banished. It was there in many of the lower budget 'B' movies that some studios specialised in and at particular moments, even within the new corporate structures, it would resurface with a vengeance.

After the 1929 Wall Street Crash and the ensuring crisis of the Great Depression, there was a four-year period when a plebeian vernacular (thanks to the newly emerged sound film), proletarian image and frank sexual morality antithetical to the then middle-class norms, crashed back onto the screens. Female actors such as Jean Harlow and Mae West played characters who were no wilting violets ready to be rescued by men or sexual innocents needing protection from the world. In *Red Dust* (1932), Jean Harlow plays a tough-talking prostitute who acts like she could drink Clark Gable under the table and she wastes little time getting him into her arms. The stories, the settings and the characters between 1929 and 1934 were a throw-back to early American cinema's working-class orientation. As historian Thomas Doherty notes of these films, they 'look like Hollywood cinema but the moral terrain is so off-kilter they seem imported from a parallel universe'.[10] It was not the corporate structures alone that shaped what came to be known as the 'classical' Hollywood cinema. Instead the plebeian, proletarian image was finally marginalised, controlled and policed by an elaborate and comprehensive censorship system that corporate Hollywood applied to itself in order to stop attacks by conservative Catholic organisations on movie 'immorality'. The possibility of state or federal censorship disrupting box office revenues led Hollywood to institutionalise its own comprehensive Motion Picture Production Code in 1934 under the command of Joseph Breen. This is a good example of how economics, corporate structures, politics, religion and culture (here mass culture vs the cultural morality of the 'respectable' middle class) work in complex ways at a particular point in history to effect a particular outcome that is 'determinate' (not haphazard or accidental) but nor is it 'pre-determined' by an 'economic base' moving all the other pieces of the jigsaw puzzle into place. Nor is this determinate outcome fixed in place for all time.

## 2.3 Revolution and Modernism

The double contradiction between intra-capitalist competition leading to monopoly capitalism and inter-class conflict between capital and labour, was also to play out on a catastrophic world scale in the form of the First World War (1914–18). Lenin argued that as monopoly capital advanced in the core capitalist countries, so it sought to export itself to other undeveloped territories looking for fresh sources of profit in cheap raw materials, cheap land, and cheap labour-power.[11] This is because continued investment in its own domestic terrain would eventually drive up workers' wages, diminish unemployment and eventually cause a crisis for capital as profit margins went down. This contradiction produces a tendency for capital to export itself to less advanced areas (something which it has been doing in recent years on a massive scale in relation to China and Asia). Lenin called this economic and political power projection 'imperialism' and it was a major driver to war. It was to have a significant offshoot in cultural theory in the form of the 'cultural imperialism' thesis, in which Hollywood capital and commodities (the films, television programmes, comics, and so forth) were seen to be dominating national audiences and markets around the world to the detriment of local industries and cultural forms attuned to specific local and national conditions (see Section 4.3).

The First World War was a disaster for both the working classes, who died in their millions, and for the bourgeoisie and their aristocratic allies. Their nineteenth-century confidence that they were the representatives of progress, reason, enlightenment and civilisation was profoundly shaken. The October 1917 Revolution in Russia, led by Lenin, Trotsky and the Bolsheviks seemed to pose, for a brief and inspiring period, an existential threat to the European capitalist order. It was the first successful working-class revolution in the world and its leaders were explicitly self-defined as Marxists. October 1917 was in some sense philosophy (the attempt to understand the world) momentarily realised (turned into action to change the world). No wonder that it inspired Georg Lukács to convert to Marxism and produce one of the great works of Marxist philosophy in the twentieth century. As he wrote in *History and Class Consciousness:*

> The self-understanding of the proletariat is ... simultaneously the objective understanding of the nature of society. When the proletariat furthers its own class-aims it simultaneously achieves the conscious realisation of the – objective – aims of society, aims which would inevitably remain abstract possibilities and objective frontiers but for this conscious intervention.[12]

However, consciously realising, as agents of history, the objective potentialities pregnant within a revolutionary situation was to be a tall order. The Russian working class was a newly formed class, largely located in St Petersburg and Moscow, and relatively small compared to the overwhelming proportion of the population that were peasants. The small geographical and social base of the Bolsheviks put a premium on the need to communicate the goals and ideals of the revolution. Film, with its ability to be intelligible to a diverse and often illiterate population, was highly valued by Lenin, and the Russian film industry was nationalised in 1919. One result of this was the famous agitation-propaganda (agit-prop) trains that toured the former Russian empire. They contained a mixture of bookshops, printing presses, telegraphy for communication, theatre groups and the capacity to produce and show films in the towns and villages they visited. Propaganda here did not mean, in the first decade or more after 1917, state-imposed 'messages' to be disseminated. The trains were genuine experiments in cultural democracy, engaging with the problems, issues and lives of the populations whom the cultural and political activists encountered and involved a genuine exchange of mutual learning. Pioneers of what would now be called 'interactive' media included the documentary filmmakers Dziga Vertov[13] in the 1920s and Alexander Medvedkin in the early 1930s.[14] The integration of film into the October Revolution transformed the medium and the Soviet filmmakers of the 1920s were in turn to be hugely influential on world cinema, not only in that decade, but for many decades to come. Sergei Eisenstein, Lev Kuleshov, Dziga Vertov, Vsevolod Pudovkin and the Ukrainian director Alexander Dovshenko, all in their different ways, championed the power and centrality of the distinctive form of editing which they became synonymous with: montage (see Section 5.2).

The Russian Revolution brought Marxism into contact with cultural Modernism – the umbrella term for all those extremely diverse experiments in cultural forms that had exploded in the early part of the twentieth century: Cubism, Dadaism, Surrealism, Futurism, Constructivism, Expressionism, and so forth. From this dialogue Modernism could acquire a new political clarity and purpose concerning the implications of formal experimentation, namely, to develop forms appropriate for the new 'content' of the twentieth century. And, conversely, Marxism could acquire a new repertoire of cultural forms in addition to (or, for some, instead of) the nineteenth-century cultural forms it had naturally inherited at the moment of its own nineteenth-century formation. We will explore one case study of this dialogue in relation to the Russian Formalists, Futurists and Marxism in more detail in Section 5.1. The potential affinity between Marxism and Modernism was explored by a number of key German theorists in the 1930s, such as Siegfried Kracauer, Walter Benjamin, Theodor Adorno and Bertolt Brecht. All were to have a profound influence on Marxist film theory.

The paradox of twentieth-century mass culture is that it was the product of new forces and relations of production unleashed by capitalism, but in many respects, it kept intact nineteenth-century cultural forms. Thus, a nineteenth-century confidence in the ability of science to produce a transparent and neutral record of reality (positivism) has been detected in the photographic-based media of the twentieth century. By contrast, one of the features of Modernist art in all its diversity, was its *self-reflexivity* or self-consciousness about its processes of representation, its own 'language', whether that was the word (e.g. Joyce or Woolf), the painting (Picasso or Kandinsky), the theatre (Meyerhold or Brecht) or film.[15] The self-reflexive nature of Modernist art was highly valued by cultural theory in the 1960s and the 1970s, although some of the theoretical and philosophical conclusions that were drawn as a result are certainly problematic from a Marxist perspective, as we shall see in Section 3.2.

Much of mass culture, at least in this early phase, resisted self-reflexivity and its accompanying strategies of breaking up and breaking down narrative structures. Instead, the more reassuring form of linear narratives predominated, 'believable' worlds, private passions, individuated characters, with the major ones having some superficial psychological depth and internally generated personal goals, were the norm. All this, it could be argued, had become rather archaic in a world of mass culture, mass communication, mass industry and a rapidly transforming urban environment. Here was a stunning example of the 'superstructure' successfully retarding (not reflecting) some of the most dynamic developments in the 'base'. Recall that, for Marx, capitalism develops the forces of production while the established social relationships contain at least the potential for undermining or dismantling capitalism. Capital also produces its own 'gravedigger', according to Marx, namely, the working class, whose political development it must also retard.

The same argument can be made at the level of culture, hence the need to retard twentieth-century (mass) culture and keep it in nineteenth-century clothes. In this context, Modernism has the potential to furnish Marxism with a cultural repertoire that could press the forces of revolution and change forward. Modernism then may be understood as articulating the characteristics of the modern world which had produced mass culture, but which mass culture typically repressed with its conventional popular formats. Of course, this argument can easily end up reproducing a new elitism and separation between mass culture and Modernism, and this is exactly what did happen in some quarters. But the best political Modernism of this period and later sought to integrate the popular and the Modernist avant-garde into a new synthesis or cultural praxis that healed the split between high and low just as Marxism attempted to reunite theory or philosophy and practice.[16]

Modernism articulates the perpetual tendency towards change. Recall our earlier discussion of how *The Communist Manifesto* recognised and celebrated capital's own tendency to melt all that is solid and established (Section 1.4). Modernism is a search for the cultural forms that express that restlessness. Modernism also articulates twentieth-century capitalism's enriched sense of mobility. The train, the bus, the automobile, the ship and the plane, the new systems of transport dovetailed with the new systems of communication to produce a distinctively modern sense of movement and stimulation which the film camera and editing perfectly embody. It is perhaps no accident that the other very early Lumière Brothers film was that of a train arriving into a station.

Modernism also works hard to articulate an enlarged sense of the world extending in all directions beyond the singular individual or place. The sense of the world as interconnected on a global basis becomes increasingly strong and seeks aesthetic representation in this period. For Fredric Jameson, this is the special vocation of Modernism to try and articulate. In the age of imperialism, where the lines of economic and political power run off in an immense and tangled network beyond the lived experience of the individual, what is or can be normally perceived (seen, touched, etc.) and the structural conditions of life, no longer coincide.[17] I mentioned earlier D.W. Griffith's 1909 film, *A Corner in Wheat*.[18] It is unusual insofar as it uses parallel editing to give some cognitive apprehension (what Jameson would call 'cognitive mapping') of 'abstract' economic relationships, namely, the power of speculators to harm the lives of people they have never had any interpersonal contact with. If we recall that such interpersonal relationships constitutes the very stuff of more conventional dramatic storytelling, we can see how *A Corner in Wheat* uses modern mass cultural forms (editing) in a way that explores modern twentieth-century capitalism. Modernism takes that potential, latent within the new mass culture medium but rarely explicitly developed, and pushes it further, for example: using montage to go beyond 'normal' perception or conventionalised rules of perspective. Marxist art critic John Berger argued in his hugely popular book *Ways of Seeing*, that the camera, especially the movie camera, challenged the implicit assumption of perspective as developed by painters, that the world can be transparently unveiled from a single point of view. With editing, and especially montage editing, the world became more dynamic, pluralised, conflictual.[19]

Finally, Modernism is a culture that gives aesthetic expression to the *mass* basis of modern life, in contradistinction to the celebration of the individual (boosted by the star system) which mass culture paradoxically kept intact. The British documentary movement of the 1930s and the 1940s may be taken as an example of this Modernist interest in the masses and the need therefore to find new forms of storytelling, new forms for the new content of life. British documentary was certainly influenced by the Soviet montage tradition, which was itself strongly infused with a documentary ethos, even in its fictional genres. The relationship between cultural forms and politics is of course highly flexible. The British documentarists were on the left but were not communist revolutionaries. Instead their interest in montage was articulated to an emerging social democratic politics. Here is John Grierson, the producer who did so much to get British documentary an institutionalised space within the public sphere, writing about the need for aesthetic forms that are adequate to the modern mass world:

> You may think that the individual life is no longer capable of cross-sectioning reality. You may believe that its particular belly-aches are of no consequence in a world which complex and impersonal forces command, and conclude that the individual as a self-sufficient dramatic figure is outmoded ... you may feel that in individualism is a yahoo tradition largely responsible for our present anarchy ... In other words, you are liable to abandon the story form, and seek like the modern exponent of poetry and painting and prose, a matter and method more satisfactory to the mind and spirit of the time.[20]

Grierson's words are themselves suffused with the spirit of the times.

The 'anarchy' of individualism that he speaks of is the free market capitalism that had crashed in 1929, but the deeper social and economic forces at work within monopoly capitalism had, arguably, already eclipsed the self-sufficient individual and the traditional narrative (or story form) as methods capable of 'cross-sectioning reality'. Grierson explicitly links the documentary tradition to modern experiments in the other arts as inspiring new modes of perceptual apprehension and social knowledge production. It was the powers of editing in film that seemed uniquely able to train and extend such new modes of visual dissection or cross-sectioning (see Section 5.2) into Jameson's cognitive mapping.

## 2.4 Western Marxism

The period between the end of the First World War (1914–18) and the Second World War (1939–45) was characterised at one pole by the consolidation of capital around monopoly together with new industrial forms of organisation and structure, and at the other pole, economic and political crises that took such diverse forms as socialist revolution or attempted revolution, the rise of fascism in Germany, Italy and Spain, the collapse of free market capitalism and the first steps towards the formation of a social democratic politics mid-way between unregulated capitalism and socialist revolution (in the USA, Britain and France, for example). Film culture was profoundly shaped by this context. It is an example of dialectical thinking that two such contradictory trends as consolidation and crisis can be seen as two sides of the same process, intimately connected and simultaneously present. But ultimately, the dominant trend was towards political and economic consolidation as the revolutionary hopes unleashed by the October 1917 Revolution were contained.

It was always the understanding of Lenin and Trotsky that the revolution in Russia could only survive as a revolution, if it ignited revolutions in the core advanced heartlands of Western Europe. Russia was too backward economically, politically, culturally and too isolated, to sustain a genuinely democratic bottom-up workers republic on its own. For a moment it looked as if the 'gamble' that historical circumstances had forced the Bolsheviks to take, might pay off – it was certainly not an irresponsible adventure. The German revolution (1918–19), the Italian factory occupations (1919–20), the Hungarian Revolution (1919) in which Lukács participated as Minister of Culture, and later the Spanish Civil War (1936–39) constituted a window of opportunity to change the balance of forces on the European continent. But these heroic assertions of collective endeavour against the established structures, all failed in the end. Inside the Soviet Union, the excitement, the energy, the dynamicism and the democratic opening that the October Revolution represented – and which had provided such creative momentum to Soviet cinema – gradually contracted. The fundamental contradiction between a small Russian working class – itself diminished by the First World War and then a civil war following the revolution – surrounded by a much larger peasantry, remained. If the latter had had a free vote, then the Bolsheviks would not have stayed in power. This contradiction meant that the Bolsheviks could only stay in power by regressing behind the most advanced bourgeois capitalist regimes in the West which were, after long struggles, gradually conceding the democratic franchise to their populations. The absence of democratic governance in fairly short order led to the rise of Joseph Stalin in the late 1920s and the consolidation in the 1930s of a new form of dictatorial and murderous state power. In another example of the dialectical development of history, where unintended consequences react back negatively on the principal actors, Stalin eliminated much of the original cadre of Bolsheviks who had led the revolution (including Trotsky). Yet neither this nor the tragic no-win situation which historical circumstances had thrust the original Bolshevik project into, entirely exempts the Bolsheviks from their under-appreciation of the importance of democracy for socialism. This debate lies beyond the scope of this book, but two key consequences of Stalinism are relevant to us. First, the cultural freedom and experimentation of the 1920s were gradually eroded and the Soviet state imposed 'socialist realism' as the official aesthetics to be followed.[21]

Second, the Soviet version of 'Marxism' was to do immense reputational damage to Marxism, which its bourgeois opponents eagerly exploited in the propaganda war. Politically it fractured the revolutionary left between those who supported the Soviet Union and those who maintained various other versions and interpretations of Marxism (as well as alternative radical traditions, such as anarchism) and who wanted to act independently of the Stalinised Communist Parties that were set up in most countries of the world. When a workers' uprising in Hungary in 1956 against the Stalinised political leadership was put down with the help of Russian forces, Communist Parties in Western Europe lost many of their members, especially their intellectuals. Nevertheless, the decline of European Communism in the West was uneven and protracted. The Italian Communist Party (PCI), the largest Communist Party in Western Europe, had over two million members in the 1950s and was a magnet for left-wing intellectuals. Most of the great directors, screenwriters and other film-workers were in or moved in political and intellectual circles close to the PCI in the post-war period after 1945. The great directors of post-war Italian cinema such as Pontecorvo, Visconti, Pasolini, Rosi, Bertolucci, Petri and many more were, at one time or another, members of the PCI.

The rise of a dogmatic Stalinised Marxism in the Soviet Union produced a distinct and opposing branch of European Marxism called 'Western Marxism'. Western Marxism differentiated itself from the Soviet version by its interest in questions of culture, education, psychology and philosophy. While this focus can be seen as symptomatic of defeat and the withdrawal of Marxism from mass working-class politics into the academy,[22] it was also a deepening and extension of Marxism's understanding of the resilience of advanced capitalism and the complexities involved in developing new attitudes, behaviour, forms of interaction, perceptions and critical thinking necessary if one wanted to break with all the negative accumulated traditions of a society based on domination and develop a society based on what Marx called 'the free association of the producers'. The emphasis of Western Marxism on cultural questions may be taken to be not only a need to theorise its situation, locked as it was within a dominant capitalism, but also, and crucially, to offer a more *democratic and liberated* version of Marxism than the Soviet version which tended to equate dictatorial state ownership with socialism.

A symptomatic figure in the transition of Marxism from a revolutionary conjuncture to a long period of capitalist consolidation which had to be theorised, was the Italian Marxist, Antonio Gramsci (1881–1937). Gramsci was a leading figure on the left who helped set up a socialist newspaper called *L'Ordine Nuovo* (The New Order) in 1919 to intervene in the working-class struggles then developing in the Turin factories. In his articles for *L'Ordine Nuovo* Gramsci stressed the importance of education, learning, clarification, persuasion, organisation, workers' democracy and the importance of culture.

A leading figure in the foundation of the Italian Communist Party in 1921, Gramsci was elected to the Italian Parliament in 1924. But by then it was the forces of reaction not socialism that were dominant after the coming to power of the Fascist Prime Minister Benito Mussolini in 1922. Gramsci was arrested and imprisoned in 1926 by the fascist state as part of its destruction of all opposition. Until his death in 1937, Gramsci compiled from prison a series of notebooks on history, politics, culture, philosophy and Marxism that were to be hugely influential in the development of Western Marxism, especially from the 1960s onwards. Gramsci's trajectory, from someone deeply involved in Marxist and mass politics that was riding a crest of revolutionary radicalism and for whom questions of state power and how to achieve it were burning practical questions, to an isolated 'academic' writer focusing on more long-term gestations of cultural, political, philosophical and historical development, may be seen as typical of the development of Marxism in the West. In a famous passage which can be taken as a justification of the need to elaborate an analysis of all the institutions beyond the coercive state in an advanced capitalist society, he wrote:

> In the East [referring to the Russian Revolution], the State was everything, civil society was primordial and gelatinous; in the West, there was a proper relation between State and civil society, and when the State trembled a sturdy structure of civil society was at once revealed. The State was only an outer ditch, behind which there stood a powerful system of fortresses and earthworks.[23]

It was a turn towards the study of the institutions of civil society and their role as a 'sturdy structure' that could withstand moments of political and economic crises that characterised Western Marxism. Gramsci essentially reworked and reconceptualised the superstructure, exploring how its two key zones – the state and culture – interacted. Civil society here refers to such institutions as the mass media, the family, educational institutions, voluntary organisations, such as trade unions, business confederations, the church, membership of political parties, everything, through to the Girl Guides and Boy Scouts, that was outside the direct arm of the coercive state (the judiciary and the police, for example) and the political executive and legislative bodies that are tied to the state. It was civil society that developed the long-term attitudes, modes of behaviour, values, habits, perceptions and preferences that tended to frame solutions to a deep crisis from *within* capitalism, as Italian Fascism had and excluded solutions that would endanger capitalism. For example, if civil society cultivates a sense of national pride and identity under threat from external enemies, then that has always been fertile soil in which right-wing politics can grow and win popular support for state power.

The role of the mass media and mass culture was already attracting the attention of Marxist thinkers, such as Siegfried Kracauer, as early as the 1920s. Successful cultural commodities were, argued Kracauer, sociologically significant evidence that was in some way speaking to the social conditions that shaped everyday lives. Trying to re-orientate the cultured elite away from the study of high culture, Kracauer insisted that the most throw-away examples of mass culture, the most 'inconspicuous surface-level expressions' of a society, provide 'access to the fundamental substance of the state of things ... The fundamental substance of an epoch and its unheeded impulses illuminate each other reciprocally.'[24] This was virtually a foundational dialectical statement for the importance of studying all aspects of mass culture (the 'unheeded impulses') from films, bestsellers, cheap detective stories, urban spaces and so forth, as signs of the 'fundamental substance of an epoch'.

Since this was a 'society of the masses' that had been shaped and formed under the leadership of the industrial bourgeoisie and their cadres of scientific managers who had revolutionised both work processes and consumption patterns, mass culture and mass society were a deeply ambivalent and ambiguous phenomenon. Gramsci characterised such developments as a 'passive revolution', that is one which had been imposed from above on the majority who had been consigned a position of passivity through a mixture of coercion, material inducements (e.g. high wages) and cultural training. Passive revolution refers to the paradox of massive change *within* the social relations of capitalism: change without real change. Gramsci recognised that America's 'Fordism' (after the revolutions in industrial organisation pioneered by Henry Ford in the motor-car business) represented 'the biggest collective effort to date to create, with unprecedented speed, and with a consciousness of purpose unmatched in history, a new type of worker and of man'.[25]

The German Marxist thinkers associated with the Frankfurt School who had to flee Germany after the rise of Nazi fascism, landed up in 'Fordist America' and were fairly horrified by what they found. For them, the 'new type of worker' was one thoroughly integrated into the mass production system. They explored the implications for critical thinking when society became 'massified' through standardised production techniques, including in the film, media and entertainment industries. Writing in the mid-1940s, Adorno and Horkheimer, the Frankfurt School's leading figures, surveyed the scene:

> The relentless unity of the culture industry bears witness to the emergent unity of politics. Sharp distinctions like those between A and B films, or between short stories published in magazines in different price segments, do not so much reflect real differences as assist in the classification, organization, and identification of consumers. Something is provided for everyone so that no one can escape ... On the charts of research organizations, indistinguishable from those of political propaganda, consumers are divided up as statistical material into red, green, and blue areas according to income group.[26]

For Adorno and Horkheimer, standardised cultural forms fostered obedience, conformity and a fear of anything different or challenging. The appearance of choice (in the market or in politics) disguised the similarities beneath the apparent diversity. For them, the culture industry helped integrate the working class into a culture of consumerism, cultivating interests in fashions and trends, celebrities and private satisfactions and aspirations that de-politicised people. Their focus on culture makes them typical representatives of Western Marxism. Their focus on the power of culture to help reproduce the existing order makes them very much theorists of 'consolidation' rather than crises. This emphasis on the power of the cultural industries to shape the consciousness of its consumers in ways that reproduce capitalism is typical of one strand of Marxist thinking. It can hardly be dismissed as nonsense, but is it dialectical enough? Is the culture which the cultural industries control and shape as unified and controlled as Adorno and Horkheimer suppose? Can we in fact dismiss differences such as between the prestige big budget film production (the A picture) and the low-budget production (the B picture)? And today, new modes of industrial organisation have arguably produced a much more differentiated cultural scene than the one Adorno and Horkheimer confronted in the 1940s and the 1950s. Ironically, their concern for the elimination of difference leads them in turn to dismiss remaining and significant differences even within the system that existed in their contemporary moment. This includes differences in the historical development of the culture industries. Writing in a philosophical register, historical differences and nuances and a plurality of practices are often eliminated from their analysis. We have already seen that we can distinguish four phases in the development of film and its relationship to the working class in America. Early American cinema had a working-class profile to its screen representations. That was eclipsed in the early 1920s by the formation of Hollywood. The working-class profile in terms of on-screen representation made a come-back between 1929 and 1934 during the economic crisis. It was then put back in its box, as it were, with the institutionalisation of the Motion Picture Production Code by Hollywood. This suggests the need for a more historically sensitive mode of analysis – operating at a 'lower' level of abstraction – as well as one more attuned to the contradictions and opposing tendencies within any social and cultural phenomenon. Gramsci's work, as we shall see in Chapter 8, is helpful here.

## 2.5 Structuralist Marxism: Barthes

In the immediate post-Second World War period the prospects of historical change seemed to congeal as the Cold War drove people to align themselves either with the capitalist West or the self-proclaimed 'communism' of the Soviet Union and the Eastern European countries that had been added to its sphere of influence with victory over Nazi Germany. In America, the Cold War was fought out by a purge of any left-leaning intellectuals across the professions, such as teachers and more famously in Hollywood itself, where left-wing directors, stars, scriptwriters, and so on were prevented from gaining employment.

The post-war economic boom saw a huge explosion in consumer goods as Fordist production techniques were adopted throughout industry and as new technologies developed during the Second World War were applied to peace-time production. Advertising expanded to help sell the goods and fund the growing output of media, such as radio, television and print. Writing in the early 1960s, Baran and Sweezy noted that expenditure on advertising in America had climbed from $1.1 billion in 1929 to $15 billion or 4 per cent of national income. They linked this to the growth of monopoly capital which had largely eliminated price competition and replaced it with marketing campaigns designed to capture the consumer's attention and desires.[27] This is certainly also true of the dominant film industry which has little price competition to differentiate products, but instead begins to have escalating marketing budgets designed to crush public awareness of competitors' goods in the marketplace.

With women, who had participated in the war effort, being driven out of the factories and back into the home, the 1950s was a moment when conservative and conformist value systems were in the ascendant. The nuclear family surrounded by the products of a consumer goods industry promoting comfort, affluence and leisure was the keystone in an ideological system that included the nation and the corporation. Together with the political class and western democracy, these institutions, or so it seemed, had delivered an economic boom that buried memories of slump and crisis from the 1930s. And this vast cornucopia of plenty and peace was ring-fenced with a nuclear force protecting the West against the supposed threat of Soviet communism.

However, in the 1950s, forces were indeed stirring that would grow in the coming decade: the civil rights struggle against America's segregated racist structures in the South began in earnest and would later develop into an assertive Black Power politics that had significant cross-fertilisation with Marxism and anti-imperialist struggles outside America. Racism in the core western countries was intimately linked to western power-projection abroad in the form of the nineteenth-century colonies and twentieth-century forms of imperialism. Anti-colonial struggles against Europe's remaining empires in Africa and Asia and anti-imperialist struggles against North America's domination of Latin America, began to take on a more militant, organised and widespread form. The French were defeated in Indochina by the Vietnamese at the battle of Dien Ben Phu in 1954 while the Algerian War of Independence against French colonial rule began around the same time. The classic cinematic account of that latter struggle was made by the Italian communist Gillo Pontecorvo in *The Battle of Algiers* (1966). At the close of the decade, the 1959 Cuban revolution overthrew the American-backed dictator Fulgencio Batista and sent shockwaves throughout the continent. A source of pride for Latin Americans, it inspired them to revolt against North America's own distinct imperialist economic and political control of the southern continent. These anti-colonial and anti-imperialist struggles would stimulate hugely significant contributions to world film culture where the combination of material scarcity, cultural ambition, an advanced intelligentsia affronted by the irrationality of the continent's inequality and foreign subjugation and the presence of mass revolutionary politics, produced a second wave of political modernism in the 1960s and the 1970s to match the 1920s and the 1930s.

In theoretical terms, an early and hugely significant breakthrough critique was Roland Barthes' 1957 book, *Mythologies*, which successfully punctured the confident promotion of capitalist value systems in the 1950s' mass media and culture. Barthes' book was the first attempt to apply the principles of structuralism to the mass media and culture. The structuralist analysis of language was pioneered by Ferdinand de Saussure before the First World War. Like his sociological contemporaries, Max Weber and Emile Durkheim, Saussure's work can be seen as a response to and reflection of the increasingly 'rational' organisation of work and society as capitalism developed. By 'rational', I mean the process by which life is subjected to systematic planning, calculation, prediction and organisation, emphasising the power of 'structures' over people and agency. Lukács linked this to the penetration of capitalist principles into social and cultural life and named it reification.[28] There are elements of this reification in Saussure's theoretical model, not least the way it insulates language from history. As Raymond Williams argued, structuralism was an 'objectivist projection of the social into a formal system, now autonomous, and governed by its internal laws'.[29]

Saussure analysed language not as a reflection of reality but as a 'structure' that had its own internal operating principles which individual utterances or users of that system had to internalise if they were to produce meaning. This emphasis on meaning being generated *not* by a relationship between language and reality, but the relationship between units of meaning or signs among themselves, is the foundation for the 'linguistic turn' in theory that was to sweep across the humanities and the social sciences after the Second World War and down to the present moment.

This was a revolution in thought and one that swept up Marxism as much as all the other methodologies. In *Formalism and Marxism*, Tony Bennett summarises structuralism's main proposition about the language-reality relationship:

> Baldly summarized, Saussure's central perception was that language *signifies* reality by bestowing a particular, linguistically structured form of conceptual organization upon it ... The 'objects' of which language speaks are not 'real objects' external to language, but 'conceptual objects' located entirely within language. The word 'ox' according to Saussure's famous example, signifies not a real ox but the concept of an ox, and it is able to do so by virtue of the relationship of similarity and difference which define its position in relation to other signifiers comprising modern English. There is no intrinsic connection between the real ox and the word 'ox' by virtue of which the meaning of the latter is produced. The relationship ... is arbitrary: that is, it is a matter of convention.[30]

This is a summary and not an endorsement of structuralism's principles. Bennett goes on to critique the static qualities of structuralism that are built into its anti-historical and anti-social conceptual architecture.[31] There is one strand of structuralism that cultural theory has become deeply invested in ever since: its endorsement of relativism. If language constructs its own meanings 'internally', then there is no way of adjudicating between different signifying systems by reference to their explanatory power vis-à-vis real phenomena independent of language or representational systems. This relativism fed into a powerful critique of film realism (see Section 3.2 and Chapter 7). Of course, specific realist practices or styles and their critical discourses must be open to challenge, but the critique of film realism was dangerously conflated with a critique of realism as a philosophical proposition (that we can evaluate representations for their greater or lesser explanatory power vis-à-vis reality).

From Bennett's outline of structuralism above, we can identify three major fallacies of structuralism:

Fallacy 1: that language is the active structuring power that signifies (makes meaning) while 'reality' is passive putty to be shaped into whatever linguistically structured organisation language desires.

Fallacy 2: that the intelligibility of 'conceptual objects', such as 'ox', has no relation to real oxen but conceptual objects acquire their meaning solely through the differentiation of the concept (here 'ox') from similar signifiers such as 'buffalo', 'horse', 'mule', 'cow', etc.

Fallacy 3: that the relationship between signs and the 'objects' they are applied to is arbitrary and that the term 'arbitrary' is equivalent to the term 'convention'.

A Marxist theory of language would respond to these fallacies with the following principles, as an absolute minimum:

Principle 1: Language is not to be conceived as dualistically separated from 'reality'; signs on one side and the isolated discrete 'things' which signs refer to on the other. Instead signs are woven into the *social production of life*. Social reality is not made up of discrete objects accorded meaning by a sign system.

Principle 2: The intelligibility of conceptual objects such as 'ox' (i.e. their ability to mean something) depends on such social practices as farming and the specific role different animals have within farming practices (ox are typically castrated cattle, so they are more docile and amenable to the harness and pulling the plough).

Principle 3: The word 'ox' is not arbitrary; the distinctions between ox and other animals derive from our social interaction and use of animals (which motivates classification). Conventions of any kind are not arbitrary, they make sense and become meaningful for communities that use those conventions in their social practices. They may not be universal, they may be questionable, they may repress or marginalise alternative ways of making sense for subjugated groups within a given community, but to say that they are *arbitrary* is to deny the *social basis* of their emergence, use and intelligibility.

Despite these conflicts between structuralism and Marxism, there were plenty of possible affinities and cross-fertilisations. Structuralism offered a systematic theory of language and culture and there was good reason to find this appealing as it at least broke with the bourgeois idealist edifice of individualism, impressionism, empiricism and psychologism when it came to trying to explain meaning. It also provided tools that undercut the cultural advantages of the middle class when it came to literary or aesthetic analysis. Typically, individualistic appeals to 'respond' to the literary text in the classroom surreptitiously smuggled in the advantages of a good middle-class family background into educational practice. What structuralism provided was a conceptual toolbox that could be learnt by anyone and did not require a long middle-class training in arts and culture 'appreciation'. If I may speak biographically for a moment, coming from a lower-middle-class background with fairly low quality 'cultural capital', as Bourdieu would say, my own intellectual development was considerably enhanced once I escaped such bourgeois modes of literary response and had access to theories such as structuralism at university.

Additionally, Saussure's distinction between the individual utterance (*parole*) and the deep structure rules that govern meaning (*langue*) could be mapped onto a Marxist distinction between the surface-level expressions of the life of a society and the deep structure *unconscious* forces that govern those expressions. Although here '*langue*' referred not to a socio-economic base but the deep structure cultural underpinning to cultural expression itself (*parole*). To put it another way, structuralism provided a model of the signifying 'infrastructure' *within* the superstructure, the system of sign rules that govern expression and meaning.[32]

It is doubtful whether Barthes would have called himself a Marxist, even in relation to *Mythologies*, which is his most Marxist-orientated work. However, his critique is very much in the Marxist tradition as he uncovers the way that the signs of mass culture constantly de-contextualise, de-historicise and falsely universalise capitalist practices and value systems. This is the bourgeois 'unconscious' or deep structure which he critiques. The first half of the book is a series of short comments on an eclectic range of mass cultural phenomena, including photographs, films, newspaper and magazine articles, advertising, exhibitions, literature and traditional cultural anthropological topics, such as food or toys.

The anthropologist Lévi-Strauss had shown how a structuralist analysis could be applied to the cultural systems of primitive societies. Barthes developed this into an analysis of modern mass culture. For example, he shows how in Joseph Mankiewicz's film *Julius Caesar* (1953), the fringe, which the film's stylists have given to all the actors, is itself a *sign* that *connotes* 'Romanness'. Connotation is the key Barthesian concept as it invites us to consider the dense web of meanings that cluster around even the simplest of signs. With the fringe we have once again the inconspicuous and the small unearthed (as Kracauer urged us to do) as a substantive unit of meaning. An additional connotative meaning or in structuralist terms 'signified' attached to the signifier 'fringe' is that it emphasises the forehead and helps direct our attention to the fact that this is a story about ideas and ideals. The sign 'fringe' also works in combination with another sign: the beads of sweat on the brow of the actors signify the great weighty moral dilemmas they are wrestling with. In another context sweat might be a signifier for a whole range of different signifieds such as heat, fever, physical exertion, fear, and so forth. But here 'sweat' combined with the 'fringe' produces the connoted signifieds around ideals and moral dilemmas. Meaning is produced by the *relationship* between signs.

Barthes mischievously suggests that there is a comical contradiction (for the European spectator at least) between the frontal lock's Southern European 'Roman' reference point and the American character actors who populate the film but whose faces seem vaguely familiar from countless gangster and cowboy films.[33] Around this time Hollywood's European competitors were pioneering strategies of representation in opposition to Hollywood. So after the Second World War, Italian cinema typically moved out of the studio setting, using real exterior locations, buildings and landscapes, natural lighting, little or no make-up and non-professional actors with a range of interesting physiognomies, drawn from the rich diversity of everyday life. Italian neo-realism of the late 1940s and the early 1950s was hugely influential in world cinema for developing a low budget model of filmmaking that could challenge Hollywood's dominance. The standardised 'Roman fringe' is utterly foreign to a film like Pasolini's *The Gospel According to St Matthew* (1964), which may be seen as a European riposte to Hollywood's biblical epics of the 1950s (and the Italian home-grown 'sword and sandal' imitations) in that it looks as if it could be set in contemporary times, if not for the absence of modern technology. This realism represents Christ as seen from a specific viewpoint (Italy, Europe, the left in the 1960s), Christ as a political warrior for the poor (hence the black gospel soundtrack) and therefore Christ as a sign whose meaning is in open dialogical contest with the dominant Catholic institutional understanding of Christ and Hollywood's own versions of the same icon.

Barthes' critique of mass culture signs spoke of a conjoining of structuralism with an analysis of ideology that was quite foreign to Saussure. Barthes' theory of signs is developed more explicitly in the second half of the book where, in a single chapter, Barthes elaborates on the theoretical underpinning to his work. Here myth – a term he used as virtually synonymous with the Marxist concept of ideology – is defined as a sign system that is suffused with the unquestioned, taken-for-granted web of associations, connotations or assumptions that dominate the mass cultural sphere that had so prodigiously expanded in the 1950s. In his later and famous analysis of an advert for the Italian food company, Panzani, Barthes showed how capitalist advertising appropriated the connotations of 'nature' and 'the natural' or 'more natural' to what was a highly advanced, mass-produced set of commodities.[34] As we have already discussed (Section 1.6) naturalising what may be open to significant dispute can be regarded as a form of ideology. It is the stilling of the critical spirit and the feel of historical contestation, the invitation to wallow blissfully in the 'immense accumulation of commodities' (Marx) that the world of mass culture lays out before us, that affronts Barthes. As he puts it in *Mythologies*:

> In passing from history to nature, myth acts economically: it abolishes the complexity of human acts, it gives them the simplicity of essences, it does away with all dialectics, with any going back beyond what is immediately visible, it organizes a world which is without contradictions because it is without depth, a world wide open and wallowing in the evident, it establishes a blissful clarity: things appear to mean something by themselves.[35]

To some extent, Barthes' critique is essentially a caveat against the dangers of conventionality, habituated thinking, easy stereotypical classifications or the surreptitious steering into certain ideological waters (those connotations again) encouraged by the mass media. The notion of unconscious internalisation of value systems is already implied by the distinction between *langue* (the system that converts the social into nature, for example) and *parole* (the utterance) and in the concept of connotations (the web of dubious associations) and would be developed further in relation to the concept of ideology.[36]

## 2.6 Structuralist Marxism: Althusser

Louis Althusser's influence on film theory and cultural studies was even more significant than Barthes and his work was more explicitly conceived within the Marxist tradition, unsurprisingly, since Althusser was a member of the French Communist Party. Althusser's work bears the traces of the influence of structuralism in a number of respects. Althusser sees language, especially theory, as having a material power and force in its own right. For in stressing the power of language to shape our understanding of reality, structuralism made language efficacious in the world. In cultural theory, the focus on systems of representation was often conceived of as a 'materialist' theory of language, in the same way that Marxism was a 'materialist' theory of society and history. Althusser did, however, improve a little on the structuralist focus on language to the exclusion of the social, by insisting that language and ideology were always inscribed into institutional power complexes or *apparatuses*. Structuralism is also evident in Althusser's appreciation of systematic theorising and in his emphasis on systems over agency. Just as structuralism focused on the importance of *'langue'* (the language system) to explain *parole* (utterance), Althusser stressed system over agency (especially individual agency). Marxism, however, may best be thought of not as a 'system theory', which tends to envisage a seamless integrated order reproducing itself, but as a theory of contradictory social practices. Above all, Althusser imported the implicit relativism and ahistorical universalism of structuralism into his philosophical outlook. I will briefly review some of the contradictions in his key essay 'Ideology and Ideological State Apparatuses' to close this chapter, bringing us to the cusp of the birth of modern film studies in the academy.

Althusser's essay 'Ideology and Ideological State Apparatuses' was finished in 1969, a year after momentous events in France in May 1968, when a ten million-strong General Strike shook the state. And yet, the crisis passed and the French capitalist state survived. Althusser's essay was an attempt to try and explain that outcome by focusing on the role ideology plays in the *reproduction* of the capitalist order. Ideological power is not the only means by which capitalist societies reproduce themselves. The 'soft power' of ideology is combined in the state with 'hard power'. Althusser distinguished between a Repressive State Apparatus (RSA) and an Ideological State Apparatus (ISA). Together they work to reproduce the capitalist social order. The RSAs includes the law, the police, the courts, the prisons, 'but also the army ... when the police ... are "outrun by events"'.[37] The RSAs function by direct physical coercion and ultimately the threat or actual use of violence. The ISAs, by contrast, include the churches, the education system (including the private schools), the family, the parliamentary political sphere, and the communications and cultural institutions.[38] They help reproduce the social order at the level of ideas, beliefs, values and the voluntary or consensual identification that people have with the social order and its key institutions.

While the RSAs form an integrated public power, the ISAs are far less visibly integrated together and typically operate in the private domain of personal life activity. But Althusser insists that we can call them *state* apparatuses because, in the final instance, the state is their condition of existence. This may be truer in some instances, such as the state church or education system, but even here, this may in fact negate his interesting observation that the RSAs are integrated into the power of the state while the ISAs typically have a looser and more arm's-length relationship to the state and each other. Althusser's essay is rather torn between two impulses as the question of the ISAs and their relationship to the state suggests. On the one hand, he veers towards a 'structuralist' emphasis on functional systems when he argues that it is the unity of the ideology of the ruling class that gives the ISAs their integrated quality. Yet he immediately seems to qualify this by arguing that the ISAs are a *site* of class struggle and the *stake* to be won in that struggle because there is greater scope to achieve positions of influence within them as a result of working-class struggles. The RSAs, precisely because they work through force under the direct control of the state, are less amenable to accommodating opposing values.[39] To put it bluntly, you will not find many leftists in the army, the police or the judiciary, but education and the media, for example, are considerably more open.

This duality in Althusser's theory of ideology is evident in the fact that he is primarily interested in discussing ideology *in general*, that is the general structure and form which all specific *ideologies* are said to have. Yet it is with specific ideologies in specific social and historical circumstances that we may find ideology as the site and stake of class struggle. Althusser's theory of ideology in general is conducted at such a level of abstraction that it tends to assume, in a structuralist and functionalist manner, a seamless system of ideological effects successfully achieved. For Althusser, ideology in general is also trans-historical and he makes this the linchpin of his analysis, which is quite different from Marx, whose intellectual energies went into developing categories that could specifically analyse capitalism. Moreover, important features that he ascribes to ideology in general and across time, seem very particular to capitalism, a confusion which threatens to universalise rather than relativise capitalism.

Althusser defines ideology as an imaginary relation to the real. The emphasis that Althusser puts on ideology as the imaginary relations to the real relations of production[40] tends to bracket off the question of how the real relations of production in turn impinge on ideology. In typically structuralist fashion, the shaping and influencing relationship is all one way, from the linguistic construction of the real *over* the real but little in the way of a dialectical shaping of language and representation by real social relations. How, for example, might social being qualify specific ideologies? How might political and economic circumstances fracture the power of ideologies? The power Althusser accords to the imaginary relations of ideology is not much corrected by his insistence that ideology is grounded in the practices and rituals of 'apparatuses' (a term that is less useful than 'institutions', I think, because it has a strong functionalist ring to it). This is because the theory of ideology is developed at a level of abstraction which is hard to then bring down into institutions and practices in the specific without major modification (and indeed rejection) of key aspects of Althusser's theory of ideology in general. While grounded, material and efficacious, the term 'imaginary' does indicate for Althusser some inadequacy, some sense that ideology is lacking, some sense that it can be distinguished from knowledge or science. For Althusser, ideology is lacking when measured against theoretical science because of the kind of identity and mode of identification it encourages – terms which may immediately hint at a transposition to film analysis where identities and identification are strongly in play but which then make film synonymous with ideology.

At the heart of ideology is the construction of the *subject* which, according to Althusser, is 'the constitutive category of all ideology, whatever its determination (regional or class) and whatever its historical date – since ideology has no history'.[41] The subject is that imaginary sense of self formed in a relationship of identification with the practices and figures of authority associated with various state institutions. We can draw together a number of characteristics, which this sense of self has, that Althusser believes are a feature of ideology in general (that is present in all particular ideologies). The subject's sense of self and their relation to the world in ideology is built on 'obviousness'. This is the unquestioning acceptance of the way things are, unquestioning acceptance that things as defined (in language) are the same as things as they must be, the sense of 'that's true!', without question, 'of course!' When things are obvious, then the 'recognition effect' of ideology is at work. To recognise this is how something is done, this is how we *must* behave, this is what this or that is for, is to stop asking questions and to accept the practices and rituals which govern our actions and beliefs. Recognition is ideological because it does not 'give us the (scientific) *knowledge* of the mechanism of this recognition'.[42] Again, as with the term 'imaginary', this recognition effect, with its strongly visual emphasis, could be transposed to film analysis. For example, self-reflexivity would become a key way of exploring 'the mechanism of … recognition' by which 'obvious' habituated conventions are called into question (see Section 5.4). Althusser's stress on the 'imaginary relation' to the real allowed him to stress the mode of address of ideology, the form which the communicative act takes. He had a particular term for this mode of address. Ideology he argues 'interpellates' subjects, that is 'hails' them, calls to them and, in answering that call, they become 'subjects' in and of ideology.[43] One of Althusser's examples of this ideological hailing is when your name is called, not even in an institutional context, such as at school, but even out in the street, and you recognise yourself in the call and turn around. In that process of self-recognition, you recognise tacitly the power of the caller to name you.[44] The example is instructive not only because of its anecdotal and abstract quality (does it make a difference if your name is called by a friend or the police, for example?) but because it indicates that, for Althusser, ideology is virtually equivalent to *making sense* of our everyday lives. For Althusser, this is a questionable affirmation of our sense of self and our quiet and unconscious support for the structures and modes of address that speak to us. The 'subject' feels that they are a 'free subjectivity, a centre of initiatives, author of and responsible for its actions'. This is an example of a characteristic of 'ideology in general' that seems to be quite specific to the capitalist mode of production (i.e. the free individual) rather than, say, something that would have made much sense to a medieval peasant. Be that as it may, within a capitalist context, Althusser's playing on the ambivalence of the term 'subject' is very effective. Althusser argues that the 'free subject', that autonomous freely choosing agent, author of their own actions, etc., is in fact *subjected* to a higher authority, the '*commandments of the Subject*', the teacher, the father, the boss, the leader, the nation, and so on with whom the subject (with a small 's') identifies as confirming their own sense of self when they are called or interpellated by some mode of address (including of course through the institutions of the media).[45] This contradiction in the ideology of capitalism was remarked upon by Marx and developed by Lukács: 'the bourgeoisie endowed the individual with an unprecedented importance, but at the same time that same individuality was annihilated by the economic contradictions to which it was subjected, by the reification created by commodity production'.[46] In calling everything into question, including all forms of language and the ways we make sense of the world, Althusser was certainly licensing a highly critical and questioning attitude. Marx himself called for the ruthless criticism of the existing order. In the library copy of Althusser's *Lenin and Philosophy and Other Essays* that I am reading, someone, a student probably, has scribbled in pencil on the page 'love as an ideology?' That is something that we are not encouraged to think about. Indeed, *romantic* love may well be thought of as an ideology, one that is especially powerful in setting expectations and behaviour for women and men in a universe of commodities. But is love in all forms and on all occasions, an ideology? Here we see the relativism that creeps in when the basis of critical thought becomes a question of intelligibility and meaning itself, *not* the contexts and social interests underpinning our ability to recognise something. In another chapter, 'Marxism and Humanism', it is even clearer that by ideology Althusser essentially means *culture*. Here he writes: 'Ideology (as a system of mass representations) is indispensable in any society if men are to be formed, transformed and equipped to respond to the demands of their conditions of existence.'[47]

Culture is precisely the means by which we make what we do intelligible to ourselves, often in highly expressive ways (see Section 8.1). But if culture is essentially ideology, then, at a stroke, all culture is equally inadequate or suspect because in its equipping of men and women to their conditions of existence it intrinsically offers an 'imaginary' relation to those conditions. In those imaginary relations, our identities are formed in unquestioning identification with the master Subjects of the ideological 'apparatuses'. By stretching the concept of ideology so widely, what it gains in encouraging a widespread scepticism about everything, it loses in terms of making evaluative judgements as to whether *anything* is better or worse than anything else. Relativism reigns.

Applied to film, one would view the entire apparatus of production and the rituals of reception (going to the cinema) and the commodity-film that is produced and consumed, as ideological. Indeed, a critique of film inspired by Althusser's critique of ideology inscribed into apparatuses, including technological apparatuses, such as the camera and the projector, and the ritual of watching films in a darkened auditorium, was founded on this basis.[48] For Althusser, only a highly theoretical 'science' that rigorously excluded any sense of 'the subject' in favour of structures, could count as non-ideological. But this notion of critical social science was so thoroughly opposed to the culture of everyday life that its elitism made it irreconcilable with Marxism. Likewise, in the field of cultural practice, only aggressively avant-garde practices that disrupted the conventions of films, of viewing or of production, would count as outside the rituals and practices of the ISAs. But even then, as soon as any intervention began to solidify into a recognisable practice, it would, logically become ideological and have to be rejected, and so on, ad infinitum into ever diminishing circles. As with the critical non-ideological science, such cultural practices are founded on highly specialised types of cultural capital whose exchange value rests on its scarcity, which is hardly a good basis for a viable Marxist cultural politics grounded in the majority (see Section 5.1 for more on this).

With Althusser's theory of ideology and apparatuses, we are now getting deep into detailed methodological questions of the kind that modern film studies emerged asking, even if its answers were not always satisfactory. It is the question of Marxism as a methodology and its relationship to the methodologies of other disciplines and how all that shaped film studies, that we turn to in Chapter 3.

## Notes

1  Jeanne Thomas Allen, 'The Decay of the Motion Picture Patents Company', in Tino Balio (ed.), *The American Film Industry* (Madison, WI: University of Wisconsin Press, 1976), p. 126.

2  Steve Ross, *Working Class Hollywood: Silent Film and the Shaping of Class in America* (Princeton, NJ: Princeton University Press, 1998), p. 19. A survey of Manhattan cinemagoers in 1910 found that 72 per cent came from 'blue-collar' backgrounds and 25 per cent from the clerical workforce.

3  Walter Prichard Eaton, 'Class Consciousness and the "Movies"', *The Atlantic*. Available at: www.theatlantic.com/magazine/archive/1915/01/class-consciousness-and-the-movies/306080/

4  Ross, *Working Class Hollywood*, op. cit., p. 74.

5  See M. Keith Booker, *Film and The American Left: A Research Guide* (Westport, CT: Greenwood Press, 1999), pp. 1–22.

6  Kay Sloan, 'A Cinema in Search of Itself: Ideology of the Social Problem Film During the Progressive Era', *Cinéaste*, 14(2) (1985): 34.

7  Ibid.

8  George Mitchell, 'The Consolidation of the American Film Industry 1915–1920, Part One', *Cine-Tracts*, 2(2) (1979): 35.

9  George Mitchell, 'The Consolidation of the American Film Industry 1915–1920, Part Two', *Cine-Tracts*, 2(3&4) (1979): 67.

10  Thomas Doherty, *Pre-Code Hollywood: Sex, Immorality, and Insurrection in American Cinema* (New York: Columbia University Press, 1999), p. 2.

11  V.I. Lenin, *Imperialism: The Highest Stage of Capitalism* (London: Lawrence and Wishart, 1948), p. 77.

12  Georg Lukács, *History and Class Consciousness: Studies in Marxist Dialectics*, trans. Rodney Livingstone (London: Merlin Press, 1971), p. 149.

13  Sheila James, 'Educational Media and "Agit Prop": The Legacy of Vertov', *Journal of Educational Media*, 22(2) (1996): 111–23.

14 Gal Kirn, 'Between Socialist Modernization and Cinematic Modernism. The Revolutionary Politics of Aesthetics of Medvedkin's Cinema-Train', in Ewa Mazierska and Lars Kristensen (eds), *Marxism and Film Activism: Screening Alternative Worlds* (Oxford: Berghahn, 2015).

15 See the excellent book by Eugene Lunn, *Marxism and Modernism: An Historical Study of Lukács, Brecht, Benjamin and Adorno* (Berkeley, CA: University of California Press, 1982), p. 34.

16 Excellent recent Marxist scholarship in this area has been done by cultural theorists such as Esther Leslie's *Hollywood Flatlands: Animation, Critical Theory and the Avant-Garde* (London: Verso, 2002) and Owen Hatherly, *The Chaplin Machine: Slapstick, Fordism and the Communist Avant-Garde* (London: Pluto Press, 2016).

17 Fredric Jameson, 'Cognitive Mapping', in *Marxism and the Interpretation of Culture* (Urbana, IL: University of Illinois Press, 1988), p. 349.

18 Available at: www.youtube.com/watch?v=WHLfjB7dSyc

19 John Berger, *Ways of Seeing* (Harmondsworth: Penguin, 2008), pp. 9–11.

20 John Grierson, *Grierson on Grierson* (Glasgow: Collins, 1946), p. 82.

21 Socialist realism looked remarkably similar in terms of its form to Hollywood filmmaking – it just had a different content – uncomplicated heroic workers instead of uncomplicated American individualists.

22 Perry Anderson, *Considerations of Western Marxism* (London: New Left Books, 1976).

23 Antonio Gramsci, *Selections from the Prison Notebooks*, (eds) Quintin Hoare and Geoffrey Nowell-Smith (London: Lawrence and Wishart, 2005), p. 238.

24 Siegfried Kracaeur, *The Mass Ornament* (Cambridge, MA: Harvard University Press, 1995), p. 75.

25 Gramsci, *Selections from the Prison Notebooks*, op. cit., p. 302.

26 Max Horkheimer and Theodor Adorno, *Dialectic of Enlightenment* (Stanford, CA: Stanford University Press, 2002), pp. 96–7.

27 Paul Baran and Paul Sweezy, 'Theses on Advertising', *Science and Society* 28(1) (1964): 20–30.

28 Lukács, *History and Class Consciousness*, op. cit.

29 Raymond Williams, *Marxism and Literature* (Oxford: Oxford University Press, 1988), p. 36.

30 Tony Bennett, *Formalism and Marxism* (London: Routledge, 2003), p. 5.

31 Ibid., pp. 57–61.

32 See Fredric Jameson's *The Prison House of Language: A Critical Account of Structuralism and Russian Formalism* (Princeton, NJ: Princeton University Press, 1972), for a discussion of the relationship between Marxism and structuralism.

33 Roland Barthes, *Mythologies* (London: Paladin, 1973), pp. 27–8.

34 Roland Barthes, 'Rhetoric of the Image', in *Image, Music, Text* (Glasgow: Fontana, 1977).

35 Barthes, *Mythologies*, op. cit., p. 156.

36 See Stuart Hall, 'The Rediscovery of "Ideology": Return of the Repressed in Media Studies', in John Storey (ed.), *Cultural Theory and Popular Culture: A Reader*, 5th edn (London: Routledge, 2018), pp. 111–41.

37 Louis Althusser, 'Ideology and Ideological State Apparatuses', in *Lenin and Philosophy and Other Essays* (London: Monthly Review Press, 1971), p. 137.

38 Ibid., p. 143.

39 Ibid., p. 147.

40 Ibid., p. 165.

41 Ibid., p. 171.

42 Ibid., p. 173.

43 Ibid.

44 Ibid., pp. 174–5.

45 Ibid., p. 182.

46 Lukács, *History and Class Consciousness*, op. cit., p. 62.

47 Louis Althusser, 'Marxism and Humanism', in *For Marx* (London: Verso, 1977), p. 235.

48 The work of Jean-Louis Baudry and Jean-Luc Comolli was influential in developing what became known as 'apparatus theory'.

# 3

# METHODOLOGIES

## 3.1 Marxism in the academy

At the same time that modern film studies really started to establish itself on university curricula in the 1960s, Marxism also came into the academy in a renewed and powerful way, in part, through new subjects such as film studies and cultural studies, or new branches of disciplines where Marxism had already established itself (political economy leads to a political economy of the media) but also quite widely across the humanities (e.g. literature and history) and the social sciences (e.g. sociology). One significant push factor in Marxism's entry into the academy was of course the wider historical context in which anti-colonial and anti-imperial struggles in Latin America, Africa and Asia (especially Vietnam but also Maoist China) combined with rising expectations in the West clashing with the first significant signs of the post-war economic boom coming to an end, producing an explosive political configuration.[1] These developments also intersected with the rise of a variety of other political constituencies based on race, gender and sexuality, whose relationships with class-based political struggles were often fraught, for both good reasons (e.g. socialist blind spots concerning the importance of combating these forms of discrimination needed self-examination) and bad reasons (e.g. the middle-class leadership of these other constituencies were often more concerned to carve out a place within capitalism than change it more fundamentally). These tensions have certainly impacted on how race, sexism and sexuality related, or did not relate, to Marxism as they fought their way onto the agenda of cultural theory.

That Marxism could enter the academy in a substantial way indicates that, like most cultural-ideological institutions, education, especially higher education where academics have historically had more professional autonomy than secondary and primary education teachers, was both the site and the stake of struggle, as Louis Althusser famously put it.[2] At the same time, Marx's base-superstructure model would alert us to the fact that Marxism's entry into academia would be difficult and problematic. If educational institutions in this period, along with media institutions, were sites of struggle (and they were), it was always an uneven one, marked by the historic and embedded structural features of advanced capitalism.

The deep divisions between intellectual and manual labour meant that intellectual activity and therefore intellectuals remained very largely cut off from working-class organisations and therefore routine encounters with working-class people. While there are academics from working-class backgrounds in academia, both then and now, they do not exist in the numbers required to give them a critical mass within higher education institutions[3] and they are under powerful pressures to assimilate and deny their working-class origins and identity when they do get in.[4] Academia is dominated by the middle class and the further one goes up the management hierarchy, the less heterogeneous are the social origins of the people occupying powerful positions.[5] Similarly, the more 'prestigious' the institutions of higher education, the more they are likely to be dominated throughout their academic ranks by upper middle-class demographics self-insulating themselves from some of the problems people are confronting beyond their milieu. For working-class students, especially in the elite universities, the environment is typically deeply alien.

This division between the intellectuals and the working classes exerts powerful deformations on intellectual practice, including avowedly Marxist intellectual practice. It is the basis, for example, of powerful social pressures towards a kind of disavowal or repression of the material base of life, or idealism (the discussion, for example, of the law, philosophy, the state, 'consciousness', culture, etc., as if they were 'innocent' of any entanglement with class relations). This makes the methodological issue of *determination* (what kind of efficacy and interrelationships do different forces have on each other and at what 'levels' of the social formation?) highly political, because *grounding* practices in conditions of unequal power raises uncomfortable questions for the dominant order.

The key question posed by Marx's methodology is how to account for the different forces in play that produce outcomes (such as films), how to weigh those forces and understand their interaction. With his synthesis of the main intellectual currents of the nineteenth century, Marx mapped out how economic and class interests, politics and philosophical questions and norms shape our lives. With some adaption we can see how this tripartite synthesis is still relevant for the study of film and the main methodologies we need to do this. We may note immediately that as the earliest discussions around it were aware, film is both an art form and an industry. As an art form it can promote a kind of thinking about life that is 'philosophical', as the new burgeoning field of film as philosophy has been suggesting, although I will reframe 'philosophy' here in more Gramscian terms. Ideally, one would want to be able to think film at both the level of the formal properties it has for creative expression and philosophical rumination *and* understand that it is a branch – albeit of a special kind – of manufacturing industry, subject to many similar economic, social and organisational features of industry in general (but also, as we shall see, with its own dynamics). Thinking these two rather distinct moments or realities of film simultaneously also requires us to consider the relationship between these two dimensions. Between the question of form and the question of industry, there is also the question of film as a remarkably sensitive Geiger counter detecting and responding to the broader milieu in which social, cultural and political relations, trends and changes are occurring. To weigh and interrelate these different levels of analysis requires trying to forge a critical synthesis out of formal analysis, political economy and the discipline that has pioneered the analysis of cultural politics, i.e. cultural studies. This is our methodological task and I believe that Marxism is one of the few intellectual resources available that has the interest and capacity to achieve this synthesis.

## 3.2 Questions of form

Right from the beginning of its emergence as a new cultural form, debates around film turned on the question of how its formal features could qualify it as an *art* form. In interrogating this legitimate question, early theorists and filmmakers were exploring the expressive possibilities of the medium, what the eighteenth-century German philosopher Kant termed in relation to art as the 'play of forms'. As *play*, art depends on a certain freedom from strict need. As the complexity of cultural forms develops, so the play of forms becomes more complex, their potentialities deepen; the photographic image that preserves and scrutinises becomes a moving image, the silent film becomes the sound film, the storytelling becomes more layered, longer and qualitatively richer, colour film adds more variables in the play of form as does the development of different lenses, and so on. Film synthesises dramaturgy from the performing arts, composition from the visual arts, storytelling structures from literature, audio possibilities from the sound recording media, as well as new temporal and spatial possibilities which editing facilitated. The expressive possibilities of the medium become broadly 'educative', they develop our cognitive and emotional range. 'The eye', writes Marx, 'has become a *human* eye when its *object* has become a *human*, social object, created by man and destined for him.'[6] The production of any objects with use value requires and in turn cultivates the humanisation of the human eye, but the visual arts expand this educative function more because the 'play of forms' has greater latitude *as play* to explore, to imagine, to experiment. For Kant, 'taste' begins when we acquire some distance from material necessity and, similarly, for Marx, culture develops as nature is humanised.[7]

Art is the transformation of historical experience into formal creative expression. This is a difficult concept to grasp, much more so than the idea that historical experiences constitutes the raw materials for the *content* of art. It is easy enough to see how slavery and racism constitute the historical raw material for films such as *Django* (2012) or *The Help* (2011). It is easy enough to see how the historical experience of consumerism and capitalism forms the raw material for films as diverse as Michael Moore's *Capitalism, A Love Story* (2009) to John Carpenter's *They Live* (1988).[8] It is harder to think of form itself as a special kind of codification of historical experiences. However, we have already referenced such things in

Chapter 2 where we discussed Modernism as a cluster of formal innovations that were responses to social, political and technological developments in the early decades of the twentieth century (Section 2.4). The British documentary film movement of the 1930s was informed by a version of Modernism that involved using montage, voice-over and an expositional logic to depict the working masses as part of an industrial landscape. But the film *Housing Problems* (1935) introduced an interesting formal innovation to this particular codification of historical experience. Using the still new capacity of sound recording technology, they interviewed men and women in their homes *talking* about the rat-infested slum conditions they lived in. Significantly, this direct-to-camera address was a formal innovation driven by John Grierson's sister, Ruby. She was critical of his way of looking at people as though they were the specimens for a natural scientist gaze, specimens whose voices were rarely heard. Here within the 'feminine' space of the home instead of the workplace, a more intimate, personal mode of engagement and address was developed in which the subjects could speak back and perhaps could feel free to speak back outside the constraints of the workplace and the eye of the employer. 'The camera is yours. The microphone is yours', Ruby Grierson was reported to have told the slum tenants. 'Now tell the bastards exactly what it's like to live in slums.'[9] Thus Ruby Grierson's (uncredited) contribution to *Housing Problems* is arguably an example of a gender and socialist politics modifying a certain middle-class distanced gaze at the 'heroic' working-class body and its industrial environment, thanks in part to new technology (the sound film). It reminds us that any given form is only one possible crystallisation of historical experiences and that social being is always multi-dimensional and not only class-determined.

It is this dialectical tension between form and historical experience which has been repeatedly lost by theories of art. Typically, the more we have penetrated into the *internal* dynamics of form and more broadly the dynamics of cultural meaning, the more the threads connecting artistic form to historical experience have become attenuated or denied altogether. The whole question of *form* is both necessary and indispensable if we are to understand film's social-aesthetic dynamic, but it is also potentially treacherous waters in which it is easy to sink into *formalism* where aesthetic questions are torn from their social and historical context.

In the 1970s, the question of film form was posed in a way that was a peculiar hybrid. It drew on the political modernism of the 1920s and the 1930s, on the one hand, which seemed to politicise the discussion of film and give it a social dimension. Indeed, many writers in the 1970s described their work as Marxist or inspired by Marxist or historical materialist modes of analysis. On the other hand, many of the approaches seemed informed by a view of form abstracted from any substantive social considerations.[10] The swirling intellectual currents that were fusing and forming at this time merged Marxism with structuralism in a decidedly ambiguous outcome. Because structuralism focuses so insistently on the internal relationships between signs, the relationship between form and social reality, which Marxism must also capture as part of a dialectic (a relationship of difference, interdependence and tension), starts to recede from view.

The events in France in May 1968 were decisive in politicising film studies. Conflicts between university students, the university authorities and the police quickly spiralled into a ten million-strong General Strike by the working class in the month of May. The state trembled and the prospect of a socialist revolution in the heart of Europe seemed briefly to be on the agenda. May 68 was brief but the energies, ideas, militancy and hope (as well as disappointments) which it generated lasted much longer. Here was a country which had a rich film tradition, some of the most respected contemporary filmmakers, a long-standing and internationally respected film journal called *Cahiers du Cinéma* which, after May, declared the need for a revolution in and through film, and some of the most influential philosophers and thinkers in the world, undergoing what looked like a near-revolutionary convulsion.[11] Shortly afterwards, in 1969, the British journal *Screen* announced that it was setting itself the task of developing film theory (as opposed to helping teachers teach film, which it had in earlier incarnations) and that the theoretical developments coming out of France would be central to that endeavour.

It was in this period that the journal developed an influential approach to film that was a combination of structuralism, post-structuralism, the Marxism of Louis Althusser and psychoanalysis (all driven by French theoreticians). This heady brew turned out to be a classic example of formalism. 'Screen theory' in this period, as it became known, has been widely discussed and extensively critiqued, not least from other Marxist positions.[12] Nevertheless, it is instructive to briefly sketch in some of its features and arguments because it is illustrative of how legitimate questions of form can rapidly collapse into formalism and because this historical episode in the development of film theory was so formative.

In terms of narrative, dominant cinema was seen by *Screen* to ruthlessly organise the spectator's view on the story content in a seamless, unified and monolithic way that resolved all the tensions raised in the film. This meant that the viewer was 'positioned', or interpellated to use Althusser's term, by the narration in a way that reaffirmed their own mastery and command over events (they have full knowledge by the end of the film), giving a sense of unity and 'completeness' vis-à-vis the story (what Colin MacCabe called 'dominant specularity').[13] This overly easy processing of story information was seen as problematic because it suggested that the world was easily comprehensible, ultimately without tensions or contradictions. This implied that the viewing subject was also without contradiction. Dominant specularity produces a non-contradictory subject at odds with 'reality' (although the nature of this reality, was little explored and tended more and more towards the reality of psychic dynamics thanks to the influence of Lacanian psychoanalysis). This stress on the need to confront 'contradiction' was ironically premised on the assumption that contradiction was always thoroughly eliminated from the dominant models of filmmaking (as with the Frankfurt School). This in turn was the result of uncoupling film from any substantive analysis of social and historical context, the ultimate source of contradictions. It also assumed that for viewers to become deeply receptive to social contradictions, formal coherence at the level of narrative structure had to be radically broken down.

The second formal feature of dominant cinema, as *Screen* conceived it, was the image itself. Narrative coherence and unity vis-à-vis the story world were said to offer a false model of the story world's relationship to the real world, thanks to the apparent capacity of the filmic image to capture what is placed in front of the camera (the pro-filmic event). The capacity of the camera to record what is placed in front of it was viewed with deep suspicion and was the basis of a virulent attack on realism as a mode of progressive film practice as well as realism as a philosophical position (that is that film could 'say something' about the real world). Again, there was a sense that the moving image, combined with synchronised sound, encouraged a view that reality was immediately accessible, there to be captured and captured by the film in front of us. Film, according to this view, offers us the real in its immediacy and 'obviousness', as if there was no 'thickness' of signs at work in the image, and this surreptitiously steers the helpless viewer in certain undeclared directions. Life-likeness or what was called verisimilitude or illusionism ensnared the unwary spectator into the compelling power of the image. The signifier disappeared into the signified, as Barthes argued.[14]

This conception of the power of the cinematic image to seduce the credulous is an old concern but was buttressed by the then new conceptual language of psychoanalyst Jacques Lacan. Lacan's concept of the Imaginary referred to that early mode of identification with the mother that the child learns prior to entering the systems of language and representation (what Lacan called the Symbolic Order). In this phase of human development, the child, struggling to achieve basic early motor co-ordination skills, invests psychologically in the power, control and size of the adult body, which is in stark contrast to the 'turbulence of the motions which the subject feels animating him'.[15] This identification is based on a misrecognition in which the infant merges with the all-powerful other. Even after we enter language systems and grow to maturity, the power of Imaginary identifications and the unity and agency they seem to offer continue to be mobilised within systems of representation (the Symbolic Order) as a kind of consolation to the turbulence of conflicting feelings (especially of powerlessness) and desires we continue to encounter. It was all too easy to graft this model of the pre-linguistic *image* seen by the infant, onto the visual image seen by the film spectator.

Finally, continuity editing also worked to integrate shots, sound and image, into a seamless unity, a persuasive 'plenitude' that minimised contradiction and affirmed the unified, non-contradictory (Imaginary) world by working towards formal cohesiveness. The match-on-action, for example, becomes a sign of a belief in individual agency and intentionality in which the character demonstrates powerful cause-effect impacts on the world. This was seen as inherently ideological. Agency and intentionality had been comprehensively denigrated by structuralism, Lacanian psychoanalysis and Althusserian Marxism which attacked such beliefs as part of a bourgeois humanist ideology that made the individual the centre of the world and bracketed off the structures which form, shape and influence us.[16] Consciousness (although not the theoretically rigorous 'scientific' consciousness of radical intellectuals apparently) and the related category of *experience* (especially working-class experience, strangely enough) were seen as almost completely mired in ideology (itself once again almost wholly conceived as the mystified belief in a unified, self-constituting subject or social agent). Instead structuralism, Althusserian Marxism, Lacanian psychoanalysis and *Screen* theory's fusion of them, insisted that we are constituted all the way down by forces (primarily language, ideology and representation) that can only be challenged by extremely difficult theoretical language and radical formal techniques in film that break our stubborn attachment to the ideology of unity, coherence and identification with characters (ego-ideals) on the 'big screen' who are the objects of our desire and emotional investments (the Imaginary in action) and whose efficacy rests on a denial of the systems of representation constructing the film-spectator relationship.

It was right to stress that cinematic form is crucial in the production of meaning, that film does not in any simple way 'reflect' the real world, and that cinematic form is a political question since meaning is constructed from a particular position or value system. It is not hard also to find a tendency in popular culture films to prematurely resolve the social problems they themselves allude to (see Chapter 6). The problem was that the model used to explore these legitimate questions was schematic, a-historical, elitist and philosophically anti-realist (as well as sweepingly dismissive of realism as an aesthetic approach). The emphasis on the importance of contradiction and the role of narrative structures in managing them, was severed from any real engagement with social and historical contexts. Signs were not seen as mediating social dynamics but rather just formal structures split between those that are alleged to promote transparency and the unity of the subject (the problematic reflectionist model) and those (celebrated and advocated) that foreground the process of artistic construction, the work of meaning-making, the difficulty of 'making sense', the conventional nature of the language that we use, and so forth. While this theorising acquired a forensic new 'productivity' in terms of analysing the complexity of meaning-making, these hints of a Marxist analysis were overwhelmed by other theoretical traditions that cut against the substance of Marxism as a methodology and cultural politics. In retrospect, this was perhaps a historical moment in the development of a Marxist aesthetic theory which it was necessary to pass through, enabling us to retain and rework what was valuable, enriching the Marxist concept of mediation with new powerful conceptual tools in relation to textual analysis, and discarding what was not.

## 3.3 Political economy

In one of the best general introductions to the political economy of communication, Vincent Mosco situates this mode of analysis within the tradition of social, economic and political analysis founded by eighteenth-century thinkers, such as Adam Smith and David Ricardo. They set out to map the new capitalist society that had established itself. But they were followed in the nineteenth century by outright critics of capitalism, especially Marx and Engels. As the title of Adam Smith's famous book, *An Inquiry into the Nature and Causes of the Wealth of Nations* makes clear, this was a mode of analysis concerned with the production and distribution of wealth and the political, social and moral consequences of that mode of production. The subtitle of Marx's major work *Capital: A Critique of Political Economy*, indicates he was not entirely satisfied with the way this science had posed the questions it sought to answer. Towards the end of the nineteenth century, however, the interdisciplinary scope of classical political economy had considerably narrowed and become closer to what we today call 'economics', which was rather less interested in the big macro social, political and moral issues raised by classical political economy, even in Smith's day. Instead 'economics' bracketed off those questions and tends to accept as given the object of its inquiry (capitalist production and markets).

For Mosco, contemporary *critical* political economy must once again widen its scope of enquiry. He defines critical political economy as having four key components: (1) it is historical (emphasising change and variability); (2) it takes as its canvas the social totality (necessarily cutting across what are today compartmentalized disciplinary boundaries);[17] (3) it is interested in political–moral questions of social justice, equity and what constitutes the public good; and (4) it embraces the concept of praxis (the reciprocal critique of practice by theory and theory by practice).[18] Together these components constitute Marxist political economy. Mosco then identifies three key dynamics within the capitalist class-economic system which political economy has studied: (1) commodification (the process of extending and intensifying the capitalist profit motive to communication practices), (2) spatialisation (the process of consolidating capital into large units with the power and resources to extend their activities and commodities across space and time); and (3) what he calls structuration. This last concept, drawn from the work of sociologist Anthony Giddens, which he also critically reworks, refers to the dynamic relationship between 'structures' and agency within those structures, that is how agents such as CEOs, producers, directors, policy-makers, cultural rights movements and consumers, mobilise the differential resources available to them within institutional and social structures, to be agents, to *do* things that act on the 'structures' and through them. Commodification, spatialisation and structuration are useful concepts helping us map the terrain of political economy. But as a discipline, political economy has come into conflict with other disciplines on the question of 'determination', that is to say, how much and how far can the kind of processes that political economy analyses, explain certain outcomes at the level of specific films.

An early encounter between political economy and those concerned with film form and representation took place with Nicholas Garnham's essay 'Subjectivity, Ideology, Class and Historical Materialism'. He took *Screen* to task in the pages of the journal, for its 'essentially idealist formulations'.[19] Idealism here meant, as it did for Marx himself, philosophies of culture that were blind to their determination by class relations and economic forces and which instead discussed culture as if it developed independently from these historically variable materialist forces. While Garnham recognised that there were different positions within *Screen*'s editorial board, the journal as a whole was characterised, in his view, by an over-emphasis on the question of ideology abstracted from the more materialist analysis of political economy or even empirical interest in concrete analysis of institutions in their historical context. Garnham argued that, for *Screen*, analysis of organisations, structures and economic contexts had become largely one of 'rhetorical gestures'.[20] One feature of a more concrete analysis would be, for Garnham, an acknowledgement that there is a 'hierarchy of determination' at work in the way social orders work.[21] If, for example, one wanted to understand why a certain cultural franchise might be renewed in a latest instalment, whether in the form of a new television series, a new issue of a comic or the latest film, what is likely to be the most important agent or force responsible, within a range of factors, for that to happen? It will not be the creative talent or consumers that are decisive, nor could the key decision-making dynamics be understood merely in terms of 'discourses', signs, language and representation. Clearly any explanation would have to look at the institutional ownership and control of the capital allocation required to make the latest instalment (i.e. the company and perhaps the banking system) and their profit-oriented calculations.

For example, Marvel Studios had sold the movie rights of the comic strip heroes *The Fantastic Four* to Fox studios in the late 1990s when Marvel was facing bankruptcy. As superhero films began to be successful in the new century (helped enormously by advances in computer-generated imagery), it was hoped that *The Fantastic Four* comic series, which began in 1961, but was facing declining sales, would benefit from successful Fox films of the franchise. However, Fox's *Fantastic Four* movie franchise had been a commercial and critical disappointment and Marvel entered negotiations with Fox to buy back the movie rights after Disney purchased Marvel Studios in 2009 (giving Marvel access to huge capital resources). Fox, however, refused to do a deal. In response, Marvel decided to bring the *Fantastic Four* comic book series to a close in 2015, thereby damaging any potential synergy benefits for Fox. When the latest reboot of the film franchise was released in 2015, it again underperformed at the box office and Fox immediately cancelled already scheduled plans for the 2017 follow-up.

Such consequences of economic ownership, control and calculation in terms of profitability and inter-corporate alliances and competition are fairly obvious to most people and one does not have to be a Marxist to acknowledge them. One of the difficulties is how far to push the *explanatory* power of such economic-class considerations in relation to culture and in what way. For example, although corporate capital can withhold funds from projects that it is wary about, for whatever reason, once the allocation of money has been made, while all sorts of control mechanisms and reporting lines are in place to keep track of any given project, can capital ownership and formal control entirely explain the representations that come out at the other end of the process? The allocation of resources establishes the broad *conditions* within which production and consumption take place. As Raymond Williams argued, class and economic determination should be thought of as a 'process of setting limits and exerting pressures'.[22] Yet in the realm of meaning-making, films do not 'belong' to capital in the same way that formally, legally and economically a film is owned by a corporate entity as a commodity. It was this 'bar' on political economy's ability, on its own, to properly account for the specificity of the production of cultural meaning, which was in turn criticised. John Hill, for example, criticised two political economists of the media, Graham Murdock and Peter Golding, for failing to get to grips with the internal 'dynamics and operations' of signification and for reducing meaning production to 'transcriptions of socio-political ideologies originated elsewhere'.[23] In other words, the specific *production* (not simply 'transcriptions') of existing socio-political ideologies by texts needs to be accounted for.

Marxist literary theorists, such as Terry Eagleton and Pierre Macherey, for example, had developed very sophisticated accounts of the generative power of texts to produce meaning in the 1960s and the 1970s and we will explore such approaches in more detail in Chapter 6. What genres a text mobilises, which narrative strategies are employed, from which perspective the events are narrated, these and other textual variables will produce the text's own *rendering* of political cultures and historical raw material that surround and influence the text. As we get into the terrain of culture, the more class-economic determinations have to be *mediated* by other categories, such as political contexts and struggles, formal inventories, such as genre and narrative, the role of powerful individual agents, such as the 'creative talent' that capitalism itself valorises (writers, directors, stars, producers) and the ethos and *strategic aims* of the organisations involved, which are more plural and shifting than, for example, simply the distinction, important as it is, between private and public ownership that Garnham and other political economists identify. This is a good example of how social reality is stratified into different layers or forces that interact in complex ways. The economic may be a *necessary condition* in a hierarchy of causal forces, but it is not a sufficient explanation of processes that take place once conditions allow new emergent activity (such as film production) to take place. 'Emergent powers', writes Tobin Nellhaus in his application of Critical Realism to theatre, 'are conditioned by lower strata' (such as ownership of economic assets and the interplay of economic forces such as competition), 'but they explain little about what the emergent power actually is and does'.[24] In part, this is because emergent practices are the product of multiple conditions and in part because a *production* creates something that did not exist before; even if only fractionally, a production changes things, adds something new to the world and therefore cannot be entirely reduced to its conditions.

For example, very similar economic conditions can foster very different cultural possibilities with very different outcomes. Marvel Studios' *Captain America: The Winter Soldier* (2014) is a far more interesting and critical political text than the Second World War setting of *Captain America: The First Avenger* (2011). This is because *The Winter Soldier* draws on the generic conventions of the political conspiracy thriller and this in turn is possible because of the present-day setting of the film. The Second World War setting of *The First Avenger* brings with it the whole accumulated history of representing the Second World War as a fairly simple fight between good and evil, democracy and fascism. It is a less complicated world, at least within this major strand of popular culture. Macherey once famously noted that 'texts' are not isolated objects but *encrusted* with a whole prior set of 'interpretations which have been attached to them and which are finally incorporated into them ... like shells on a rock by the seashore'.[25] We can also say the same about how texts are preformed and shaped by the prior iterations of similar material, similar representations and broader cultural patterns that may contract possibilities for critical voices more on some fronts than others. Such 'determinations' are not reducible to political economy alone, although it is always a factor.

Political economy is often unfairly charged with being 'reductive' almost as a reflex action response by those more concerned with aesthetic and formal questions. Yet in many ways, the most functionalist theories (those that argued that film 'functioned' to reproduce the social order) came from the formalists gathered around *Screen* rather than political economy. Garnham's model of political economy was certainly characterised by a high degree of sensitivity to the contradictions of this mode of production. And, as a result of these contradictions, he was certainly aware of the possibility for the economic logic of capitalism to be checked, interrupted or contained (within limits) by a variety of social, cultural and political logics.

> Because capital controls the means of cultural production in the sense that the production and exchange of cultural commodities become the dominant forms of cultural relationships, it does not follow that these cultural commodities will necessarily support, either in their explicit content or in their mode of cultural appropriation, the dominant ideology.[26]

This points to an important contradiction between the desire to make money and the ideological preferences of the dominant social order. This is a contradiction which savvy filmmakers can turn to their advantage. Take Andrew Niccol, who made the science fiction film, *In Time* (2011), which portrays a future where people are genetically programmed to stop ageing at 25 but drop dead if they run out of the currency which keeps them alive. That currency is 'time' which those who have little time work hard for it while those who have hundreds of years on their biological clock are the elites. The 'timekeepers' (or police) help to protect the status quo. In an interview, Niccol was asked how a film so obviously critical of the capitalist system could be made by a large capitalist corporation (20th Century Fox).

> You're not going to tell them that, are you? I'm not going to ... Listen, if you go in with a pitch and you say no character's over twenty-five years of age and there's a ticking clock in every scene, they just go 'where do I sign?' They don't read the script. Fortunately.[27]

This example of structuration illustrates an important contradiction or potential source of tension within the capitalist production process, as Garnham argued:

[A]rtisanal modes of labour organization ranging from individual craft production, i.e. the authorship of a book, to a small group, i.e. the independent
film company or record producer, remain common and important within the
cultural sphere. Such residues have been the focus for struggle against the logic
of capital and have produced a powerful anti-economic cultural ideology …[28]

Hans Magnus Enzensberger explained why artisanal modes of labour organization
survived. The 'culture industry' he noted, 'thrives on a stuff it cannot manufacture
by itself. It depends on the very substance it must fear most, and must suppress
what it feeds on: the creative productivity of people.'[29]

Garnham argued that the relative autonomy of creatives at the point of production
could be reconciled with the needs of capital because the latter control the means of
mass reproduction and distribution of the 'authorial product', as well as being a
powerful player in determining how much return creative labour gets in terms of
royalties.[30] Yet a working reconciliation does not mean that all the tensions between
the direct cultural producers and the imperatives of capital are resolved any more
than it does in any other work shaped by the capital-labour struggle.

Along with this potential contradiction between producer autonomy and
control of distribution and capital allocation, Garnham also identified other key
contradictions in the political economy of the capitalist culture industries. For
example he noted that although innovation is necessary since cultural products
must have something new and different about them to attract audiences,
innovation is also highly risky because of the volatility of audience demand for
products, or, as they say in the industry, 'nobody knows anything' about what
may or may not succeed. Corporations therefore try to mitigate against this by
trying to standardise products to a degree, using tried and tested formulas, stars
who seem able to pull in an audience, spreading their bets across a repertoire of
films, hoping that at least some will be successful and pouring huge amounts of
money into marketing.[31]

Another contradiction is the tendency towards monopoly and how that develops
corporations that struggle to respond to new trends and market opportunities.
Capital has tried to respond to this contradiction by the development of what I call
subsidiary and subcontractor capitalism. On the one hand capital is amassing into
fewer and larger corporate behemoths who have ultimate control over the allocation of capital to resource projects. On the other hand, this tendency towards
monopoly is combined with a tendency to organise the production process around
a plurality of smaller production units working in complex relations with the Big
Media corporations, either as wholly or partly owned subsidiaries or subcontractors,
who do the research and development necessary to bring the Big Media companies
*ideas* to produce into commodities.[32]

While being attentive to differences within a heavily corporate and commodified
culture, we have already seen (in Section 2.2, for example) that changes in structures of ownership and control do establish the broad conditions within which
trends are established. Political economy, Graham Murdock has argued, 'is

concerned to show how different ways of financing and organising cultural production (and production in general) have traceable consequences for the range of discourses and representations in the public domain and their accessibility to audiences'.[33]

Political economy can, when appropriately mediated by other methods, trace out major determinants of ownership, financing and organisational strategising on the kind of films that get made, but political economy also provides evidence of other important impacts in terms beyond the actual product, around distribution and audiences. Critical political economy's interest in economic power can explain both the prevalence of certain models of filmmaking and also the reach which those models have vis-à-vis audiences. That reach crosses national boundaries and so raises questions of asymmetries of cultural exchange that have important implications for both self-understanding and the understanding of others (e.g. other cultures, other countries, etc.). Finally, critical political economy of film can also analyse how power reproduces itself by tracking how revenue streams are distributed and controlled and by whom.

While political economy is not committed to any simple model of isomorphism between the capitalist profit motive and the production of pro-capitalist value systems, there are those pressures and constraints that Williams spoke of. If there is *no* discernible probability that certain corporate class features of the cultural industries shape both production outcomes (including meanings and values) and, just as crucially, the differential profile such outcomes have in the public sphere and access to audiences, in certain ways, then the Marxist wager that social life is in broad terms explicable as the outcome of a determinant hierarchy of forces and powers, is redundant. We need not worry about capitalist ownership of cultural resources because it hardly matters. Instead we can adopt a 'liberal' methodological position in which these different factors are all more or less equally weighted or believe in the surface appearance of a plurality of providers, or, worse, a position that agrees with corporate capitalism's useful fiction that the consumer is sovereign and that the reason Hollywood dominates global box offices and cinema screens is because that is what the audiences want to see to the exclusion of everything else.

In terms of understanding cultural production, we have seen that it is problematic to reduce film to the economic-class interests that formally own commodities, and we have seen the dangers of discussing film form politically but abstracted from a methodological framework that can really engage with substantive historical, social and political contexts (the problem of formalism). The missing link between economic-class questions and formal analysis can be found on the terrain of culture (broadly conceived), history, society and politics. These provide the essential mediating categories that help us understand the *determinate* but not *mechanistically determining* relationships we need to explore so that we can attend to the specificity (but not complete autonomy) of film. It was this terrain that was being explored in the 1970s in a new way by the Centre for Cultural Studies at Birmingham University, under the leadership of Stuart Hall.

## 3.4 Cultural studies

Film form and film industry mediate (reconfigure) what is happening in the wider culture. This means we must engage with the issues that the study of culture and its various categories raise. The development of British Cultural Studies provides another site of key debates within which Marxist cultural theory flourished in the 1970s. Stuart Hall has traced the emergence of Cultural Studies out of the preceding work of Richard Hoggart, namely, his book *The Uses of Literacy*, Raymond Williams, especially *Culture and Society* and *The Long Revolution*, and E.P Thompson's classic work of historiography, *The Making of the English Working Class*. [34] Hoggart's book extended and modified an earlier and somewhat conservative and elitist or canonical literary criticism founded by F.R. Leavis, by applying a 'reading' to the living, everyday, working-class cultures of his youth and the 1950s amid what he saw as the erosion of that culture by the advance of mass culture. In its opening up of cultural questions to both the everyday and working-class culture (albeit one under threat from mass culture), it was an essential democratising move. Williams' initial contribution was to similarly situate the 'literary' as part of broader social transformations wrought by industrialisation and the growing claims of the working class as part of making the polity more democratic. [35] He also famously argued that '[c]ulture is ordinary: that is where we must start'. [36] Thompson's Marxist historiography helped pose the question of the cultural production of an entire class, particularly in relation to forgotten histories, erased voices and rebellions against class superiors. [37]

The Centre for Contemporary Cultural Studies at Birmingham University was founded in 1964 by Richard Hoggart, and Stuart Hall took over as director four years later. By the early 1970s, Marxism was seen as one of the key methodologies that the Centre had to engage with and try and develop as a form of cultural analysis. The Centre extended Hoggart's work on *living working-class cultures* in a definite historical materialist direction. This was a 'break into a complex Marxism' as Hall put it. [38] The work on working-class sub-cultures, for example, situated class cultures in relation to precise points of pressure and transformation, such as urban and housing redevelopment, automation of traditional jobs, changes in the labour market, as well as the more Hoggartian terrain of mass culture (especially music, youth-culture rituals and the representation of youth cultures in the mass media in variously demonised forms). Sub-cultures were seen as the symbolic working out along generational lines of the pressures and contradictions that were impacting on working-class cultures and lives at a time of change. [39] The attention to the relative diversity of cultural practices (Mods, Rockers, Skinheads, Casuals, etc.) as a set of possible options within a determinate set of shifting conditions, broke with older models of Marxist thinking about the relationship between an assumed *unified class and an assumed unified culture* produced by that class. A more diverse sense of working-class cultures was emerging.

The method of critical ethnography which values the ways the subjects of study articulate their own understandings of their experiences and practices was also central to the Centre's work.[40] Whether by participant observation and/or the semi-structured detailed interview, such qualitative methods have subsequently been influential and valuable in the study of audiences and their reception of cultural products.[41] They have also been used in the study of production cultures and practices in film and television. The latter has expanded considerably, largely under the discipline of the 'cultural or creative industries' which may be seen as a fusion in some ways between political economy and cultural studies.[42] A cultural studies approach to production tends to lean more towards sociological analysis than political economy. Cultures of work, professional norms and negotiations of internal issues and external pressures and how subjects themselves conceive their activity, tend to predominate. Janet Woollacott's reflections on the Open University's production study of the James Bond film, *The Spy Who Loved Me* (1977) stressed the role of the 'Bondian' in the production process.[43] The 'Bondian' is the knowledge of the Bond formula which the production team have and their awareness of its prior evolution through the films and the books. Woollacott shows that this formula was not static but changing and that the production team were aware of their own transformation of the Bond formula in *The Spy* while maintaining its identity. For example, she shows how the 'Bondian' began to self-consciously incorporate an element of the Women's Liberation movement into its leading female star (Barbara Bach in *The Spy*) or how a comic element was increasingly introduced into Roger Moore's version of Bond, around sexuality and the use of technology. Using interviews with the production personnel, Woollacott stressed the team's active and, in many ways, conscious transformation of values and ideologies associated with Bond.[44]

Whether investigating audiences, cultural producers or sub-cultures, cultural studies necessarily stressed the importance of 'experience'. But this also raised difficult questions. The popular and potentially deeply ideological understanding and appeal to 'experience' may validate uncritically the 'world' of the subject and their response and understanding of that world. A rendition of 'experience' as the unvarnished truth of a situation is clearly problematic from a Marxist perspective which makes the philosophical distinction between forms of appearance (where experience is experienced) and real relations and conditions (less visible but determining forces shaping experiences). From this perspective, not all the conditions and forces impinging on people's experiences *are* necessarily immediately available to their consciousness and their vocabulary. To reach back down to the roots of experience tends to require a critical or reflective decoding of experience which is political and philosophical all at once. On the other hand, experience and what one learns from experience are clearly an indispensable part of making history as well as making culture. One way of qualifying the question of 'experience' in cultural studies was to draw on structuralist accounts of meaning making. As Hall noted in a famous essay, the French structuralism tradition did not easily fit together with the 'culturalist' tradition more closely associated with British thinkers such as Hoggart, Williams and Thompson. The latter stressed experience, testimony and agency and very often was the basis for a democratic revalidation (including by radical documentary film practices) of formerly excluded and marginalised class cultures; the other stressed the 'structure' of language and representation over agency (collective or individual) and displaced 'consciousness' with the sense of a cultural *unconscious* (Barthes' concept of myth, that would quickly become the category of ideology and imaginary relations in the work of Althusser).[45] Woollacott's analysis of the production team of *The Spy Who Loved Me* can be seen as an attempt to credit the category of 'experience' with some conscious validity while still retaining some role for the concept of ideology as a critique of the limits of experience.

The Centre was also drawn to the study of the daily mass media more, such as the press and television. In the 1950s, much of the British left was highly dismissive of the popular mass media, especially its dominant American forms. The British Communist Party advocated folk songs and folk dance as a bulwark against American cultural imperialism at this time.[46] By the 1960s, these media were seen as important organs in the production and construction of popular attitudes and they needed to be seriously engaged with rather than dismissed. Here was one of the enduring legacies of cultural studies. The validation of the everyday culture of ordinary people led to the study of popular culture as an important site where a broader cultural politics was fashioned. It was on this terrain that 'the people' gathered around particular clusters of taste and attitudes and representations and it was here too that the theoretical understanding of popular culture and the political struggle to democratise it and develop its stifled critical capacities had a real urgency and relevance. News programmes on television that were reporting on intense conflicts between workers and bosses during the 1970s, became key case studies in the process of meaning-making. As Hall noted:

> Because meaning was not given but produced, it followed that different kinds of meanings could be ascribed to the same events. Thus, in order for one meaning to be regularly produced, it had to win a kind of credibility, legitimacy or taken-for-grantedness for itself. That involved marginalizing, downgrading or de-legitimating alternative constructions.[47]

The patterning, the systematic framing of certain issues in certain ways to achieve legitimacy, credibility and a 'taken-for-grantedness', speak of Hall's interest in the work of the Italian Marxist Antonio Gramsci, whose concept of hegemony we will discuss in Chapter 8. Briefly, hegemony refers to the complex struggle to win leadership on the moral and political questions of the day, to win the terms on which problems and issues are debated. Those who control the material and intellectual means of production are significantly advantaged in this respect, but their leadership has to be won on each and every front. What Althusser had called the 'obviousness' of ideology (see Section 2.6) is an indication of who has been able to make their ideas seem self-evident. Gramsci contrasted those who could set the terms of any debate with the everyday world of 'common sense', which is fragmentary and contradictory, containing a mix of 'philosophies' or conceptions from many different sources. It is the task of revolutionaries to help develop the common sense in a more coherent, systematic and self-conscious way, breaking 'common sense' away from its current alignment with the political and moral leadership of the bourgeoisie. This broader sense of cultural formations helped shift the theoretical focus of cultural analysis away from merely 'textual analysis' and instead situate meaning-making within contexts of production, cultural contexts and consumption. Cultural studies theorists developed models around what they called 'the circuit of culture', which could include production, normative and official regulatory apparatuses (such as film censoring bodies), questions of identity (e.g. national identity), representation (textual analysis) and consumption.[48]

Broader contextualisations of cultural texts, Chris Robé has argued, are particularly apposite for radical or revolutionary film and media practices that emerge out of political protest movements, labour movements, community projects, and so forth and which suggest the social origins of problems and the collective possibilities of addressing those problems.[49] Yet the development of a cultural studies–influenced film studies has been more sporadic than one would have hoped. The initial dialogue between *Screen* and the Birmingham School where a cultural studies influence on film studies might have happened was highly conflictual. Ros Coward, for example, suggested that *Screen*'s interest in Lacan could 'provide a more genuinely materialist account of the process of representation' than the Birmingham School.[50] Language and systems of representation (discerned by textual analysis) for Coward and *Screen* were primary and references to class were seen as 'reductionist'. The Birmingham School shot back that their attempts to situate representation in relation to complex class and institutional contexts had been parodied by Coward because 'the overall thrust of her critique is to suggest that the culture/class relation is not only "problematic" – it is a non-starter'.[51] But elsewhere, and especially in the pages of the American film journal *Jump Cut* (run by John Hess, Chuck Kleinhans and Julia Lesage), one sees the consistent development of a more cultural studies–inflected leftist and broadly Marxist film criticism. This American tradition was concerned to situate films in their social, historical, cultural, political and industrial contexts rather more than *Screen*'s on-going neo-formalism. Unusually, *Jump Cut* has sustained a politically committed understanding of film and media culture that has not always been evident elsewhere.[52]

In fact, as cultural studies developed into the 1980s and beyond, the category of class as economic logic and socially lived experience and practice, was increasingly marginalised from its concerns, in line with the broader victory of the political right, the apparent elimination of any historical rival to capitalism once the Soviet Union collapsed in the early 1990s and the displacement (rather than combination) of class by a variety of other political concerns focused on gender, sexuality and race. The trajectory of cultural studies in this period brought another critical intervention from Nicholas Garnham. He had argued that cultural studies and Hall's work in particular, had, since its inception, not engaged seriously enough with political economy.[53] But now he accused it of very largely abandoning the crucial question of determination and economic power altogether. Symptomatic of this was a shift away from questions of production to a celebration of the apparently emancipatory, liberating potential in the cultural consumption of popular culture.[54] Under the influence of post-structuralism and ethnography, the active reader or audience who could deconstruct textual ideologies now came to the fore as a reaction against the neo-formalist conflation of audiences with spectator positions derived solely from textual analysis. The study of popular culture had become its more or less straightforward celebration, which was not at all what Raymond Williams had meant when he struck the first blow for democratising culture with his 'culture is ordinary' formulation.

Political economist Graham Murdock argued that much of the ethnographic work conducted under the banner of cultural studies was not sufficiently engaged with the lives of the people who were being studied and that this facilitated a tendency towards a romantic celebration of popular resistance to the products of the mass media.[55] He called for a shift away from the 'expressive individualism' that seemed to be flourishing in certain quarters of cultural studies and a move back to questions of citizenship which could pose the question of the cultural rights necessary to participate effectively in the public sphere so that change could come about through a process of democratisation, rather than the 'natural law' of capital and the market. Murdock's call for cultural studies to re-orientate itself to citizenship, cultural rights, public spaces and the resources needed to facilitate democratic change, seems much more in line with the original impulses of cultural studies and offers a bridge between its early democratisation discourse and political economy's focus on the questions of economic ownership and resource allocation that could enhance democratisation in the cultural sphere.

This re-orientation of the question of determination around broad cultural rights and the quality and inclusiveness of conversations within our public spheres, certainly has relevance for the study of film although it is a perspective rarely heard in film studies. We need in fact to see film as part of the public sphere (those conversations that enhance our capacity for reason and democracy) in order to properly appreciate its actual and potential importance. Such questions are obviously relevant to a genre like the documentary which has had a significant revival in recent years, but it is also important for fiction films as well. Whose stories get told, who gets represented and how in which media (film, television, press), whose idioms and cultural practices flourish on the screen, who gets to work in the film industry as writers, directors and actors, for example, are all significant questions which tie questions of representation and access and meaning making to a broad conception of the political economy of the media. Framed in this way, film is part of a broader multi-media environment producing representations as part of the formation of opinion, understanding and debate. This is the institutional production of that reflective aspect *on experience* that *could*, for example, help people interrogate the iterations of failed models and oppressive practices. Just as easily, standardised modes of framing things can lock us into those models and practices which reproduce existing inequalities.

For a critical culture to develop, experience itself has to be seen *as a production*. This was the argument made by Negt and Kluge in their book, *Public Sphere and Experience*, [56] a more Marxist version of Jürgen Habermas's famous work on the public sphere. Unable to see their experience as a *production*, the worker has a 'technical' relationship to experience, seeing it as fundamentally unalterable, experience can only be made better by adapting oneself to the context (today becoming a highly 'flexible' worker, for example). The worker sees this as maximising their chances within the structures that structure their experience.

> [The worker] encounters a concept of experience derived from the natural sciences, which, in that narrow sector of social practice whose object is domination over nature, has a real function and suggestive power. He will take this scientific body of experience, which is not socially but rather technically programmed, as the form per se in which experience is secured. This will lead him to "understand" that there is nothing he can do with "experience", that he cannot alter his fate with its help. It is an issue for his superiors in the workplace and for specialists.[57]

This technical relationship to experience is instrumental and calculative, it lacks critical and creative dimensions. It is particularly encouraged by school, by the workplace and today it must be said, by the university sector pursuing an 'employability' agenda and constructing a neo-liberal subjectivity for staff and students alike. When film works critically, it acts as a rendering of historical experience into an aesthetic experience, one that has great potential to help people *re-evaluate* their *individual* experiences and responses to ideological discourses. The aesthetic experience does this by translating individual experiences back into social experiences, making them a topic for public debate and dialogue as a precondition for progressive change. Ideology, by contrast, tends to work the other way under capitalism, rendering what are social and collective experiences into individual ones primarily.

Cultural studies' focus on the broader politics of cultural values, habits, practices, perspectives, and so forth also helps us situate film in the wider cultural contexts that account for how and what film is responding to in its formal strategies, representations and the conversations it generates. Representations of class, gender, race and sexuality in film are impossible to adequately conceive without thinking about how they relate to the way class, gender, race and sexuality are thought about, represented and practised (often in conflicting ways) beyond film as well as within it. So, it is clear that cultural studies' perspectives and methodologies are important to add to political economy and textual analysis of form and the specific language of film. Structures of ownership and control intersect with questions of form and culture just as form moulds historical experiences as mediated by cultures in specific ways, and may well borrow from the modes of expression to be found in those cultures themselves. Understanding film then requires a methodological synthesis of formal analysis (but not formalism), critical political economy (but not economic reductionism) and the study of popular culture (while avoiding uncritical celebrations of popular culture).

# Notes

1  Sohnya Sayres *et al.* (eds), *The Sixties Without Apology* (Minneapolis, MN: University of Minnesota Press, 1984).

2  Louis Althusser, 'Ideology and Ideological State Apparatuses', in Louis Althusser, *Essays on Ideology* (London: Verso, 1993), p. 21.

3  David E. James and Rick Berg, *The Hidden Foundation: Cinema and the Question of Class* (Minneapolis, MN: University of Minnesota Press, 1996), p. 3.

4  See the autobiographical reflections by a number of commentators in Sally Munt (ed.), *Cultural Studies and the Working Class: Subject to Change* (London: Cassell, 2000).

5  Biographical note: I went to a comprehensive secondary school where there was a far greater social mixing of classes than I find in the university sector, which is, in terms of academic staffing, a far more homogeneous social experience than my school days.

6  Eric Fromm, *Marx's Concept of Man* (London: Continuum, 2004), p. 107.

7  For a discussion of the relationship between Kant and Marx(ism), see Michael Wayne, *Red Kant, Aesthetics, Marxism and the Third Critique* (London: Bloomsbury, 2016).

8  In fact, there is an IMBD list of such films with Moore's film at number 1 and Carpenter's listed last at 22. See www.imdb.com/list/ls003681183/

9  See Sarah Neely, 'Sisters of Documentary: The Influence of Ruby Grierson and Marion Grierson on Documentary in the 1930s', *Media Education Journal*, 55(Summer) (2014): 29. Available at: http://ames.scot/resources/pdf/MEJ55.pdf

10 See, for example, Dana Polan's critique of the neo-formalism of Noel Burch in *Jump Cut*, 26(December) (1981). Available at: www.ejumpcut.org/archive/onlinessays/ JC26folder/DistantObserver.html. Burch's critique of the dominant codes of representation was very influential at this time.

11 The classic account of the relationship between May 68 and film is Sylvia Harvey's *May 68 and Film Culture* (London: BFI, 1980), which looks at the impact that May 68 had on film *theory*. But see also Paul Douglas Grant's *Cinema Militant: Political Filmmaking and May 1968* (New York: Wallflower Press, 2016), which, as the title suggests, focuses on the relationship of May 68 to film*making*.

12 See, for example, Simon Clarke *et al.* (eds), *One-Dimensional Marxism: Althusser and the Politics of Culture* (London: Allison and Busby, 1980), and Terry Lovell's *Pictures of Reality: Aesthetics, Politics and Pleasure* (London: BFI, 1980). For a more recent reappraisal, see Warren Buckland, 'The Politics of Form: A Conceptual Introduction to "Screen Theory"', in Yannis Tzioumakis and Claire Molloy (eds), *The Routledge Companion to Cinema and Politics* (London: Routledge, 2016.

13 Colin MacCabe, 'Realism and the Cinema: Notes on Some Brechtian Theses', *Screen*, 15(2) (1974): 12.

14 For a brilliant application of Barthes' critique of narrative representation to film, see Julia Lesage's essay, '*S/Z* and *Rules of the Game*', *Jump Cut*, 12–13 (1976–77): 45–51. Available at: www.ejumpcut.org/archive/jc55.2013/LesageRulesOfGame/index.html. However, note also that important contextual analysis is excluded from a purely Barthesian approach.

15 Jacques Lacan, 'The Mirror-Phase as Formative of the Function of the I', in Slavoj Žižek (ed.), *Mapping Ideology* (London: Verso, 1994), p. 94.

16 For a valuable critical reappraisal of humanism, see David Alderson and Robert Spencer (eds), *For Humanism* (London: Pluto Press, 2017).

17 Vincent Mosco, *The Political Economy of Communication* (London: Sage, 2009), p. 29.

18 Ibid., pp. 37–8.

19 Nicholas Garnham, 'Subjectivity, Ideology, Class and Historical Materialism', *Screen*, 20(1) (1979): 121.

20 Ibid.

21 Ibid., p. 127.

22 Raymond Williams, 'Base and Superstructure in Marxist Cultural Theory', *New Left Review* 82 (1973): 4.

23 John Hill, 'Ideology, Economy and the British Cinema', in M. Barrett (ed.), *Ideology and Cultural Production* (London: Croom Helm, 1979), p. 114.

24 Tobin Nellhaus, *Theatre, Communication, Critical Realism* (Basingstoke: Palgrave, 2010), p. 27.

25 Interview with Pierre Macherey in *Red Letters*, 5(Summer) (1977): 7. *Red Letters* was the British Communist Party's literature journal.

26 Nicholas Garnham, 'Contribution to a Political Economy of Mass-Communication', *Media, Culture and Society*, 1 (1979): 136.

27 Tommy Cook, Interview with Andrew Niccol, available at: http://collider.com/a ndrew-niccol-in-time-the-host-interview/122279/

28 Garnham, 'Contribution', op. cit., p. 139.

29 Hans Magnus Enzensberger, 'The Industrialization of the Mind', in Reinhold Grimm and Bruce Armstrong (eds), *Critical Essays* (New York: Continuum, 1982), p. 5.

30 Nicholas Garnham, 'From Cultural to Creative Industries', *International Journal of Cultural Policy*, 11(1) (2005): 20.

31 Ibid., p. 19.

32 Mike Wayne, 'Post-Fordism, Monopoly Capitalism and Hollywood's Media Industrial Complex', *International Journal of Cultural Studies*, 6(1) (2003): 82–103.

33 Graham Murdock, 'Cultural Studies at the Crossroads', in Angela McRobbie (ed.), *Back to Reality? Social Experience and Cultural Studies* (Manchester: Manchester University Press, 1997), p. 68.

34 See, for example, Stuart Hall, 'Cultural Studies and the Centre: Some Problematics and Problems', in Stuart Hall *et al.* (eds), *Culture, Media, Language* (London: Routledge, 1996).

35 Raymond Williams, *The Long Revolution* (Cardigan: Parthian, 2013).

36 Raymond Williams, *Resources of Hope: Culture, Democracy, Socialism* (London: Verso, 1989), p. 3.

37 E.P. Thompson, *The Making of the English Working Class* (Harmondsworth: Penguin Books, 2013).

38 Hall, 'Cultural Studies and the Centre', op. cit., p. 25.

39 Phil Cohen, 'Subcultural Conflict and Working-Class Community', in Stuart Hall *et al.* (eds), *Culture, Media, Language* (London: Routledge, 1996).

40 Hall, 'Cultural Studies and the Centre', op. cit., p. 24.

41 There is a debate whether spending a couple of hours with someone in an interview situation and/or observing them can be called 'ethnographic', a term which in its anthropological origins has been associated with the building of long-term engagements and even immersion. See G. Turner, *British Cultural Studies: An Introduction* (London: Routledge, 2003), pp. 130–4, for a discussion of this.

42 See David Hesmondhalgh's *The Cultural Industries* (London: Sage, 2002) for an excellent example of this kind of synthesis.

43 The Open University became another major centre for Cultural Studies, first under the leadership of Stuart Hall, who moved there from Birmingham and then, latterly, under Tony Bennett.

44 Janet Woollacott, 'The James Bond Films: Conditions of Production', in James Curran and Vincent Porter (eds), *British Cinema History* (London: Weidenfeld and Nicholson, 1983).

45 Stuart Hall, 'Cultural Studies: Two Paradigms', *Media, Culture and Society*, 2 (1980): 66. Published in the second issue of the newly established journal, Hall's discussion of two paradigms did not discuss their relationship to critical political economy, an absence which did not escape Nicholas Garnham's attention. His article, 'Contribution to a Political Economy of Mass Communication' had been published in the first issue. The two articles represented the schism between critical methods.

46 Roy Sear, 'Youth and Heritage', in *Britain's Cultural Heritage* (Bury St Edmunds: Arena Books, 1952), p. 59.

47 Stuart Hall, 'The Rediscovery of Ideology', in John Storey (ed.), *Cultural Theory and Popular Culture* (London: Routledge, 2009), p. 121.

48  Paul du Gay, Stuart Hall, Linda Janes, Hugh Mackay and Keith Negus, *Doing Cultural Studies: The Story of the Sony Walkman* (London: Sage/Open University, 1997).
49  Chris Robé, 'Materializing Cultural Struggle in Film and Media Studies', *Culture, Theory and Critique*, 55(1) (2014): 17–33.
50  Rosalind Coward, 'Class, "Culture" and Social Formation', *Screen*, 18(1) (1977): 79.
51  Iain Chambers, John Clarke, Ian Connell, Lidia Curti, Stuart Hall and Tony Jefferson, 'Marxism and Culture', *Screen*, 18(4) (1977): 113.
52  *Jump Cut* is available free online at: www.ejumpcut.org/home.html
53  Garnham, 'Contribution', op. cit., p. 131.
54  Nicholas Garnham, 'Political Economy and Cultural Studies: Reconciliation or Divorce?' in John Storey (ed.), *Cultural Theory and Popular Culture* (London: Routledge, 2009).
55  Murdock, 'Cultural Studies at the Crossroads', op. cit., pp. 60–1.
56  Oskar Negt and Alexander Kluge, *Public Sphere and Experience: Toward an Analysis of the Bourgeois and Proletarian Public Sphere* (Minneapolis, MN: University of Minnesota Press, 1993).
57  Ibid., p. 6.

# 4

# PRODUCTION

## 4.1 The general structure of a film industry

We must find ways of relativising the capitalist mode of production, using theory, history and comparative case studies. Marxism is crucial to this endeavour. In his notes on the method of critical political economy, as he was preparing to write *Capital*, Marx argued that really 'concrete' analysis required the development of a network of concepts that are sensitive to the historical specificity of capitalism. This is a little counter-intuitive, as we might expect the 'concrete' to be associated with either empirical data of observable phenomena or, if involving concepts at all, the sort of concepts which are available to people in everyday life. For example, we may begin with an apparently 'concrete' widely used and easily understood concept such as 'population' and underpin it with some empirical statistics (size, composition, regional distribution, etc.), but Marx insists,

> population is an abstraction if I leave out, for example, the classes of which it is composed. These classes in turn are an empty phrase if I am not familiar with the elements on which they rest. E.g. wage labour, capital, etc.[1]

For Marx, then, analysis proceeds by moving from abstractions to the 'concrete'. The concrete is understood not as empirical data (although it does not of course exclude empirical data) but rather as a complex conceptual framework to discover the 'rich totality of many determinations and relations'.[2] As his examples suggest (wage labour, capital, etc.), the 'concrete' requires a conceptual mapping of capitalism. Abstractions, however, are useful in identifying the common elements of a phenomena across different historical periods. For example, Marx opens Part three of *Capital*, volume I, with a celebrated discussion of what is common to *all* labour in *all* human history. This is where he famously differentiates human labour from the instinctual labour of insects like the spider and the bee (although he was here building on the thoughts of Kant).[3] He then moves on to examine what happens to the historically variable *creativity and imagination* of human labour once it becomes a commodity under capitalism (a topic of some interest to us). This is a movement from abstraction (what all human labour has in common) to the concrete – the concepts necessary to analyse what has happened to human labour under the historically specific conditions of capitalism. Similarly, 'production' is an abstraction, but a 'rational abstraction' says Marx, as long as we are aware that further historical specificity with the appropriate conceptual tools, must be the real further work.[4] Marx has some interesting things to say about production and consumption *in general* as we shall see, but we can start with our own 'rational abstraction' which is the general structure of *any* film industry. We can also give the analysis more concrete specificity by indicating how different *modes of production* shape the general structure of film industries in different ways.

The general structure of any film industry can be mapped out as in Figure 4.1. All film industries involve four main phases:

1. Production
2. Distribution
3. Exhibition
4. Consumption.

One of the advantages of distinguishing between the general structure of the film industry and specific modes of production (which include distribution, exhibition and consumption) is that it helps us to not conflate the dominant model for film production (the capitalist mode of production) with filmmaking *per se*, just as we need not conflate what happens to wage-labour under capitalism, with labour in general. In terms of film-making as a 'rational abstraction', we can say that all filmmaking requires, for example, a period of production, the temporal starting point of which may be quite fuzzy when we include pre-production and research

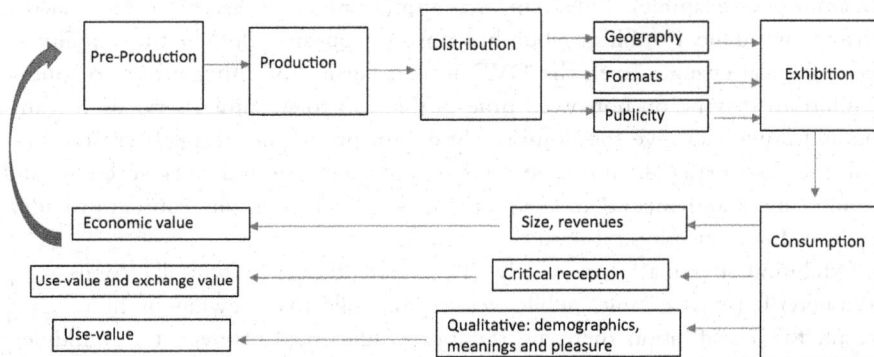

FIGURE 4.1 Film production as a 'rational abstraction'

and development phases, such as developing a script. When the planning phase and other materials essential to the making of the film, such as a script, actors, locations, and so forth have been prepared, the actual production phase begins when the recording of material into the audio–visual form intended for the final film commences. At this point, more significant resources for the undertaking have to be drawn on or invested. The origins of these resources may range from finance capital all the way through to the spare time which a community sets aside to represent itself in the cinematic form. This range reminds us that film production sits inside wider modes of production which in turn are likely to shape which technical forces of production are available to the production team (equipment, money, skills and expertise, etc.). Production requires the co-ordination and co-operation of people. Hardly anyone, even the most revered auteur, makes a film entirely on their own. But the nature of the co-ordination and co-operation will vary depending on the mode of production in operation.

Once the production and post-production phases are over (that is, editing and other post-production procedures, such as audio, sound effects and colour correction) and a finished product has been made, then any film needs to be distributed, it needs to travel in space, in time and today across different formats. The finished film produces a prototype or master copy from which other multiple copies are made. These copies have to be transported in some form in space, which means that the film has some geographical reach and the number of copies produced and circulated gives an indication of how many people it may be reaching. Distribution is also the phase where publicity materials are prepared for the film. Whatever mode of production in question, *all* films have to try and present themselves to the public, stimulating their interest and curiosity so that they are willing to at the very least invest their spare time (itself a relatively scarce resource) and watch the film (but typically of course, also invest some spare money as well). Distribution formats were once only available as celluloid film prints transported in distinctive circular cannisters. Today distribution is typically a digital file, formats vary depending on where the film will be shown (theatrical, in which case a large Digital Cinema Package format will be used or a smaller file suitable for downloading or online streaming, for example). Video tape was another mode of distribution format (for private or public exhibition) but has now disappeared due to the rapidity of technological change. Even the DVD format (again, for either private or public exhibition) may be on borrowed time in the shift to streaming services. Streaming and download give the dominant mode of production (capital) greater control over the material, over availability of the material and over access to and monitoring of audiences than VHS tape or DVD, which is why content providers want to phase out physical hard copies of films.

Exhibition sites may vary widely. The word 'theatrical' typically conjures up commercial, purpose-built, public venues for collective viewing of films. Even within this classification there are significant differences between the 'multiplex' and smaller 'independent' theatre chains. But there are many other types of public exhibition possibilities now that digital formats and cheap projectors (whether installed or portable) can turn venues that are also cafés, theatres, community centres, libraries, museums, and so forth into film exhibition sites. However, even this is not new. Labour movements and political parties have been running film societies showing alternative films since the First World War. There have even been mobile projection vans as well. Between 1917 and the Second World War, films from the Soviet Union were particularly popular on such alternative distribution and exhibition networks.[5] The Cuban film, *For the First Time* (1969) documents a mobile film projector team reaching a very remote village in Cuba after the revolution in 1959 and screening Charlie Chaplin's humanist anti-capitalist classic *Modern Times* (1936). This was the first time some people in the village had ever seen a film. By 1964, such mobile projectors had produced 48,000 screenings and attracted nearly 8 million Cuban spectators.[6]

The contemporary diversity of sites increases the possible diversity of different types of consumption, beyond the dominant entertainment experience offered by the multiplex.[7] This public theatrical mode of cinema viewing has, since the 1950s, had to work with other modes of exhibition that are more private in their orientation. Television as a medium was initially seen as a major threat to the Hollywood majors but they soon learned to work with the new medium, selling their archive to television and making original content for the new medium. Video then turned television from a broadcast or cable distributor of film content into a monitor for content played by a VHS cassette recorder until this technology was displaced by DVD and Blu-ray discs and players. Hollywood initially opposed the development of video technology, fearing that it would loosen control over copyrighted content (it did). In the contemporary moment, new streaming technology via the television or now the computer or other devices (such as the mobile phone) is again transforming the industry and allowing new entrants to come into the film distribution and production market because they can by-pass the lock on distribution to theatrical exhibition which the Hollywood majors have, not only in the US, but all over the world.

Finally, there is the audience for the film which is the moment of consumption. We can think about the audience quantitively (how many people see it and/or buy it and generate revenues for it); we can think about the audience qualitatively (audience demographics and what meanings, pleasures, uses they make of the film); we can also distinguish between regular audiences and a film's reception by critics, that is the specialised professionals whose job it is to review and evaluate films (we can make this distinction from ordinary filmgoers because this is a specialised and influential role within the social division of labour which may contribute to both the cultural level of reception, influencing its use-values, as well as revenue for producers by promoting a film to audiences).

Marx made some very interesting comments on the relationship between production and consumption in general. First, production creates a product that furnishes consumption material that can be consumed. Without production, 'consumption would lack an object'[8] but without consumption, production would also lack a fully realised purpose. Production also shapes the object in ways that cue how it *should* be consumed. Production 'gives consumption its specificity, its character, its finish'.[9] A film designed to initiate political debate and encourage political activism and change is a very different product from one which is produced in order to be consumed as only entertainment along with a big bag of expensive popcorn (although, of course, the 'political' is here too, although in a different way). Production, however, not only provides material for a need, it also 'supplies a need for the material'. Here Marx is pointing to the broader cultural consequences of production and he takes artistic production specifically as his example:

> The need which consumption feels for the object is created by the perception of it. The object of art – like every other product – creates a public which is sensitive to art and enjoys beauty. Production thus not only creates an object for the subject, but also a subject for the object.[10]

Thus, the most dominant model for the global film industry is the Hollywood model and this means that Hollywood is the most powerfully placed player to produce a 'subject' for its preferred object (the film as a certain kind of commodified film experience). The difficulty of finding audiences for alternative models of film and alternative national cinemas is in part because the dominant model produces audiences that are trained to want what that model produces and be indifferent or unaware of other possible models or types of film experience or modes of production.

## 4.2 Modes of production and social formation

The general structure of film as an industry that involves production, distribution, exhibition and consumption can now be made more concrete by noting that *how* the process of production, distribution, exhibition and consumption happens is shaped by the *mode* of production in question. A mode of production is 'a way or manner (a mode) of producing', notes Louis Althusser.[11] The term 'mode' indicates that it is 'a series of systematically regulated operations'[12] in which the labour process is organised so as to interact with and transform raw materials using instruments of production. These forces of production are organised and regulated by the social relations of production, although the forces of production also do have *potentialities* that may cut against the social relations of production (for instance, digital technology widens access to the means of production and distribution which capital would prefer to monopolise). Together, the forces and relations of production form the mode of production.

Marx used the term mode of production to give a schematic mapping of the development of human history, from primitive communal forms of property of the hunter-gatherer societies, through to the slave-based modes of production of the ancient world, through to the feudal mode of production in Europe turning on the key relationship between lord and peasant and then, finally, the capitalist mode of production, in which the main social and economic relationship turns on the capital-wage-labour dynamic. In the latter case, the social basis of the forces of production has potentialities that cut against the relations of capitalist production, producing crisis (over production, lack of 'effective demand', etc.) and possibly revolutionary transformation of the mode of production. We have seen Marx's idea that theory moves from the abstract to the concrete by developing a theoretical network of concepts attuned to the historical period. This 'concrete', however, remains at the quite epochal level of 'the mode of capitalist production'. We do need to descend further into historical specificity for an actual analysis of real situations and not read off real social and historical reality *against* the epochal mode of production analysis of the type Marx mapped out in *Capital*. One of the things we find when we do descend down into real historical situations is the presence of *different* modes of production co-existing at the same time, something which Althusser stressed. To theorise this, Althusser made a distinction between modes of production and the 'social formation'. In any actual social formation, different modes of production may co-exist in specific historically concrete situations, but with one mode of production dominating over the others:

> Every concrete social formation is based on a *dominant* mode of production. The immediate implication is that, in every social formation, there exists more than one mode of production; at least two and often many more. One of the modes of production in this set is described as *dominant*, the others as dominated.[13]

Althusser's idea of different modes of production combining in social formations is an elaboration of Marx's insights:

> In all forms of society there is one specific kind of production which predominates over the rest, whose relations thus assign rank and influence to the others. It is a general illumination which bathes all the other colours and modifies their particularity. It is a particular ether which determines the specific gravity of every being which has materialized within it.[14]

Thus, in the period of the capitalist mode of production, other modes of production also co-exist with it but are dominated by it. Applying this notion of mixed modes of production to the film industry, it is clear that the capitalist mode of production, unsurprisingly, dominates the sector. The US film industry, which dominates the global industry and accounts for most of its investment and profits, generated $43.4 billion revenue in 2017 and four-fifths of that total was secured by the seven largest capitalist film conglomerates in the world. These include Disney (18.2 per cent), NBC Universal (16.4 per cent), Warner (16.2 per cent), 21st Century Fox (12.9 per cent) and Sony (12.1 per cent).[15] This represents a tremendous expropriation of social wealth by private interests. One way in which this capitalist mode of production 'assign[s] rank and influence' to any other modes of production is simply by grabbing the lion's share of available resources and marginalising other modes of production. The fact that there are mixed modes of production, however, despite the inequality, is important, not least because it helps us *relativise* the dominant mode of production. Despite its self-identity as the only possible mode of production, the presence of other modes sources different practices and values that can help critique the dominant mode of production.

The capitalist mode of production exemplified by the dominant US industry does itself have significant internal complexity, as we shall see, but there are also arrangements for the regulation of the film production, distribution, exhibition and consumption process that it may make sense to think of as bleeding into other modes of production. We may, for example, want to think about state-led modes of production, such as Britain's early documentary film production, which was located initially in the Empire Marketing Board, then the General Post Office and finally during the years of the Second World War, the Ministry of Information. Cuba's film industry after the 1959 Revolution became a statist mode of production, ensuring that the industry could develop independently of the market and Hollywood's global domination. We may want to identify art cinema as a distinct mode of production as well (with its mix of state and, generally speaking, small capital funding) or the avant-garde which tends to push art film strategies further and often combines this with less conventional technical divisions of labour, smaller teams and budgets that are often drawn from the personal finances of the filmmakers or small arts grants rather than capital (big or small). Then there is a range of other film practices, such as revolutionary Third Cinema and Fourth Cinema (indigenous people's cinema), which situates film in relation to revolutionary movements or moments of resistance. They have often challenged the dominant technical division of labour for filmmaking since task fragmentation and hierarchical structuring of power relations within the production team are inextricably connected to the capitalist mode of production.[16] However, their prime mark of difference from other modes of production is their challenge to the established social division of labour which has typically positioned film in relation to either 'entertainment' or 'art'; instead Third Cinema and Fourth Cinema situates film in relation to political responsibilities, intervention and revolution and at its best overcomes divisions between politics, art, pleasure, the spectator and the streets.[17] Unsurprisingly, it is typically a poor or insecure cinema, sometimes a guerrilla cinema made on the run from state power, although it may be supported at times by revolutionary states.

How do we define a mode of film production? We may define a mode partly in terms of funding sources and the ethos behind those sources, partly in terms of whether they mimic the dominant technical division of labour in the filmmaking process, partly in terms of its place within the social division of labour (with art cinema and the avant-garde frequently conceived as a middle-class cinema, for example), and partly in terms of an evaluation of the actual films themselves. We may see not only that there are different modes of production in play simultaneously, but precisely because of that, it could be possible that within a *single* film there may be characteristics of different modes of production combined. Mike

Leigh's £14 million *Peterloo* (2018) was largely funded by Amazon Studios, definitely a representative of the capitalist mode of production. Leigh himself is very much an art cinema film director (whose cultural esteem Amazon wanted to be associated with), using for the most part the standard technical divisions of labour for filmmaking. However, he is famously known for the scope he gives to actors to build up their own characters and improvise (a bias towards the artistic side of the production process that fits with the ethos of art cinema). This modification in the technical division of labour is a sign that we are in art cinema territory. Leigh's two previous forays into historical drama were classic examples of art cinema *content* insofar as they were both about artists. *Topsy Turvey* (1999) is about the musical and theatrical writers Gilbert and Sullivan, while *Mr Turner* (2014) is a film about the British nineteenth-century painter, J.M.W. Turner. By contrast, *Peterloo* deals with an episode of British class history that has been largely erased from official historical accounts (state violence towards the working class) and thus speaks to a more Third Cinema type of filmmaking in theme and, in the case of *Peterloo*, form as well.

## 4.3 The dominant mode of production

When thinking about the various sources of funding for film production, the most salient fact is that the dominant capitalist mode of film production attracts investment in order to make a profit within a system of competitive accumulation. This last part is very important, because making a profit alone is not enough; within a system of competitive accumulation, the prospect of *how much* profit could be made in one production relative to investing in another production is absolutely key. This system of competitive accumulation wrenches the system ever upwards towards whatever the average rate of profit is at any point in time. It means that the prospect of a modest profit is less attractive than the prospect of a larger profit and that skews the entire dominant mode of production towards certain kinds of projects. Film is a commodity and for the investors that means what is paramount about it is the surplus value (or return on investment) that can generated. Commodification is the process by which more and more value can be squeezed out of a commodity.[18] Product placement, for example, has become increasingly institutionalised within the Hollywood production process and is indicative of the intensity with which film capital in the Hollywood industry squeezes value out of the commodity and its place within a broader culture of consumerism.[19]

Labour is also a commodity, of course (the capital-wage-labour relation) and squeezing this commodity is central to the production of surplus value. Squeezing labour-power as a commodity is in some ways the same in the film industry as in any other kind of work situation; it 'is organized according to industrial principles that economize at every step in a sprawling creative process, constantly seeking efficiencies and accelerating workflows'.[20] This amounts to making labour work longer and/or harder and/or bearing down on the real value of wages. The organisation of time, especially production time, is key to controlling costs. This is why the dominant technical division of labour organises the shoot according to efficiency savings rather than in the chronological order of the narrative. The scope for shooting in chronological order is wider in the art cinema mode of production, such as with Alfonso Cuarón's recent *Roma* (2018). Ken Loach also tries to shoot in chronological order whenever possible.

Marx identified two broad ways that capital can squeeze more value out of labour-power. Making labour work longer hours, more intensely and for less money constitutes the production of what Marx called absolute surplus value (an overall increase within a given time period). The meaning of this term only becomes apparent by contrast with the second way in which capital produces surplus value. Here capital increases the *productivity* of labour by combining labour power with new innovations in machinery and technology. Marx called this the production of relative surplus value. Relative surplus value increases surplus value by decreasing the amount of time the worker works to cover their wage and increasing the amount of time that labour works for capital (surplus labour = surplus value). With machinery and automation, labour can produce *quantum leaps in output* by changes in the technical basis of production (which is different from making workers work harder with the *existing* technologies). Relative surplus value means the worker produces more in less time and produces enough value to cover their wage more quickly than hitherto. Outside film, labour-intensive commodity manufacturing has declined as automated machinery has displaced the jobs once performed by numerous hands.

However, film labour is less susceptible to being displaced by automated machinery (fixed capital) and assembly line processes, as Michael Chanan notes. Film requires 'the exercise of creative initiative and aesthetic judgement in a collectivized form, which [makes] real controls over the labour process, of the kind exemplified by Henry Ford's production line, impossible'.[21] While film can be commodified, as an aesthetic and cultural product, there are severe limits to automating creativity in ways that produce surplus value (although experiments in Artificial Intelligence may mean that even this frontier will be breached in the not-too-distant future, for example, in relation to scriptwriting). Technological innovations have produced some economies of course but by far their most significant impact is to increase the repertoire of creative decision-making the production process requires. To take one rather humble example, the impact of the zoom lens is a complex aesthetic-critical debate and set of practices, not primarily efficiency savings.[22] This builds in points of resistance to the exploitation and commodification process that can be leveraged further by creative and craft labour against capital. As numerous writers have noted, the film production process involves the serial production of prototypes, meaning that neither the final product *nor* the process of production are ever identical. According to Curtin and Sanson:

> Unlike an integrated assembly line, motion picture production is a large-scale industrial enterprise that is distinguished by the collaborative production of prototypes, each one the outcome of thousands of creative choices. Movies are *made* not mass produced.[23]

Technological developments in film production have not increased productivity (more output per hour of labour) very significantly, and this is true across any complex cultural practice as Michael Chanan notes: 'Productivity in the chamber music sector has been stagnant, while in the manufacturing sector it has rocketed, with a consequent rise in the relative cost of artistic performances.'[24] However, aside from productivity, it has become technically possible to produce films more cheaply in terms of, say, the size of a crew and the supply of labour that can skilfully use the technology. But this is an avenue which the dominant players are reluctant to pursue as high production budgets are a barrier to entry that cements the position of monopoly cultural capitalists. Big budget spectaculars, with their immense promotional budgets and synergies with other merchandise, are also where the film industry can make huge profits. Here is another significant difference between aesthetic artefacts and, say, car making, where driving down the price per unit of output is central to the economics of the business.

The process of production and the product that comes out of the process are differentiated (if only modestly) because the use-value of the cultural product is significantly *qualitative and singular*, or to put it in a way that mainstream economists would understand, audiences will not pay for exactly the same product again and again, since the elements of novelty, surprise, pleasure, stimulation and post-screening reflections on the film experience would quickly degrade. (I leave aside the consumption mode of *fans* who will re-consume the same film again and again. All we can say here is that this mode of consumption is a complex one exhibiting both a kind of fetishism and an anti-consumerist stance against disposability.) This need for the qualitative and the singular makes capital peculiarly dependent on 'talent'. It also introduces significant areas of risk and uncertainty for investors since demand for the product in which they have invested is uncertain. There has to be some difference between one film and another, but is it the right kind of difference to make money? Of course, the capitalist mode of film production has introduced various attempts to standardise creative elements that have proved popular in order to predict and control demand: certain techniques of narrative storytelling, genres, the use of film stars or making adaptations from previously successful or high profile pre-existing materials (books, plays, television programmes, previous films – remakes, sequels, prequels, etc.). Formulas are effective, to an extent, but demand still remains uncertain. What should be a sure-fire hit (e.g. a story of the young Han Solo years) turns into a *relative* flop, the low budget horror film that is a political allegory, becomes a global hit.[25]

All the literature on film production cultures emphasises that this uncertainty of demand and the novelty of each production process give some leverage to creative talent. For example, the industry constructs an image of the audience (what it wants, etc.) as a way of organising production.[26] Decision-makers in various stages of production (scriptwriters, directors, stars, producers, etc.) vie for their image of the audience and its tastes and needs to dominate. Track record and therefore reputation are crucial here. Cultural production is typically characterised as 'craft-like, non-routine, unpredictable, formed of temporary organizations, and characterized by ambiguity, informality and negotiation'.[27] The embedding of craft-like artisanal labour-skills within the production process, even in the most capital-intensive sectors of the film industry, makes aesthetic-cultural production significantly different from other manufacturing sectors where craft skills have long been absorbed into fixed capital (technology). Yet such relatively 'loose' control over artistic labour[28] is coupled with strict control over distribution, through which the all-important revenues flow.[29]

Marx described labour under capital as variable capital. It is variable because labour can always be worked harder or longer or more productively with the help of machines as a way of extracting more value from it. Marx called machines fixed capital because their value is already fixed and they cannot produce more value. For example, a capitalist film producer may buy an expensive film camera at its value or perhaps picks one up at a price that is less than its value, perhaps because another capitalist producer has gone out of business and sold it cheaply. In the latter case, value is distributed from one capitalist to another. But in neither case can the film camera produce *new* value. Its existing value (the product of the workers who made it) in both cases can only be distributed incrementally into new commodities (e.g. a film) by human labour power which then also adds new value to the commodity in the process of working for a wage.

Additionally, though, we may say that creative labour is variable in a different, qualitative rather than merely quantitative sense as well: creative labour provides the variety which makes the cultural commodity useful to people in some way or another. The moment of production, as opposed to distribution and exhibition, is where the 'magic' of *variable creative labour* happens, whether it is the particular performance of an actor or the decisions the set designer has made. In the end, capital wants to quantify all this variable creative labour into an abstract quantum: profit. But it cannot do without this creative qualitative dimension that makes the commodity useful to filmmakers (creative expression) and audiences (consuming use-values). Right here we have that tension and contradiction between use-value and exchange-value in the commodity that Marx identified. 'Could commodities themselves speak,' he noted wryly, 'they would say: Our use-value may be a thing that interests men. It is no part of us as objects … we are nothing but exchange-values.'[30] While capital needs these crucial creative variable inputs, it would also like to control such inputs in a way that would, paradoxically, negate what it is that they add to the cultural commodity. It is around such contradictions that tussles between capital and labour routinely take place in the creative production process.

In terms of sources of investment, obviously the large studios have their own funds to invest, or they can borrow money from the banks. In terms of finance capital, hedge funds have increasingly invested in US film production, often on a slate basis (investments covering a number of films rather than just one). Relativity Media for example, which has co-produced such films as *Zero Dark Thirty* (2012), *Les Misérables* (2012) *The World's End* (2013), *The Woman in Black* (2015) and *Jane Got a Gun* (2016), had investment partners such as Citibank, Merrill Lynch and Deutsche Bank, although the company has had a troubled recent history and has been in and out of bankruptcy.

In Europe, funding from state-backed public bodies remains a crucial source of investment, with one study finding that as much as 93 per cent of European fiction films have *some* funding from these sources.[31] This suggests that if a 'pure' capitalist mode of production was in operation, European cinema, as we know it, would collapse. Funding that comes from bodies that in whole or part have a cultural remit, will be shaped by the ethos of the respective institutions. Broadcasters also have a very significant role in funding European films, accounting for approximately 25 per cent of financing (although only 11 per cent if France, a major defender of the principle of a national film culture, is excluded).[32] Again, broadcasters, whether public or private, have their own organisational ethos and interests. Another form of state assistance, however, coming in the form of tax exemptions, is much closer to a market model of public assistance because it by-passes the need for a cultural policy explicitly seeking to develop certain priorities for a politics of cultural subvention (such as engaging with under-represented social groups or diversifying the national identity). Predictably tax exemption is the model of public assistance favoured by neo-liberal UK policy-makers. For 2015/16, for example, 64 per cent of all UK public funding came from tax exemptions that companies could claim for investing in film production,[33] a policy designed to attract investment from large US multi-nationals.[34] This *subsidy* to Big Capital by the public purse is of course part and parcel of the capitalist mode of production in this sector, as in others. Production has become increasingly mobile and international with different exchange rates, labour rates, government subsidies and tax rebates, hurling nations, regions, cities and film labour into competition with each other to attract film capital investment.[35]

At the other end of the scale, digital technology has opened up the possibility of crowdfunding films through platforms such as Kickstarter, Indiegogo and Seed and Spark. Money that is raised in this way is not generally investment capital seeking ROI (returns on investment) but gifts paid out of spare revenue. While there may be promises of T-shirts and names on the credits, etc., these are not financial returns but forms of thanks. Investments of this kind are done for reasons other than pecuniary and that means that the filmmakers are free from the kind of controls and obligations which capital investment attempts to impose. Along with the wider access to formal or informal education and training as well as the automation, simplification and lower costs that digital technology brings to various aspects of the film production and post-production process, crowdfunding has made low-cost film production viable for more people than ever before. However, if 'anyone' can now make a film, only some players have the capacity to distribute that film in ways that can garner a mass audience and recover investment.

Earlier I suggested that distribution has three key dimensions: (1) geographical reach and numbers; (2) formats; and (3) publicity. Let us take each in turn.

## Geography

In terms of geographical reach and numbers, Hollywood reigns supreme over the world's theatrical outlets. It has been able to use its huge home market (huge in terms of the number of theatres and cinemagoers) to produce the most expensive films in the world, recover its costs in a home market which it dominates and in which foreign films have only the most marginal place, and then sell its own produce abroad, undercutting local productions where necessary, building up a global and powerful distribution network. A paradox of filmmaking is that it has a relatively high cost to produce the master copy (thus raising barriers to entry) but the reproduction costs are very low (thus facilitating the dominant player's dominance). As Guback notes: 'Duplicates require little additional investment and wide distribution hastens the flow of revenue to producers who are obliged to repay loans from banks and financiers.'[36] In short, Hollywood had every incentive and every advantage to push its product globally, and it is well known that Hollywood films worked in turn as adverts for the American manufacturers, from jeans, to cigarettes, to cars.[37]

Hollywood's global distribution power has always been profoundly political as well as economic. Its powerful trade association, the Motion Picture Association of America (MPAA) has aggressively lobbied governments around the world to prevent any infringements on Hollywood access to national markets and they have been able to call on the US state to apply significant pressure on governments around the world. In the late 1980s, for example, the MPAA was able to get the Canadian government to drop a government bill that would have given Canadian films some access to a market they can hardly enter. The market in question? Their own.[38] The French meanwhile provided backbone to the European position in the negotiations around the General Agreement on Tariffs and Trade in the early 1990s. The American negotiators (and Hollywood) wanted all forms of cultural protectionism banned under a free trade agreement. Eventually the agreement was signed but cultural goods were excluded from it, allowing national governments to provide some protections and subsidy to their film and television industries.[39] Today, typically more than half of theatrical revenues which Hollywood accumulates happens outside the US market. Foreign markets for Hollywood are the growth areas, especially the coveted Chinese film market which is on the cusp of surpassing North America in terms of box office and number of movie-goers.[40]

Hollywood's spatialising power inevitably generates concern. Film has been part of a general media penetration of foreign markets around the world, which, because of the links between media and broader goods and trends, has been labelled a form of 'cultural imperialism'. No doubt the conflation of cultural goods with economic, military and political domination has unfortunate consequences, since culture has a semiotic plasticity that cheap labour markets, truncheons, tear gas and legal force do not. But the phrase has a valuable polemical purpose: namely, to remind us that film and other media goods (television, press, radio, comics, video games, etc.) shape identities and perceptions, and that if one country has a dominant role in the media systems of another, or in the case of Hollywood, many others, thus restricting the ability of those nations to produce media that emerge from their own specific historical and social conditions, then that is indeed a very significant problem. It is not a question of being against cultural exchange of course, still less is it 'Anti-American', but rather a question of the massively asymmetrical relations of cultural exchange and the larger political-economic systems they are embedded in.

The classic early critique of cultural imperialism was produced by Ariel Dorfman and Armand Mattelart in *How to Read Donald Duck: Imperialist Ideology in the Disney Comic*, a work of ideological critique rather than political economy. They argued that Disney's penetration of the Chilean media space promoted stereotypical representations of the developing world, apologetic forms of imperialist intervention in fantasy geographies outside the capitalist West, promotion of capitalist values and ideological erasure of the sphere of production. They were writing (in the early 1970s) in a specific historical moment that gave this critical assault on Disney comics a real wider political import. At that time, Chile had democratically elected the first explicitly Marxist head of state in the world: President Salvador Allende. This was a moment when, as Dorfman and Mattelart note in a later edition of the book, that 'the whole of the Chilean people were recovering the industries that during the twentieth century had been the means of enrichment for Mr Rockefeller, Grace, Guggenheim, and Morgan'. This recovery was 'intolerable' for US capital and the US state and so they 'organized a plan … to overthrow the constitutional government of Chile'. An economic war was launched against Chile by the US government, while the CIA aided and abetted the capitalist class and their supporters within the country. Still, the US continued to send 'planes, tanks, ships and technical assistance for the Chilean armed forces' who would overthrow the Chilean government in 1973. They also continued to export 'magazines, TV serials, advertising, and public opinion polls for the Chilean mass media' to prepare:

> the climate for the bourgeois insurrection … Each day, with expert U.S. advice, in each newspaper, each weekly, each monthly magazine, each news dispatch, each movie, and each comic book, their arsenal of psychological warfare was fortified … In the words of General Pinochet, the point was to "conquer the minds" while in the words of Donald Duck (in the magazine *Disneylandia* published in December 1971) … the point was to "restore the king".[41]

On September 11, 1973, the Chilean military, with support from Washington and the CIA, overthrew Salvador Allende in a coup in which he was killed.[42]

## Formats/material forms

In this chapter on political economy, as in the book as a whole, it is my intention to try and demonstrate what a Marxist film theory specifically brings to our analytical methodologies. Hence my focus on the concept of *mode of production* which more mainstream economic analyses do not engage with. The question of formats is also a good example of the need for a specifically Marxist terminology. Actually, 'formats' is a term from conventional economics, and we would be better advised to substitute for it the Marxist concept of *material form*. With the concept of material form, we focus on the interaction between *technology* and *social relations*. For instance, the dominant commercial industry made 35mm film the 'quality' material form for feature film production to raise barriers of entry into the industry and to ensure audiences did not develop a taste for low budget aesthetics. Today film, as in the celluloid base on which the cultural product film was made, has been driven to the brink of extinction by the capitalist economic drive for efficiencies, irrespective of the particular aesthetic qualities that the material form of celluloid has. Digital is cheaper to shoot on, cheaper to distribute and cheaper to exhibit (cinemas no longer need multiple skilled projectionists). The changing material forms constantly change the terrain on which the struggle within and between different modes of production takes place. Thus, 16mm and other formats became the material form that defined a range of alternative and oppositional film practices for many years. Nick Macdonald, for example, made his film *The Liberal* War (1972), an anarchist critique of American imperialism in Vietnam, on 16mm film in his own apartment, using mass media materials (newspapers, books, photographs), toy soldiers, simple animation techniques, a letter board and a sock puppet to represent the US South Vietnamese client regime. The development of VHS tape and DVDs, while it opened up important ancillary markets to theatrical releases, also posed the problem for the big studios of value leakage through unlicensed copies of their property. This is particularly acute outside the West. In Latin America, for example, the vast masses outside the middle class cannot afford to watch Hollywood movies in the expensive mall cinemas, and so in the informal economy, vendors circulate the latest films, often at the same time as they hit the big screen. The contradiction is one of Hollywood's own making. It has globalised its culture as the model of filmmaking, as the universal culture, which to be outside of is to be in some way outside a universal human conversation, yet access is governed by ability to pay and in Latin America, where inequality has been protected and reinforced by North American business and political interests, that ability is certainly not universal.

The possibility of piracy is one reason why release patterns have changed since the 1980s.[43] Whereas once upon a time, new releases would go first to the big prestige cinemas in the city centre, and then on into suburban locations, now there is almost always a broad release of films at the same time. Theatrical receipts are increasingly 'front loaded' with a significant chunk of overall theatrical profits coming early in the release period. This in turn speeds up the transition of the film commodity from theatrical formats (Digital Cinema Package) to domestic consumption formats. The latter, in the form of television and DVD sales, are now responsible for the lion's share of profits which Hollywood makes overall across formats but the theatrical release still functions as an important 'shop window' for ancillary markets. 'Theatrical box-office figures are seen as a measure of how the film can be valued and exploited as a ... property over its life cycle, and across different formats,' writes Philip Drake.[44] The mutating material forms through which value flows and accumulates and the speed of transition from one to the other are part of the acceleration of the circulation process by which the commodity transforms itself into money and hopefully profit (capital).

The development of Netflix shows how important the material form of the commodity is for business models and opportunities. Originally (starting in 1998), Netflix was a hybrid technology and rental mail-order business. It combined a website that offered a catalogue of films produced by others where customers made their choices with a postal system for delivery of the product in the form of a DVD. In other words, not only the internet but also the slimmer/lighter and therefore cheaper to post material form of the DVD made this business model possible. But in 2007, as broadband internet and digital content technology developed, Netflix switched the epicentre of its business away from DVDs and Blu-ray discs to streaming film and television programmes direct to customers' computers or televisions. By 2018, Netflix was spending $8 billion on producing its own original films and television series and in 2019 joined the Motion Picture Association of America, confirming that it had arrived as a major player and competitor in Hollywood without ever buying a single cinema theatre or television network. The material form of the commodity, which opens up the chance of using data analytics culled from customer choices to recommend further titles, has an impact at every level of production (and consumption). The rise of Netflix has led, for example, to further rounds of consolidation/merging within Hollywood, with Rupert Murdoch recently selling 21st Century Fox to Disney for $71.3 billion.

## Publicity

The dominant commercial model will see advertising of films across newspapers, television, billboards, magazines, radio, theatre trailers, social media, websites as well as tie-ins with other products. This kind of publicity makes it very hard for films without this level of financial backing to be visible not only in theatrical markets but in the ancillary ones as well.

> By choosing to emphasize the high cost blockbusters which must appeal to mass audiences and therefore must be given elaborate and expensive marketing campaigns as well, the major producer-distributors limit the movie themes and treatments that can find their way to the screen.[45]

Rising marketing costs are symptomatic of a lack of price competition in the film industry just as it is in other markets dominated by oligopolies. Publicity budgets now in Hollywood are typically half as much as the production budget for the film, adding $30 million in costs to a $60 million production budget. As well as limiting movie themes and treatments, skewing visibility to those with vast financial resources, escalating costs are a barrier to entry and limit the number of successful players (producers and distributors) in the sector.[46] The textual products of publicity under the dominant capitalist mode of production seek to offer the potential spectator the promise of a certain cinematic experience as determined by genre, star and possibly director. The film poster constructs what John Ellis calls the 'narrative image' of the film, a set of intriguing enigmas, hints, suggestions and possibilities that will only be answered by actually watching (and purchasing access to) the film.[47] Typically, photographic stills of individual characters (played by the main stars) and the situations that they encounter in the film are depicted in collages as a kind of promise of pleasure for exchange. The poster designed for the British release of the film *The Godfather* (1972) by American graphic designer S. Neil Fujita is (unusually for Hollywood) a restrained (uncluttered) image of the leading star, Marlon Brando in profile with a blood red tint on his face against a black background (Figure 4.2). The poster's minimalism and high contrast use of black shadows and red tint may be read as mobilising certain classed codes of taste that suggest that this is a serious work of art. The puppeteer motif next to the title in large text is borrowed from the novel and was also designed by Fujita, thereby drawing on the already existing cultural presence and esteem of Mario Puzo's bestseller (published in 1969). Brando's brooding presence and formidable power (underlined by the rectangular framing of the image) similarly capitalise on his enormous star persona and along with the title of the film makes the question of power as much about the individual as about the role itself.

Compare this with the Cuban-originated film poster advertising the same film (Figure 4.3). It was designed by Antonio Pérez González Ñiko using the silk screen technology typical of Cuban film posters, with their stark and bold use of colour (or here mainly black and white). Notice how the image and presence of the film star are not used at all. Notice too that there is no intertextual link to the preexisting commodity (the book via the puppeteer motif). Even the title is relatively less prominent. Notice too, and in line with the Cuban film poster tradition, that there is no use of photographic stills, with its strong promise of what the actual film experience might offer. Instead of foregrounding the individual character and star or 'experience' the film may offer, this poster foregrounds what is rather marginal in the American/British publicity for the film, the *institution and ideology* of Catholicism and its historic fusion with armed violence. This in turn of course speaks to the broader historical and cultural experience of Latin America with its Spanish conquistadores and Catholic missionaries. But not only is this poster attuned to the specific cultural context into which the film is now entering, the Cuban poster also clearly emerges from a mode of production that has different priorities and value orientations than the capitalist Hollywood publicity machine, with its focus on selling and its individualising and psychologising of what are properly broader historical, cultural and institutional structures. These two posters represent the symbolic production of two different modes of production and, as Marx noted, modes of production that 'produce' (cultivate) different 'subjects' for the product, that is to say, different modes of consumption, which Julianne Burton has shown us, revolutionary Latin American filmmakers have for example, pioneered.[48]

## 4.4 Organisation and ownership

There are two features of the dominant mode of production that I want to briefly discuss in this section. First, how the *organisational* structure of the dominant mode

**FIGURE 4.2** The British release poster for *The Godfather*

**FIGURE 4.3** The Cuban release poster for *The Godfather*

of production (led by but not restricted to Hollywood) has changed at the point of production. Second, how *ownership* structures have changed in recent decades. In both cases, the political and state context that regulates the capitalist market has been a significant determinant in shaping developments. We have seen that capitalism is shaped by two powerful forces that dialectically interact with each other. Competitive accumulation means competition between capitalist firms (as well as intensifying competition between wage-labour). This tendency can never be completely squeezed out of the capitalist system but it does also tend towards its own negation for the simple reason that competition is bad for profits. It makes sense for capitalists to try and drive competitors out of the market, or buy them up and raise barriers to entry for potential new competitors. Competition leads inexorably to the centralisation of capital into fewer units of capital that have concentrated huge quantities of capital. With some minor qualifications concerning the organisation of production, this 'law' (tendency) of capitalism holds good for the film industry. The erosion of competitive markets by the tendency towards oligopolistic control is a major embarrassment for capitalist economic theory and practice since it undermines what Wasko calls the 'common myths about our economic and political system, especially the notions of pluralism, free enterprise, competition and others'.[49] Marxist political economy, therefore, makes the centralisation and concentration of capital a major theme of its critique, not least because there is a direct link between the diminishing bargaining power of the labour force and increasing corporate domination of the industry.[50]

However, there are also significant broader cultural-political implications. Although the nature of film production means that it will never be tied systematically into the daily news agenda that shapes the institutions of politics and which makes news production such an obviously important feature in debates about the public sphere and the need to have diverse sources involved in it, film nonetheless has a role to play in the public sphere(s). It ruminates and reflects on the cultures we inhabit and provides audiences with the chance to perhaps have deeper reassessments of those cultures than the daily news output provides. Thus, for the same reason that campaigners have argued that the tendency towards centralisation and concentration in the news media (press and television) is detrimental to the public sphere, so too we can argue that is also true in the case of the film industry.

In the classical era of the Hollywood studios (broadly from the 1920s through to the 1950s), the industry was largely owned and controlled by the so-called Big Five and the Little Three. The Big Five were vertically integrated companies that owned studio lots on which they made their films with workers (including stars) on long-term contracts; they had their international distribution networks and they owned key 'first-run' cinemas in the main urban locations where films would be showcased before wider releases. They were integrated vertically within the supply and value chain of a single sector from idea to the final product's exchange with the consumer.

The Big Five were:

1.  MGM
2.  Warner Brothers
3.  20th Century Fox
4.  Paramount
5.  RKO

The Little Three were:

1.  Universal
2.  Columbia
3.  United Artists

The Little Three produced and distributed their own films but did not own chains of cinemas so they were not fully vertically integrated all the way through the value chain.

The fortunes of these eight companies have been quite tumultuous, with MGM and United Artists having a particularly difficult post-classical Hollywood time for several decades and RKO dying as a film production business in 1959 and its back-catalogue devoured by its various competitors. The shift from the classical Hollywood period to a post-classical one was triggered by the US state's anti-trust action after the Second World War. Concerns about Hollywood's oligopolistic structures had been brewing since the early 1920s and they now came properly to court with the charge that the majors owned and controlled around 70 per cent of the nation's first-run theatres.[51] After a complex legal battle involving appeals, the Supreme Court ruled against the Hollywood majors in 1948 and they were compelled to begin divestment of their ownership of the first-run theatres. The most significant effect though of the decision was to be at the production end of the value chain. Divestment encouraged more independent production to enter the business because there was a greater chance of their film commodity being able to access audiences on revenue-generating terms following the majors' partial loss of control. Competition from television in the 1950s added to the new sense that demand for the older type of cultural film commodity was uncertain. Cultural changes in the 1960s where older studio personnel lost touch with an audience that was differentiating itself strongly in generational terms and becoming more pluralised in terms of emergent identities (around feminist, gay, black and counter-cultural identities, for example) lent further impetus to the need to source story material from production outfits outside the majors.

In retrospect, Hollywood was at the forefront of some broader trends within the cultural industries and within the organisation of manufacturing production more generally. There was arguably a broader shift underway in the *mode of development* within the capitalist mode of production. Capitalism has historically seen significant shifts from one mode of development to another without thereby ceasing to be capitalism. We may define a mode of development as characterised by a certain ensemble of social-technical and organisational relations. The agricultural basis of early British capitalism shifted to industrial capitalism, for example. That spread internationally and became, with America as the leading industrial nation, the basis for Fordism, as Gramsci analysed (see Chapter 2). The transition away from Fordism has been given various names, such as flexible specialisation (by small capital), flexible mass production (by big capital), post-Fordism, postmodernism, etc. Although such shifts have become associated with technical developments such as the digital communications and the computer revolution, the key determinant in triggering changes in Hollywood's organisational structure was, as we have seen, political intervention, but probably the key determinant continuing the proliferation of outsourcing to external production companies was a combination of political and the above-mentioned cultural trends.

The economist Michael Storper, in line with a lot of excited talk in the 1980s about how capitalism was 'deconcentrating', wrote about 'vertical disintegration' in Hollywood.[52] But although there has been a significant proliferation of production outfits in Hollywood (a model that was also reproduced within the UK television industry in the 1980s and the 1990s), the commodities were still owned and significantly controlled by the major Hollywood studios through their crucial distribution pipelines as well as investment clout.[53] As the more pro-capitalist politics of the current period got under way with the Presidency of Ronald Reagan in the 1980s, the major studios moved *back* into exhibition as anti-trust laws were weakened.[54] After News Corporation bought 20th Century Fox in 1985, other major studios were absorbed by larger conglomerates. Sony bought Columbia Records and Films in 1988 and 1989 respectively. The Japanese electronics firm Matsushita bought Universal in 1990 and Viacom bought Paramount in 1994. At the same time, cross-media ownership rules were also radically relaxed, allowing large corporations to own both film and television sectors. In *Multinational Corporations and the Control of Culture*, Armand Mattelart's 1976 book, the author notes that when the International Telephone and Telegraph Corporation (ITT) tried to buy ABC (American Broadcasting Company) in the US in 1967, the Federal Communications Commission (FCC) blocked the deal on the grounds that this might compromise ABC news' journalistic independence.[55] Today no such concerns are to be found within the FCC and numerous other regulators around the world. The ownership structure of the film industry and its integration into the larger media and communications corporate structures are constantly changing but at the time of writing it currently looks as described below.

## The Big Five

1.  *Walt Disney* is now a conglomerate monster following its absorption of 21st Century Fox in 2018. Apart from its own film studio, its other film production holdings include Pixar, Marvel Studios, Lucas Films and The Muppets Studio (this is called horizontal integration, when a firm owns different firms in the same stage of the supply chain). It has cross-media holdings in ABC and the sports network ESPN. It has the Disneyland parks and resorts and interests in publishing, merchandise and music.

2.  *Warner Brothers* (or now Warner Media) was bought by the American Telephone and Telegraph Company in 2018 for $85 billion. A telecommunications behemoth, this purchase is another example of vertical integration insofar as it gives AT&T, which specialises in hardware delivery systems, huge critical mass in terms of audio-visual content. With Warner Brothers AT&T now has the film library archive of a major Hollywood studio, Warner Brothers Pictures, its wholly owned film production subsidiaries, New Line Cinema and Castle Rock Entertainment, the DC comics and film franchise and its television entities HBO, Turner Broadcasting and Cartoon Network.

3.  *Universal* was sold by its parent company General Electric to the telecommunications giant Comcast in 2011. Comcast has extensive interests in the internet and telephone systems, in cable and pay TV. Along with Universal, Comcast gained a number of subsidiaries such as Focus Features (a production and distribution company), a label within Focus called Gramercy Pictures, Dreamworks, Amblin, the British (but wholly owned subsidiary) Working Title Films, as well as a stake in the international distribution network, United International Pictures. In television, Comcast also owns the NBC network, Telemundo and a 25 per cent stake in Euronews. In 2018, it paid £30 billion to buy Sky broadcasting from Rupert Murdoch, giving it 27 million subscribers across Europe.

4.  *Columbia* was purchased from Coca-Cola by the Japanese electronics firm Sony in 1989 and is part of the Sony Pictures Motion Picture Group, which also includes Tri-Star Pictures, Screen Gems, Destination Films, Stage 6 and Affirm Films, the latter specialising in productions aimed at evangelical Christians. Through these acquisitions Sony has both film production and distribution capacity. Sony also had companies that specialise in special effects, animation, and digital distribution networks as well as extensive television production interests internationally.

5.  *Paramount* came out of the classic studio period in crisis and was bought by Gulf and Western in 1966. Gulf and Western was essentially a holding company for an assortment of distinct companies in automobile manufacturing, aluminium and brass manufacturing, mining, clothing, sugar and cigar making (with capital investments in Latin America), as well as some new investments in the cultural industries (records and video games). In an example of the growing economic power of the cultural industries, Gulf and Western divested itself of these non-entertainment companies, bought television stations and theme parks with the cash raised from these sales and renamed itself Paramount Communications in 1989. In 1994, Paramount was acquired by Sumner Redstone's Viacom, which is in turn controlled by National Amusements (also run by Sumner Redstone). National Amusement is a chain of theatres but they also own CBS television and through Paramount such entities as MTV Films, Nickelodeon Movies, Comedy Central Films and BET films, which targets African-American television audiences.

We may note that the film industry is now part of giant media and communications conglomerates that typically have interests in news production as well as fictions and entertainment. Their preference for simple stories of heroes and villains that draw on the least robust and critical currents within the popular culture, their cultivation of morality tales that are uncoupled from social and economic class interests, can, I think, plausibly be seen to cross-fertilise into news production, where once again simple narratives of good guys and bad guys, moral tales divorced from material contexts predominate, serving to keep public thinking about political matters in a generally immature state.[56] To take one example: there is a striking similarity between fictional President Thomas J. Whitmore, played by Bill Pullman, giving his speech in

*Independence Day* (1996) and George W. Bush's 2003 'Mission Accomplished' speech on the flight deck of the *U.S.S. Abraham Lincoln* (Figure 4.4). The fictional president was a former fighter pilot and 1991 Gulf War veteran who had to lead the human race in a desperate fight against alien invaders and who gives a famous speech rousing the troops towards the end of the film. The real US president, George W. Bush led the US to a second Gulf War against Iraq in 2003 and was landed on the *U.S.S. Abraham Lincoln* as a co-pilot in full jet fighter gear to declare victory. This stage-managed propaganda exercise looks to have been almost directly inspired by such Hollywood spectacles as *Independence Day*.

Returning specifically to the concentrated power of the film majors, the hundreds of production companies are minnows, essentially subcontractors to the big studios. The vast subcontractor network allows the important research and development work in creative ideas (and the time and money spent in doing that) to be externalised. Various deals between subcontractors and studios, such as first look deals, partial equity stakes, distribution only deals, etc., tie the production 'independents' to the major studios.[57] Particularly successful subcontractors can typically be bought up by the studios to become wholly owned subsidiaries if need be.[58] As well as being economically serviceable to Big Capital, the post-Fordist organisational structure of the production sector serves an ideological purpose by suggesting that there is a great deal of diversity and plurality in the film industry (all those company logos that appear at the beginning of the film) at the level of ownership and control. But when we reconstruct the power relations behind the appearance-forms of the commodity world, we can see how misleading that is.[59]

**FIGURE 4.4** US President George W. Bush declaring 'Mission Accomplished' after the 2003 invasion of Iraq

Many stars have their own production companies, as do many leading producers. Surplus capital within the bourgeois family can also be used to set up new and often powerful production entities. Annapurna, for example, was founded in 2011 by Megan Ellison, whose father is the billionaire Larry Ellison, head of the Orwellian-sounding Oracle Corporation. With this kind of financial backing, Annapurna was able to invest in a number of director-led films such as *Her* (Spike Jonze, 2013), *American Hustle* (2013) and *Joy* (2015), both directed by David O'Russell, *Detroit* (Kathryn Bigalow, 2017), *If Beale Street Could Talk* (Barry Jenkins, 2018), *Phantom Thread* (Paul Thomas Anderson, 2017), *Vice* (Adam McKay, 2018) and, as distributor, *Sorry To Bother You* (Boots Riley, 2018). Many of these films have been critical successes and, in terms of the use-value for the audiences who saw these films, important cultural experiences. The culturally driven motivation of Annapurna is not unusual even if the scale of the resources available to the company is. However, use-value must be trumped by exchange-value in a system that values accumulation for the sake of accumulation. Even with pockets as deep as the Ellison family has, the logic of capital still exerts itself in the last instance. At the end of 2018, Annapurna was reportedly in financial trouble and undergoing a scaling back of ambitions and operations.[60] The problem is that films that audiences may regard as 'good' do not necessarily cut the capitalist mustard. *Vice*, for example, which reminded audiences of the moral and political corruption of the George W. Bush-Dick Cheney presidency, barely recovered its $60 million budget. *Detroit*, which told an important story about police violence and racism, fell some way short of recovering its $40 million budget. Depending on other distributors to reach audiences is always risky as they are often committed to other projects in which they have more of an equity stake. This is why Annapurna moved into the distribution side of the business in the domestic US market with *Detroit*, but that in turn increases their exposure because distribution is expensive. Annapurna picked up another film for distribution which it did not produce, *Sorry To Bother You*. It was written and directed by Boots Riley, better known as the Marxist lead singer of the rap group, The Coup. While music's low capital costs of production and distribution make The Coup's anti-capitalist songs feasible, the material-economic nature of the film commodity raises higher barriers to entry for such radical messaging. This low-budget $5 million film had been funded by Significant Productions (co-owned by the black actor Forest Whitaker) and among others, Cinereach, a not-for-profit organisation that also contributed funding for Raoul Peck's documentary *I Am Not Your Negro* (2016). Annapurna were able to generate $18 million at the US box office for *Sorry To Bother You*, but the film struggled to find international distribution deals. It was eventually given a very desultory distribution by UIP (owned by Universal and Paramount), recovering less than $700,000 in the six countries UIP gave it to. The film, a satire on capitalist exploitation and racism, had its exposure to a world-wide audience significantly curtailed by … capitalism and racism.

## 4.5 Hollywood's domination of the British theatrical film market

It is only when we look at Hollywood's oligopoly control of markets at the point of exchange that we can really begin to appreciate how systemically the dominant mode of production skews revenue and resources back to the already powerful. Hollywood dominates theatrical box offices around the world. The British Film Institute provides an annual statistical yearbook that charts Hollywood's domination in the UK film business. Critical political economy typically has to rely on statistical data produced by industry or industry-related or government sources. What it must then do is provide the *critical* commentary on those statistics which is typically missing from the documents produced by organisations too embedded into the mode of production to gain critical purchase on it.

Tables 4.1–4.5 are from the *BFI Statistical Yearbook 2017*, looking back on 2016. They provide a devastating picture of Hollywood domination.

Table 4.1 shows the top 20 films released in the UK and Republic of Ireland in 2016. In the distributor column we see that Walt Disney distributed four of the top ten films, Warner Brothers distributed three of the top ten, Universal two of the top ten and 20th Century Fox (before its absorption by Disney), one of the top ten. Only one other distributor features in the top 20 box office films (eOne Films with two hits), the rest are dominated by the aforementioned companies (20th Century Fox takes four more spots, Walt Disney three and Universal one). Given this domination of the crucial distribution pipeline by US companies, it is hardly surprising that every single film in the top 20 box office hits is registered to the USA as 'country of origin'. However, we also see that the top four films and others in the top 20 are also registered British films as well. This is because they have qualified for UK Film Tax Relief, which, as noted above, is a favourite way of providing public subsidy to filmmaking under a neo-liberal model. It hands all the initiative and, as we shall see, most of the resources, to large US media corporations. In order to qualify for tax relief, US corporate productions have to pass a 'cultural test' to qualify as suitable for taxpayer subsidy. This test is designed to facilitate US corporate investment. The test requires getting 18 points to qualify, but you get six points (one-third of the required total) just for the film being predominantly in the English language. You can get four points if 80 per cent of the special effects work takes place in the UK.

If we look at Table 4.2, we see that 19 out of the top 20 UK qualifying films at the box office had US backing (the exception being *The Danish Girl*). A number of these films have what you might describe as British 'cultural content' at the level of story, such as *Fantastic Beasts*, *Bridget Jones's Baby*, *The Jungle Book*, *Absolutely Fabulous*, *London Has Fallen*, *Alice Through the Looking Glass*, *The Legend of Tarzan*, *Eddie the Eagle*, *Dad's Army*, and *Grimsby*. Either they derive from British authors, and/or are set in Britain, and/or started life as British TV programmes, and so forth. Other films do not have much in the way of British cultural content but have qualified for reasons such as using British studios, production houses, employing British actors, directors, and so forth. It is hard to see

**TABLE 4.1** Box office results for the top 20 films released in the UK and Republic of Ireland, 2016

| | Title | Country of origin | Box office gross (£ million) | Number of opening weekend cinemas | Opening weekend gross (£ million) | Distributor |
|---|---|---|---|---|---|---|
| 1 | Rogue One: A Star Wars Story★ | UK/USA | 65.9 | 689 | 17.3 | Walt Disney |
| 2 | Fantastic Beasts and Where to Find Them★ | UK/USA | 54.6 | 666 | 15.3 | Warner Bros |
| 3 | Bridget Jones's Baby | UK/USA/Fra | 48.2 | 639 | 8.1 | Universal |
| 4 | The Jungle Book | UK/USA | 46.2 | 595 | 9.9 | Walt Disney |
| 5 | Finding Dory | USA | 43.0 | 589 | 8.1 | Walt Disney |
| 6 | Deadpool | USA | 38.1 | 544 | 13.7 | 20th Century Fox |
| 7 | Caption America: Civil War | USA | 37.0 | 605 | 14.5 | Walt Disney |
| 8 | Batman v Superman: Dawn of Justice | USA | 36.6 | 612 | 14.6 | Warner Bros |
| 9 | The Secret Life of Pets | USA/JPN | 36.6 | 591 | 9.6 | Universal |
| 10 | Suicide Squad | USA | 33.6 | 574 | 11.3 | Warner Bros |
| 11 | The BFG | USA | 30.8 | 680 | 5.3 | eOne Films |
| 12 | Trolls★ | USA | 24.6 | 610 | 5.5 | 20th Century Fox |
| 13 | Zootropolis | USA | 24.0 | 579 | 5.3 | Walt Disney |
| 14 | The Girl on the Train | USA | 23.7 | 608 | 7.0 | eOne Films |
| 15 | The Revenant | USA/HKG/Taiwan | 23.4 | 589 | 5.3 | 20th Century Fox |
| 16 | Jason Bourne | UK/USA | 23.4 | 561 | 7.6 | Universal |
| 17 | Doctor Strange | UK/USA | 23.2 | 603 | 9.3 | Walt Disney |
| 18 | Moana★ | USA | 19.3 | 556 | 2.2 | Walt Disney |
| 19 | X-Men: Apocalypse | USA | 18.3 | 598 | 7.3 | 20th Century Fox |
| 20 | Alvin and the Chipmunks: The Road Chip | USA | 17.1 | 590 | 4.3 | 20th Century Fox |

Source: *BFI Statistical Yearbook 2017*, p. 26. Available at: www.bfi.org.uk/sites/bfi.org.uk/files/downloads/bfi-statistical-yearbook-2017.pdf

Notes:

Box office gross = cumulative total up to 19 February 2017

★Film still on release on 19 February 2017

in what sense though *Rogue One*, *Jason Bourne*, *Passengers*, *The Conjuring 2*, *Now You See Me 2* and *The Huntsman* could be described as 'British'.

If we wanted to find out how much public subsidy is at stake through the Film Tax Relief scheme, we could Google it and find regular annual reports in the trade press. Alternatively we could go direct to Her Majesty's Revenue and Customs (HMRC) and look at the published accounts. Table 4.3 gives an interesting breakdown of the number

**TABLE 4.2** Box office results for the top 20 UK qualifying films released in the UK and Republic of Ireland, 2016

| | Title | Country of origin | Box office gross (£ million) | Distributor |
|---|---|---|---|---|
| 1 | Rogue One: A Star Wars Story★ | UK/USA | 65.9 | Walt Disney |
| 2 | Fantastic Beasts and Where to Find Them★ | UK/USA | 54.6 | Warner Bros |
| 3 | Bridget Jones's Baby | UK/USA/Fra | 48.2 | Universal |
| 4 | The Jungle Book | UK/USA | 46.2 | Walt Disney |
| 5 | Jason Bourne | UK/USA | 23.4 | Universal |
| 6 | Doctor Strange | UK/USA | 23.2 | Walt Disney |
| 7 | Absolutely Fabulous: The Movie | UK/USA[#] | 16.1 | 20th Century Fox |
| 8 | Passengers★ | UK/USA | 12.7 | Sony Pictures |
| 9 | Miss Peregrine's Home for Peculiar Children | UK/USA | 12.3 | 20th Century Fox |
| 10 | London Has Fallen | UK/USA | 11.0 | Lionsgate |
| 11 | The Conjuring 2 | UK/USA | 11.0 | Warner Bros |
| 12 | Alice Through the Looking Glass★ | UK/USA | 10.0 | Walt Disney |
| 13 | Me Before You | UK/USA | 9.7 | Warner Bros |
| 14 | The Legend of Tarzan | UK/USA | 9.2 | Warner Bros |
| 15 | Eddie The Eagle | UK/USA/Ger[#] | 8.7 | Lionsgate |
| 16 | Dad's Army | UK/USA[#] | 8.7 | Universal |
| 17 | The Danish Girl | UK/Ger/Den/Bel | 7.5 | Universal |
| 18 | Now You See Me 2 | UK/USA | 6.3 | eOne Films |
| 19 | The Huntsman: Winter's War | UK/USA | 5.3 | Universal |
| 20 | Grimsby | UK/USA[#] | 5.3 | Sony Pictures |

Source: BFI Statistical Yearbook 2017, p. 27. Available at: www.bfi.org.uk/sites/bfi.org.uk/files/down loads/bfi-statistical-yearbook-2017.pdf

Notes:

Box office gross = cumulative total up to 19 February 2017

★Film still on release on 19 February 2017

[#]UK qualifying film made with independent (non-studio) US support or with the independent arm of a US studio.

of films that have been awarded tax relief, the amount of money awarded and, importantly, the difference between big-budget films and low-budget films. Looking at the 2016–17 period, we see the following picture. There were 75 large-budget films that were awarded £323 million of tax relief. There were also 555 low-budget films awarded £91.9 million. This is very revealing because it shows how the big-budget films (overwhelmingly US-funded) take the majority share of the publicly funded subsidy. The percentages show that under 12 per cent of the films awarded took nearly 79 per cent of the Film Tax Relief for that year, leaving the remaining 555 films with just 21 per cent of the subsidy between them. We see here the skew towards the already economically powerful that is typical of the class-stratified structure that is capitalism.

In Table 4.4, we are given the top 20 UK independent films – although 'independent' here includes films made by an independent arm of a US studio. On the distribution side, we can see a little bit more diversity, with nine companies represented in this top 20 as opposed to only five represented in the top 20 box office hits. We also

**TABLE 4.3** Number of claims and amount of relief paid on receipts basis, from 2006–7 to 2016–17

| Year claim paid | Large films | | Limited budget films | | Total | |
|---|---|---|---|---|---|---|
| | Paid | | Paid | | Paid | |
| | Number | Amount | Number | Amount | Number | Amount |
| 2006–07 | – | – | – | ★ | ★ | ★ |
| 2007–08 | 15 | 62.3 | 100 | 41.4 | 115 | 103.7 |
| 2008–09 | 25 | 88.9 | 200 | 56.2 | 225 | 145.1 |
| 2009–10 | 25 | 76.7 | 285 | 52.1 | 310 | 128.8 |
| 2010–11 | 35 | 148.6 | 280 | 50.7 | 315 | 199.3 |
| 2011–12 | 45 | 154.5 | 350 | 62.8 | 395 | 217.3 |
| 2012–13 | 35 | 155.9 | 325 | 48.9 | 360 | 204.8 |
| 2013–14 | 55 | 171.6 | 365 | 68.7 | 415 | 240.8 |
| 2014–15[p,r] | 60 | 183.8 | 450 | 75.1 | 510 | 258.9 |
| 2015–16[p,r] | 60 | 255.9 | 475 | 82.7 | 535 | 338.6 |
| 2016–17[p] | 75 | 323.0 | 555 | 91.9 | 630 | 414.9 |
| **Total** | 430 | 1,621.1 | 3,375 | 630.6 | 3,810 | 2,251.7 |

Source: HMRC Management Information System (MIS) and BFI HMRC. Available at: www.gov.uk/government/statistics/creative-industries-statistics-july-2017

Notes:

1. Companies have a period of one year to submit returns after the end of the accounting period and another year to amend or withdraw a claim. Therefore, the data for 2014–15 and 2015–16 have been revised and data for 2016–17 remains provisional and subject to change due to claims not yet received.

2. Finance year ending 31st March.

r. Revised

p. Provisional

★Value suppressed as cell count is less than 5

Zero values are represented as –

Statistics in this table are consistent with HMRC's policies on dominance and disclosure.

Numbers: actual; Amounts: £million.

start to see that there are now films being represented that are either UK-only registered or are co-productions with European companies. We also, I think, start to see British cultural content that is more diversified, less stereotypical, sometimes more challenging material in that it is less familiar or more politically explicit or just more idiosyncratic than those that featured in Table 4.2. We also see that none of the top 20 UK independent films made it into the top 20 box office hits at the UK/Republic of Ireland box office and that only the top five made it into the top 20 box office for UK

**TABLE 4.4** Box office results for the top 20 UK independent films released in the UK and Republic of Ireland, 2016

|  | Title | Country of origin | Box office gross (£million) | Distributor |
|---|---|---|---|---|
| 1 | Absolutely Fabulous: The Movie | UK/USA[#] | 16.1 | 20th Century Fox |
| 2 | Eddie the Eagle | UK/USA/Ger[#] | 8.7 | Lionsgate |
| 3 | Dad's Army | UK/USA[#] | 8.7 | Universal |
| 4 | The Danish Girl | UK/Ger/Den/Bel | 7.5 | Universal |
| 5 | Grimsby | UK/USA[#] | 5.3 | Sony Pictures |
| 6 | Eye in the Sky | UK/RSA | 5.1 | eOne Films |
| 7 | A Street Cat Named Bob* | UK | 4.3 | Sony Pictures |
| 8 | Brotherhood | UK | 3.7 | Lionsgate |
| 9 | David Brent: Life on the Road | UK | 3.6 | eOne Films |
| 10 | Florence Foster Jenkins* | UK/Fra | 3.2 | Pathe |
| 11 | I, Daniel Blake* | UK/Fra/Bel | 3.2 | eOne Films |
| 12 | Swallows and Amazons | UK | 3.1 | StudioCanal |
| 13 | A United Kingdom* | UK/USA/Cze[#] | 2.4 | Pathe |
| 14 | Bastille Day | UK/Fra/USA[#] | 2.0 | StudioCanal |
| 15 | High-Rise | UK/Bel | 2.0 | StudioCanal |
| 16 | Our Kind of Traitor | UK/Fra/Lux | 1.3 | StudioCanal |
| 17 | My Scientology Movie | UK/USA[#] | 1.1 | Altitude |
| 18 | The Infiltrator | UK/USA | 1.1 | Warner Bros |
| 19 | The Girl with All the Gifts | UK | 1.1 | Warner Bros |
| 20 | Youth | UK/Ita/Fra/Swi | 1.0 | StudioCanal |

Source: comScore, BFI RSU analysis *BFI Statistical Yearbook 2017*, p. 28. Available at: www.bfi.org.uk/sites/bfi.org.uk/files/downloads/bfi-statistical-yearbook-2017.pdf

Notes:

Box office gross = cumulative total up to 19 February 2017

*Film still on release on 19 February 2017

[#]Film made with independent (non-studio) US support or with the independent arm of a US studio. The table does not include UK qualifying US inward investment titles such as London Has Fallen and Now You See Me independent companies through UK-based SPVs qualifying films. We see also that the box office gross has dropped considerably compared to Table 4.1 and Table 4.2, with 14 of the films listed recovering less than £5 million and five of them less than £1.5 million.

Table 4.5 provides confirmation of what we may have already suspected – that Hollywood distributors dominate the share of the UK (and Republic of Ireland) box office. With only 19 big budget releases, Disney commanded a 23.2 per cent share of the market and a box office gross of over £300 million. Together with the three other main distributors, the Hollywood majors seized 68.5 per cent of the market share. Most of the remaining share of the market is carved up between other major corporate entities, such as Sony, Paramount, Lionsgate, and so forth. Only 4.1 per cent of the market is left for 97 other distributors! So, what we see here is that while there are many companies involved in the distribution game, the top four seized 68.5 per cent and the top ten grabbed nearly 96 per cent of market share, leaving 97 smaller companies distributing 675 films between them. What these numbers tell us is that the big players have managed to massively concentrate wealth and shift the financial risks involved in filmmaking onto the majority of smaller companies who are scrambling around looking for crumbs from the master's table. Such is life inside the capitalist mode of production.

**TABLE 4.5** Distributor share of box office, UK and Republic of Ireland, 2016

| Distributor | Market share (%) | Films on release in 2016 | Box office gross (£ million) |
| --- | --- | --- | --- |
| Walt Disney | 23.2 | 19 | 300.7 |
| 20th Century Fox | 15.7 | 42 | 204.3 |
| Warner Bros | 15.6 | 38 | 201.9 |
| Universal | 14.0 | 38 | 181.3 |
| eOne Films | 8.4 | 42 | 109.2 |
| Sony Pictures | 6.6 | 33 | 86.0 |
| Paramount | 5.4 | 13 | 69.7 |
| Lionsgate | 4.0 | 28 | 52.4 |
| StudioCanal | 1.5 | 82 | 20.1 |
| Entertainment | 1.5 | 7 | 19.2 |
| Sub-total (top 10 distributors) | 95.9 | 342 | 1,244.8 |
| Others (97 distributors) | 4.1 | 675 | 52.9 |
| **Total** | **100.0** | **1,017** | **1,297.7** |

Source: comScore *BFI Statistical Yearbook 2017*, p. 107. Available at: www.bfi.org.uk/sites/bfi.org.uk/files/downloads/bfi-statistical-yearbook-2017.pdf

## 4.6 Flashback

In the early 1970s, the British film industry was in crisis. Studios were closing, film production slumped, casualisation of the workforce was endemic and Hollywood capital withdrew from the UK. In response, the film trade union Association of Cinematograph, Television and Allied Technicians (ACTT) developed a policy demanding public ownership of the film industry and under workers' control. The ACTT's 1973 report *Nationalising the Film Industry* (Figure 4.5) argued that state control was not sufficient:

> Whitehall is a substitute neither for Wardour Street nor for Hollywood. Our demand is for an industry in which workers themselves are responsible for

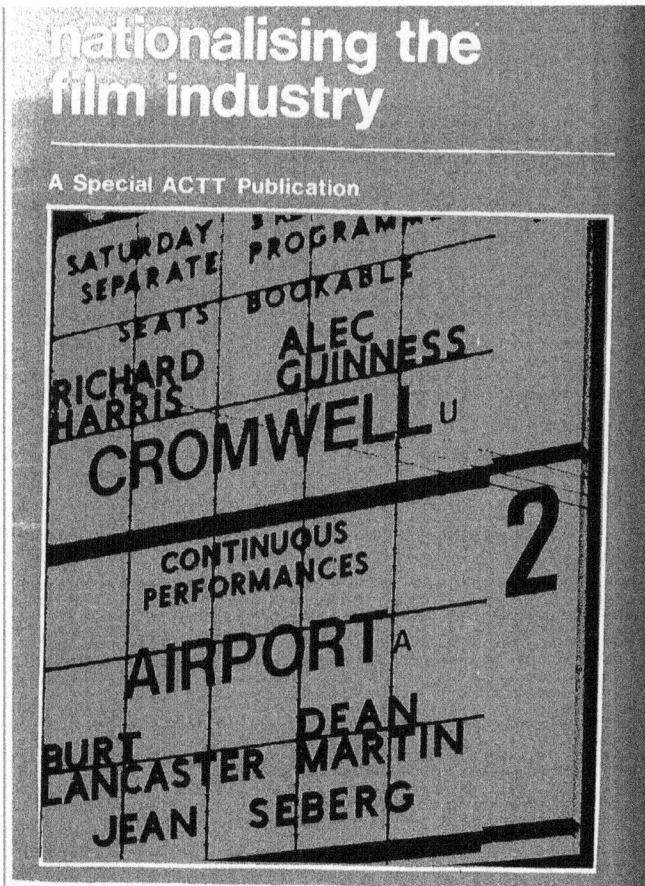

**FIGURE 4.5** Front cover of the ACTT's 1973 report calling for workers' control of the film industry

Source: Reproduced with kind permission of BECTU.

the management of the industry. Government appointed boards of management are replaced by elected management committees. The fundamental power within the industry rests with those who know its potential and its limitations. It rests with those who work in the industry and without whom it could not exist.[61]

## Notes

1 Karl Marx, *Grundrisse* (Harmondsworth: Penguin Books, 1993), p. 100.
2 Ibid.
3 Karl Marx, *Capital*, vol. I (London: Lawrence and Wishart, 1983), p. 174.
4 Marx, *Grundrisse*, op. cit., p. 85.
5 Stephen G. Jones, *The British Labour Movement and Film, 1918–1939* (London: Routledge & Kegan Paul, 1987).
6 David Kunzle, 'Public Graphics in Cuba: A Very Cuban Form of Internationalist Art', *Latin American Perspectives*, 2(4) (1975): 91.
7 There is, for example, a burgeoning sub-field within film studies looking at different types of festival curation.
8 Marx, *Grundrisse*, op. cit., p. 91.
9 Ibid., p. 92.
10 Ibid., p. 92.
11 Louis Althusser, *On the Reproduction of Capitalism* (London: Verso, 2014), p. 22.
12 Ibid.
13 Ibid., p. 19.
14 Marx, *Grundrisse*, op. cit., pp. 106–7.
15 David Robb, 'U.S. Film Industry Topped $43 Billion in Revenue Last Year, Study Finds, But It's Not All Good News', available at: https://deadline.com/2018/07/film-industry-revenue-2017-ibisworld-report-gloomy-box-office-1202425692/
16 See Julianne Burton's 'Film Artisans and Film Industries in Latin America', in Michael T. Martin (ed.), *New Latin American Cinema: Theory, Practices and Transcontinental Articulations* (Detroit: Wayne State University Press, 1997), p. 174.
17 See Mike Wayne, *Political Film: The Dialectics of Third Cinema* (London: Pluto Press, 2001).
18 '*Commodification* is the process of transforming things valued for their use into marketable products that are valued for what they can bring in exchange,' writes Vincent Mosco in *The Political Economy of Communication* (London: Sage, 2009), p. 127.
19 Janet Wasko, Mark Phillips and Chris Purdie, 'Hollywood Meets Madison Avenue: The Commercialization of US Films', *Media, Culture and Society*, 15(2) (1993): 271–93.
20 Michael Curtin and Kevin Sanson, *Voices of Labour: Creativity, Craft and Conflict in Global Hollywood* (Berkeley, CA: University of California Press, 2017), p. 1.
21 Michael Chanan, 'Swallowing Time: On the Immaterial Labour of the Video Blogger', in Ewa Maierszka and Lars Kristensen (eds), *Marxism and Film Activism* (Oxford: Berghahn Books, 2005), p. 241.
22 See Nick Hall's *The Zoom: Drama at the Touch of a Lever* (New Brunswick, NJ: Rutgers University Press, 2018).
23 Curtin and Sanson, *Voices of Labour*, op. cit., p. 3.
24 Chanan, 'Swallowing Time', op. cit., p. 245.
25 *Get Out* (Jordan Peele, 2017), for example, was made for $5 million and made over $431 million. *Solo: A Star Wars Story*, made less than $100 million at the box office. While that might sound like a lot of money to ordinary people, Lucas Films do not go into production to generate that kind of revenue.
26 Garth Jowett and James M. Linton, *Movies as Mass Communication* (Thousand Oaks, CA: Sage, 1980), p. 29.

27  Johanne Brunet, 'The Social Production of Creative Products in the Television and Film Industry', *International Journal of Arts Management*, 6(2) (2004): 6.

28  David Hesmondhalgh, *The Cultural Industries* (Thousand Oaks, CA: Sage, 2002), p. 22.

29  Nicholas Garnham, 'Contribution to a Political Economy of Mass-Communications', *Media, Culture and Society*, 1 (1979), .139.

30  Karl Marx, *Capital*, vol. I (London: Lawrence and Wishart, 1983), p. 87.

31  Martin Kanzler, 'Fiction Film Financing in Europe: A Sample Analysis of Films Released in 2016', European Audiovisual Observatory, 2018, p. 56. Available at: www.obs.coe.int/en/web/observatoire/industry/film

32  Ibid., p. 68.

33  *BFI Statistical Yearbook 2017*, p. 224. Available at: www.bfi.org.uk/sites/bfi.org.uk/files/downloads/bfi-statistical-yearbook-2017.pdf

34  David Steele, 'Rethinking the Focus of UK Film Support: Is Subsidising US Studios a Safe Strategy for UK Film Production in the Coming Decade?' *Cultural Trends*, 24(1) (2015): 74–9.

35  Curtin and Sanson, *Voices of Labour*, op. cit., p. 9.

36  Thomas H. Guback, 'Hollywood's International Market', in Tino Balio (ed.), *The American Film Industry* (Madison, WI: University of Wisconsin Press, 1985), p. 463.

37  See Lee Grieveson's *Cinema and the Wealth of Nations: Media, Capital and the Liberal World System* (Berkeley, CA: University of California Press, 2018). Grieveson discusses British concerns that Hollywood was eroding interest in British manufacturing goods from the 1920s onwards in Britain and across the Empire (see especially Chapter 8).

38  Manjunath Pendakur, 'Hollywood and the State: The American Film Industry Cartel in the Age of Globalization', in Paul McDonald and Janet Wasko (eds), *The Contemporary Hollywood Film Industry* (Oxford: Blackwell, 2008), p. 188.

39  Toby Miller, 'The Crime of Monsieur Lang: GATT, the Screen, and the New International Division of Cultural Labour', in Albert Moran (ed.), *Film Policy: International and Regional Perspectives* (London: Routledge, 1996).

40  Deloitte, *China's Film Industry: A New Era* (Deloitte, 2017), p. 2. Available at: www2.deloitte.com/.../deloitte-cn-tmt-china-film-industry-en-161223.pdf

41  Ariel Dorfman and Armand Mattelart, *How to Read Donald Duck: Imperialist Ideology in the Disney Comic* (London: International General, 1991), p. 9.

42  The classic cinematic account of the Chilean revolution and its tragic end is provided by Patricio Guzman's *The Battle of Chile* (1975/6) which was smuggled out of Chile after the coup.

43  Garth Jowett and James M. Linton, *Movies as Mass Communication* (Thousand Oaks, CA: Sage, 1980), p. 47.

44  Philip Drake, 'Distributing and Marketing in Contemporary Hollywood', in Paul McDonald and Janet Wasko (eds), *The Contemporary Hollywood Film Industry* (Oxford: Blackwell, 2008), p. 64.

45  Jowett and Linton, *Movies as Mass Communication*, op. cit., pp. 64–5.

46  Toby Miller, et al. *Global Hollywood* (London: BFI, 2001), p. 151.

47  John Ellis, *Visible Fictions: Cinema, Television, Video* (London: Routledge 1992), pp. 32–3.

48  Julianne Burton, 'Film Artisans and Film Industries in Latin America', in Michael T. Martin (ed.), *New Latin American Cinema: Theory, Practices and Transcontinental Articulations* (Detroit: Wayne State University Press, 1997), p. 175.

49  Janet Wasko, 'Revisiting the Political Economy of Film', in Tannis Tzioumakis and Claire Molloy (eds), *The Routledge Companion to Cinema and Politics* (London: Routledge, 2016), p. 64.

50  Susan Christopherson, 'Hard Jobs in Hollywood: How Concentration in Distribution Affects the Production Side of the Media Entertainment Industry', in Dwayne Winseck and Dal Yong Jin (eds), *The Political Economies of Media* (London: Bloomsbury, 2012).

51  Ernest Borneman, 'United States versus Hollywood: The Case Study of an Antitrust Suit', in Tino Balio (ed.), *The American Film Industry* (Madison, WI: University of Wisconsin Press, 1985), p. 452.

52 Michael Storper, 'The Transition to Flexible Specialisation in the US Film Industry: External Economies, the Division of Labour and the Crossing of Industrial Divides', *Cambridge Journal of Economics*, 13(2) (1989): 273–305.

53 Asu Aksoy and Kevin Robbins, 'Hollywood for the 21st Century: Global Competition for Critical Mass in Image Markets', *Cambridge Journal of Economics*, 16(1) (1992): 1–22.

54 Charles Acland, 'Theatrical Exhibition: Accelerated Cinema', in Paul McDonald and Janet Wasko (eds), *The Contemporary Hollywood Film Industry* (Oxford: Blackwell, 2008), pp. 85–6.

55 Armand Mattelart, *Multinational Corporations and the Control of Culture: The Ideological Apparatuses of Imperialism* (Hemel Hempstead: Harvester Press, 1979), pp. 140–1.

56 David Cromwell, *Why Are We the Good Guys? Reclaiming Your Mind from the Delusions of Propaganda* (New York: Zero Books, 2012).

57 Janet Wasko, 'Financing and Production: Creating the Hollywood Film Commodity', in Paul McDonald and Janet Wasko (eds), *The Contemporary Hollywood Film Industry* (Oxford: Blackwell, 2008), p. 49.

58 Thomas Schatz, 'The Studio System and Conglomerate Hollywood', in Paul McDonald and Janet Wasko (eds), *The Contemporary Hollywood Film Industry* (Oxford: Blackwell, 2008), p. 29.

59 Mike Wayne, *Marxism and Media Studies: Key Concepts and Contemporary Trends* (London: Pluto Press, 2003), pp. 61–73.

60 'Annapurna Upheaval', *The Wrap*, available at: www.thewrap.com/annapurna-upheaval-megan-ellison-reevaluating-film-division/

61 ACTT, *Nationalising the Film Industry: Report of the ACTT Nationalisation Forum* (London: ACTT, 1973), p. 6.

# 5

# FORM

## 5.1 The Formalist debate

The workers and students revolts in France, in May 1968, sparked interest in the debates on culture and art during that earlier twentieth-century upheaval, the Russian Revolution in October 1917. *Screen*, for example, published articles from the Russian journals *Lef* and *Novy Lef*, [1] while Sylvia Harvey's book, *May 68 and Film Culture*, is the classic account of the recovery and reworking of the debates between the two historical conjunctures. The debates from the Russian Revolution seemed to map pertinently onto the 1970s' debates concerning the extent to which it was necessary to break with dominant cinematic forms, exemplified by Hollywood. A renewed appreciation of the cultural politics of form underpinned this debate. As we saw in Chapter 2 and Chapter 3, it was realised that visual and audio representation or form shapes the way spectators engage with the 'content' of a story, what we see and how we evaluate what we see (and hear). Furthermore, form may encourage certain skills and capacities and discourage others. For example, formal experimentation may try and wean spectators away from modes of decoding that encourage fairly simple allegiances with certain characters, values, authorities and institutions. Formal experimentation may try and sustain a more complex 'working through' of the issues which the story content is mulling over, rather than hurry to firm up for the spectator what is the 'right' position to take in alignment with this or that character or issue. Another important contribution which formal innovation can make to the cultural and political skills of the audience is the ability to make links and connections, to handle material in a layered manner, historically, for example, by playing with temporal structures or socially by extending the context for events by bold editing decisions (montage is particularly important here).

Finally, there is the argument that was frequently made by the Modernists after the 1917 Revolution that new political and social content in life needed new artistic forms to properly express them, for example, urban life and the working class who had entered the stage of world history. Such new artistic forms would not arise spontaneously just because reality was changing, however. Instead, as Sylvia Harvey argued, 'These changes had to be brought about within artistic production by those who were conscious of the specific histories of the modes of artistic production within which they worked.'[2] Still, the theoretical justification of formal innovation may overestimate the extent to which actual practice achieves the goals espoused and the theory after May 68 probably underestimated the extent to which more established and widely disseminated forms also permit degrees of cognitive and emotional complexity. It is perhaps also the case that dominant cinema itself has become significantly more complex in the last 50 years or so since May 68, in part, because dominant cinema has absorbed some of the experiments initially tested out by the Modernist avant-garde throughout the twentieth century. It is worth revisiting the debates that emerged following the 1917 Revolution because they raised important questions concerning the relationship between cultural forms and social change, the relationship between the working class and the existing bourgeois culture, the relationship between the working class and the radical middle-class intelligentsia and the contribution of Marxist theory to an understanding of culture and artistic production.

After the October 1917 Revolution there were four main collective protagonists in the debate: (1) the Futurists, who were an influential strand of Modernist artistic practitioners working mostly in literature and especially poetry, many of whom became communists after the October Revolution; (2) the Formalists, who were literary scholars influenced by Saussure's linguistic revolution; (3) Proletkult, a mass movement dedicated to developing proletarian culture; and (4) the Bolsheviks, who had led the Russian Revolution and who had to respond intellectually and in policy terms to these other groups. The relations between the four groups was complex, full of overlaps and contestation. The intellectual and political problems they were addressing were more complex still and the debates were not helped by fierce polemics between and within the camps. We must remember that these labels, while useful as rough and ready ways of organising the tendencies of the participants, like all labels, disguise the heterogeneous strands within them. Proletkult, for example, had a minority Modernist wing within it while the Bolsheviks had a range of positions in relation to Proletkult, the Futurists and the Formalists. The most sophisticated responses to these debates coming from the Bolsheviks, however, can be found in the work of Leon Trotsky, who made a series of interventions into these debates, collected in his book *Literature and Revolution* and his fellow Bolshevik, Aleksandr Voronsky, editor of the journal, *Red Virgin Soil*, whose book (another collection of essays) *Art as the Cognition of Life*, remains a classic high point of Bolshevik thinking on culture and revolution.

The Russian Futurists were part of a Europe-wide Modernist movement that had existed before the revolution. Their 1912 manifesto, characteristically entitled

'A Slap in the Face of Public Taste', called for the Russian classical literary tradition, such as Pushkin, Tolstoy and Dostoevsky to be thrown overboard from the 'steamer of modernity'.[3] For Futurist supporter Nicholas Gorlov, the movement was a 'rebellion against old content and old forms, the destruction of an old aesthetic'.[4] For Gorlov, the classical leanings of the leading Bolsheviks meant that they were 'political revolutionaries whose aesthetic instinct is a good fifty years behind their political consciousness'.[5] The Futurists wanted to be recognised by the Bolsheviks as *the* cultural movement that best aligned with the new revolutionary government. But their attitude to history and tradition was deeply problematic from a purely Marxist perspective. In their rejection of the past, the Futurists were rejecting the cultural traditions that were a condition of their own existence. For example, like the nineteenth-century Realists, they wanted to relate to their own contemporary moment and, like the Russian Symbolists from the turn of the twentieth century, they wanted to experiment with language and the acoustic play of words. Yet with their typically Modernist stress on rupture with the past, the Futurists disavowed their own cultural inheritance and lineage. In his response to the claims of the Futurists, Trotsky was friendly but critical. He reminds them, thinking of the Romanticists, that 'revolt' is actually the historic trademark of new schools of bourgeois culture, as a semi-pauperised wing of the intelligentsia rebel against 'the closed-in and caste-like aesthetics of the bourgeois intelligentsia'.[6] The Russian Revolution cemented the leftist orientation of the Futurists but the anti-historical optic of the Futurists was profoundly incompatible either with Marxism or any sensible cultural history. As Alexandr Voronsky argued:

> Modern innovation, "energetic word development", stress patterns, the density of phrases, dynamicism, liberation of rhyme, and so forth – all this is at best a series of innovations which differ in no way from those that occurred sometime in the past. No matter how significant or modern they may be, they are completely interwoven with the solid roots of the old art. What about the new content, and new world outlook? All the urbanism, industrialism, cosmism, and so forth, which the proletarian writer tries to employ in order to set himself apart from the art of the past, is simply a product of bourgeois urban culture, and doesn't go beyond its limits ... in England we find the writer Wells. All of his wonderful science fiction comes from the dynamo, the airplane, chemistry and physics. Everything that our poets and writers are arguing about has already been done by this mechanized science fiction writer.[7]

Proletkult, as the name implies, was concerned to develop the culture of the proletariat. It was set up in 1918 and had close organic links to the Bolsheviks. Anatoly Lunacharsky, who was the first Commissar for Education (Narkompros) after the revolution, had long been interested in the broader cultural and educational needs of the working class and along with his brother-in-law, Alexander Bogdanov, had run schools outside Russia for Russian workers since 1909. Proletkult was a heterogeneous organisation dedicated to education as much as artistic expression, and it included within it a Modernist strand much influenced by Constructivism, which was to the visual arts what Futurism was to literature. In Moscow, where there was of course a concentration of the cream of the Russian intelligentsia, Proletkultists espoused, like the Futurists, the importance of an artistic revolution to match the social and political revolution. At Moscow's Proletkult theatre, Sergei Eisenstein learned his craft as a set designer and then director of formally experimental plays before entering into film production.[8] Yet this strand of Proletkult was very much in a minority. Outside the metropolitan centres a more conservative cultural politics asserted itself. Bogdanov himself stressed simplicity of form, accessibility and the importance of 'new content', i.e. the working class itself.[9] Unlike Futurism, Proletkult was a genuinely working-class organisation with close links to the factories and whose membership reached around 500,000 by 1920.[10] However, like Futurism, it was also increasingly sceptical of the value of the bourgeois cultural heritage and aspired to build up working-class or proletarian culture internally largely from its own direct experience and conditions.[11] Like the Futurists, Proletkult wanted to be seen as the exemplary model for a cultural politics in revolutionary Russia and claimed that they were building a proletarian culture. Unlike the Futurists, however, Proletkult left little in the way of a lasting cultural legacy outside its minority Modernist strand. Its depictions of the working class were often sentimental and heroic, a feature that was to later feed into the culture of Stalin's Socialist Realism.

The lasting cultural legacy of the Modernist middle-class intelligentsia was underpinned by the time, education and upbringing to absorb the best that bourgeois culture had built up across Europe in the preceding five hundred years. Already in his mid-teens, Sergei Eisenstein was familiar with Dumas, Racine, Corneille, Mallarmé, Shakespeare, Dickens, Hugo, Zola, Poe, Tolstoy and Dostoevsky.[12] This rich and deep cultural knowledge that fed his social criticism and satirical vision, was the basis for his own major contributions to film culture in the 1920s. The Futurist rejection of the cultural past because it was out of date and the Proletkult rejection of the cultural past because it was the culture of the bourgeoisie, missed the essential Marxist point: just as a socialist revolution is only possible on an advanced material basis built up by the bourgeoisie, so a socialist culture also requires a deep and extensive, if *critical* absorption and transformation of the cultural achievements of the bourgeois class. For Trotsky, the proletariat needs elements of bourgeois culture, but it had not had the time to absorb them, in part, because its historic subaltern position as a 'non-possessing class' excluded it from that culture, in part, because of the particular poverty of culture which the Russian working class had endured, with basic literacy skills, for example, very restricted, and, in part, because since 1917, the proletariat had been engaged in a battle for survival, such as the civil war with the counter-revolutionaries, whom Trotsky, as leader of the Red Army, had played a key role in defeating. So, for Trotsky, it was premature to speak of rejecting the past in the name of experimentation or building a proletarian culture.[13] Grand statements about a revolutionary culture, or proletarian culture produced by a tiny minority, cannot short-circuit the patient and extensive work of cultural capacity building or what Trotsky calls 'culture bearing, that is, a systematic, planful and, of course, critical imparting to the backward masses of the essential elements of the culture which already exists'.[14] Calls to recognise a proletarian culture in the making is for Trotsky anti-historical wishful thinking; it is 'not Marxism, but reactionary populism' and instead he cautions patience and a commitment to the necessarily long-term process 'to raise the cultural level of the working class'.[15] Finding the time to write about literature and art in between the more pressing matters of the revolution's survival indicates that Trotsky thought these matters were important. But he wisely argued that 'the actual development of art, and its struggle for new forms are not part of the Party's tasks, nor is it its concern',[16] that is to say it should refuse to make any short-sighted endorsement of this or that tendency.

The Formalists were a loose network of scholars, theorists, linguists and literary analysts organised primarily around the Moscow Linguistic Circle, where Roman Jakobson was the key figure and the Society for the Study of Poetic Language (Opoyaz), where Viktor Shklovsky was predominant. Their main concern was to establish a 'scientific' analysis of literature that broke with the subjective and impressionistic language of the past, with its eclectic mix of references to the artist, their genius, their biography, their psychology, eclectic historical reference points, talk of 'feelings', 'sensations' and 'images', etc., etc. None of this was a basis for an objective, scientific analysis that focused on the *language* of literature itself, the words on the page. What made these words on the page 'literary' was what concerned the Formalists and what made them literary was their formal properties that distinguished them from ordinary everyday language. The label 'formalists' was applied to the Formalists by their Marxist critics and the label stuck. Boris Eykhenbaum complained, 'We are not "formalists" but rather, if you like, "specifiers."'[17] What they wanted to specify were the principles of literature, but as we shall see, the Formalists were indeed formalists. Yet their anti-historical focus on language to the exclusion of everything else did bring dividends in a new awareness of how literary form (and artistic forms in general) construct meanings and perspective. One of the key concepts that emerged out of their work, that would become crucially important for politicised artistic practices, was that of *Ostrananie* or 'making strange'. In his essay, 'Art as Device' (or 'technique'), Shklovsky argued that what made literature literary was its ability to disrupt 'the economy of mental effort' which everyday language acquired through habitual use and responses. This economy – necessary for everyday life in so many ways – dulls us to the processes by which we achieve a meaningful relationship to the world. For Shklovsky, the artistic use of language should reverse this everyday automatization using the special devices or techniques that artistic language use has developed.[18] The Formalist concept of 'making strange' feeds into the concept of self-reflexivity which we will discuss in more detail later in Section 5.4.

Many of the Formalists were inspired by the poetic work of the Futurists, and the Futurists in turn acquired new conceptual understandings of their practice from the Formalists. But the Formalists were quite unable to explain the emergence of a formal development such as the Futurists, since they bracketed off all other social forces impinging on the work of art. Trying to justify this, Eykhenbaum made a distinction between genesis and causality. 'To indicate the genesis means to recognise and identify the connection between phenomena but not the *causality* which explains them.'[19] A literary form like Futurism may be connected with social developments, but for Eykhenbaum, the *causality* which explains the development of Futurism is the internal modifications in literary language itself. It should be clear that this is radically unsatisfactory and what the Futurists lacked was something like a concept such as *mediation*, which would explore how connections between form and wider social conditions pass through into the 'internal' system of artistic form and its causalities.

Trotsky skewered the absurdity of the Formalist's anti-historical assumptions, noting that they could not explain the development of Futurism as a response to the development of urban city culture, but instead, according to Formalism, 'the new form, originating arbitrarily, forced the poet to seek appropriate material and so pushed him in the direction of the city!'[20] Urbanism and city culture are clearly the 'content' that is secreted in the form of Futurism and in the visual arts, Constructivism. Social life is the content that provides the key motivating forces for the new forms. This is the best way of thinking about the relationship between 'form' and 'content', with the latter understood not as the theme of an individual text but as the social conditions of life which the text is responding to in its theme and form.

Trotsky's critique of the Formalists illustrates the strengths of Marxism against the bourgeois tendency to isolate distinct practices from the totality of social production. At the same time, while Trotsky is strong in broad terms in dismantling the Formalist position, when it comes to analysing specific artistic practices, his own language betrays the underdeveloped state of the Marxist theory of culture and art at that time. Eykhenbaum was right that Trotsky oscillated between collapsing back into the old bourgeois language of discussing art or he has to make (unacknowledged) concessions to Formalist ideas and language about the relative autonomy of literary technique.[21] It was not until the work of scholars such as V.N. Vološhinov's 1929 *Marxism and the Philosophy of Language* and Mikhail Bakhtin's work from the 1930s onwards, that Marxism was in a position to begin to absorb the key lessons and language of Formalism and combine it with a theory receptive to the social and historical conditions of artistic production.[22] For example, Vološhinov reversed the structuralist emphasis on an *a priori* and a-historical language structure (*langue*) or ideology and grounded analysis in the combination of signs that make up specific utterances woven into social practices. This makes the category of 'ideology', for example, less prone to becoming a static, fixed abstraction (see Chapter 6).

## 5.2 Montage dialectics

We have already seen how in the years between the First and Second World Wars, revolutionary upheavals crossed with capitalism's own transformations of everyday life (industrialisation, urbanisation, mass communications, etc.) constituted the historical 'content' of the forms associated with Modernism (see Section 2.3). Modernism expressed modern life in its very artistic forms. In film, the rhythm, the dynamicism, the speed and the geographical scale of modern life seemed to prioritise the centrality and importance of editing. I discussed how D.W. Griffiths' 1909 film *A Corner in Wheat* (see Section 2.3) used parallel editing to make connections between the actions of Wall Street speculators and ordinary Americans who had no interpersonal contact with them. In short, the form was responding to the impersonal forces connecting people across time and space. In the context of the Russian Revolution after 1917, it was precisely this political power of film to develop emotional and intellectual responses that burst out of the classical unities of time and space that filmmakers and theorists of this still new medium wanted and needed to explore.

One of the most important early film practitioners and theorists was Sergei Eisenstein, whose films and theoretical reflections are associated with *montage*. Sergei Eisenstein was a brilliant polymath who turned away from becoming an engineer and who threw himself into the Russian Revolution of 1917 (his father joined the counter-revolutionaries). He went into experimental Proletkult theatre and then emerged to produce a series of classic films that transformed the medium. For Eisenstein, editing, and a particular approach to editing, namely, montage, were fundamental, as he considered film montage to be the culmination of hundreds of years of artistic development. He found the principles of montage in earlier examples of prose literature, in painting, in poetry, theatre and music. It was the beating heart of everything dynamic and energetic in the aesthetic experience, in the 'play of forms', to cite Kant.

Eisenstein's compass and the influences on his thought were remarkably wide, but certainly he drew on Marxist philosophy, especially the concept of the dialectic (see Section 1.7), to fashion a vision of art that struck a blow against classical and bourgeois theories of art as serene contemplation of harmonious relationships. Art, he wrote, is:

CONFLICT
As the essential basic principle of the existence of every work or art and every form.[23]

So alien and odd to the dominant artistic traditions is this idea of conflict being at the root of aesthetic form (because it is so potentially subversive an idea) that we must pause for a moment to consider it. Conflict at the level of form exists right at the heart of the *moving* image. The perception of movement when single frames are passed through the projector at speed involves the superimposition of one shot over the other, so that the impression of movement arises from the retained impression in the mind's eye of the object's first position against the object's now perceived second position.

> The incongruity in contour between the first picture that has been imprinted on the mind and the subsequently perceived second picture – the conflict between the two – gives birth to the sensation of movement, the idea that movement has taken place.[24]

The perception of movement arises from the *conflict* between positions. In the film that made him famous, *Battleship Potemkin* (1925), Eisenstein produced such an impossible 'animation' from the static. Using three single shots of three marble lions, one sleeping, one waking and the third on its feet, he animated them by cutting them rapidly together to give the impression of one *single* marble lion sleeping, waking up and standing up. The difference between the positions/postures/contours can, I think, be legitimately thought of as *tensions*, as differentials that are also connected to produce an action (the lion awakes) and a political idea (the lion awakes is a metaphor of the proletariat awakening and striking back against the old Tsarist authorities who have just massacred the people on the Odessa Steps during the 1905 uprising). Here the conflict between *forms* (the marble lion in different poses) stirs up affective and intellectual awareness of the *social* conflict. Thus, we make a leap from Sensation to Idea.

But, Eisenstein teaches us, formal conflicts are present at every level of film. Tensions between graphic lines, such as the bodies of the people gunned down on the Odessa Steps lying across the horizontal lines of the steps; tensions between planes of action (foreground, middle-ground, background), volumes in space, figure movement, lighting, between sound and image, frame and object, and so forth. One key issue in subsequent film theory in the 1970s was precisely to what extent films should foreground awareness of *formal* tensions to undergird awareness of *social* tensions. My feeling is that there should and must be a connection between formal tension and social tension, but that does not automatically privilege radical avant-garde forms over more 'classical' forms of storytelling. As we shall see in this chapter and others, that is a simplistic binary that is unhelpful.

As a political Modernist, Eisenstein conceived of the theatre and film as a series of psychological shocks or explosions: clusters of stimuli going off in the mind of the spectator. This is what he meant by the notion of a montage of attractions, where an 'attraction' in the theatrical or filmic experience is 'every aggressive moment in it, i.e., every element of it that brings to light in the spectator those senses or that psychology that influence his experience'.[25] This is typical of Modernism as an artistic force, bent on aggressively shaking the spectator up instead of giving them a peaceful contemplative experience.[26] These conflicts *within* the shot are then orchestrated by the powers of editing into what Eisenstein characterised as collisions between shots, generating further stimulation of conflict, the further stirring up of feelings and, just as importantly, cognitive openings and insights.

Eisenstein identified emotional or tonal montage (that is the emotional 'tones' of a shot) as an important feature of the cinematic experience. What he called 'intellectual montage' referred to the power of film to provide cognitive openings (or mappings) and insights into various aspects of social relationships. Cognitive openings and insights are generated by editing's ability to make connections, to construct temporal and spatial connections in the 'world' of the film. In particular, montage bursts out of the unity of time and space beloved of a more classical aesthetics. In *October (Ten Days that Shook the World)* (1927), Eisenstein cuts between the trench warfare of the First World War and other social and institutional spaces to map the determining relationships at work on the soldiers. First, he cuts between a truce between Russian and German soldiers which sees them fraternising before cutting to government headquarters. A close-up of a statue of an eagle (symbol of imperial power) and a jump-cut of a civil service flunkey delivering a piece of paper, is enough to sketch the scene before cutting back to the trenches, where bombs are now suddenly falling. The inference is that the bourgeois Russian government remains committed to the continuing slaughter. Then as the Russian soldiers take cover in the trenches, Eisenstein cuts to a completely different space as a large artillery gun in an armaments factory is lowered by a winch mechanism to the floor. As the camera watches, the weapon descends from a low-angle shot, we cut back and forth to the Russians in the trench looking up at the mortar fire raining down on them. The cutting creates a *false* eye-line match and it appears as if they are looking at the gun as if it were descending on them.

This rupture from specific temporal-spatial relations of the scene of the trenches works to metaphorically suggest the soldiers being crushed by the 'machine' of war. The specific and particular scene is thus contextualised in a larger arena of social and political relationships thanks to the spatial and temporal relations constructed by the editing and its power to turn particular images into metaphors (like the lions) of larger meanings. The montage of attractions between the soldiers and the government and the armaments factory reveals the social relationships of an imperialist war that cost the lives of millions of working-class young men across Europe.

Pudovkin did something similar in *The End of St Petersburg* (1927) with a brilliant montage between the frenzied slaughter at the war front with the frenzy of the speculators making money on the Russian stock exchange. This montage is a perfect synthesis of intellectual *and* emotional or tonal montage. The delirious delight of speculators at making money is crashed against the fear and horror of the battlefront, a collision that gives the intellectual critique of the link between capitalism and war a stirring emotional underpinning through the obscene clash of emotional tones experienced by the protagonists (delirious greed and fear) between the two dramatic spaces.

As we saw in Chapter 2, Modernism converged with Marxism because it helped develop aesthetic forms that could correspond to the extensive lines of social and economic forces running off in all directions from the simple photographic depiction of a particular thing in time and space. The German Marxist philosopher Walter Benjamin once recalled this remark from his friend, the Marxist playwright Bertolt Brecht, on the matter:

> The situation is complicated by the fact that less than at any time does a simple *reproduction of reality* tell us anything about reality. A photograph of the Krupp works or GEC yields almost nothing about these institutions. Reality proper has slipped into the functional. The reification of human relations, the factory, let's say, no longer reveals these relationships. Therefore something has actually to be *constructed*, something artificial, something set up.[27]

This analysis of the problem of discovering the real in the mere reproduction of it, in sticking to immediate temporal-spatial relations in front of the camera, succinctly summarises the Marxist critique of aesthetics which do not manage to bring into the frame the deeper forces at work that determine what we see in front of us (in an image or indeed in a reified reality). By occluding those forces, the perceptible is in danger of being naturalised, accepted as both an inevitable fact and then, quite easily, as a positive value as well. Marxism regards reality as stratified between forms of appearance (e.g. a depiction of a factory) and deeper structuring social realities (e.g. exploitation). The solution Brecht suggests, to artificially pose or build up something to break through reification also commanded a wide degree of support among more adventurous Marxist cultural practitioners of the day.

Institutional and social contexts are important factors in assessing the political meaning of aesthetic forms. There is nothing *inherently* liberating about montage. Indeed, the technique was rapidly appropriated by advertising to help sell commodities. Montage, wrote Eisenstein, works by 'chains of associations that are linked to a particular phenomenon in the mind of a particular audience'.[28] That, of course, is precisely what advertisers do when they link chains of positive associations to a particular commodity in order to make it psychologically appealing to consumers. Does the ease with which advertising appropriated montage mean that it is essentially a technique of manipulation? Again, we have to think of the institutionally inscribed intentions and context of the form in question. Advertising sells commodities and in order to do that it must *contract* the mind of the viewer to the self and the satisfaction of their own personal desires (commodity fetishism) and sever our sense of social interconnectedness (reification). Montage bent to revolutionary purposes does not sell a political message, but tries to expand the cognitive and emotional reach of the viewer, since progressive political change requires thinking in socially connected ways. Of course, montage is not the only strategy that can do this, but it is one way that has succeeded.

As mass culture and the mass media expanded in the twentieth century in the form of films, television programmes, cartoons, photo-journalism, magazines, music, newspapers, advertising and so forth, the relevance of montage as a liberating aesthetic method for filmmakers and audiences increased. Montage provided the means by which the ideologies of individualism, consumerism, tacit racism and sexism, class hierarchy, status acquisition and sometimes the sheer stupidity of capitalist culture, could be subjected to critique. The mass media become an enormous archive to be raided, its materials deconstructed by pulling them out of their original contexts and creating new contexts within a work that simultaneously deconstructs their value systems, subjecting them to critique, subjecting them to a kind of active rewriting or talking back, so that filmmakers and audiences are no longer powerless recipients of their dubious messages, but active political subjects once more. Esfir Shub was one of the pioneers of this montage method. In her film, *The Fall of the Romanov Dynasty* (1927), she drew on documentary archives from newsreels, industrial footage and even home movies from the Czar's private collection, using careful cutting and ironic and critical intertitles to turn the material against its original uses and intentions and reconstruct the historical background leading to the 1917 Russian Revolution from a revolutionary perspective.

One filmmaker who developed montage in this new post-Second World War context of borrowing and reworking was the Cuban filmmaker, Santiago Alvarez. Like Eisenstein, Alvarez's best work was developed in the context of revolutionary change, this time in Cuba in the 1960s following the successful overthrow of the American-backed dictator Fulgencio Batista in 1959. His short film *LBJ* (1968) is a masterwork of what Eisenstein called intellectual montage, that is, thinking philosophically and politically through images (and sounds). In 18 minutes Alvarez dissects the social and political malaise of the USA, linking the series of political assassinations in the 1960s (John F. Kennedy and Robert Kennedy, and Martin Luther King) to the historic racist violence woven into the fabric of the culture. This was the decade in which the black civil rights struggle was confronting state violence and violence from racist and even fascist forces within American society, especially in the former slave states of the South. In response, Alvarez turned the visual culture of American society against itself through brilliant juxtapositions. To take just one example of *LBJ*'s multi-layered and complex critique: Alvarez links the then President Lyndon Baines Johnson's carefully constructed image as a cowboy (shades here of George Bush junior's presidential image 30 years later) through various photographs, to the western genre. Cue Alvarez appropriating a standard Hollywood film in which the cavalry are engaged in a shoot-out with the Indians. Alvarez distorts the image by squashing its proper widescreen ratio, slowing it down and bringing up the contrast. All of this increases the *formal* tensions in the way Eisenstein would have approved because they also foreground social tensions. But something else is also going on here. Alvarez is alerting us not to simply consume this image as if it were just innocent entertainment. Instead, deploying a strategy from Brecht, the original film material is *defamiliarised*, made strange. In this way, Brecht and Alvarez examine the politics of habitualised responses within aesthetic forms (building on the Russian Formalists). In *LBJ*, Alvarez focuses on the Indians getting shot and falling off their horses and then in a masterpiece of political editing cuts to and zooms in on a photograph of a black child's face and then eyes, *as if* he were looking at the film that Alvarez has just re-cut extracts from (the music associated with the film, i.e. 'exciting' adventure music carries on over this photograph). As with Eisenstein's false eye-line match between the soldiers in the trench and the artillery gun appearing to descend on them, here a convention from continuity editing (eye-line match) is used and subverted to construct through images and sounds a complex truth about how American history and society have been plagued by racist violence and tensions *across time and space*. Only montage could compress this argument and make it comprehensible, as if in an illuminating flash of lightning (what Walter Benjamin called the dialectical image) with a single cut between two shots drawn from radically distinct source materials. One cut, two shots and a whole continent of racial violence is lit up. We can call this form of reworking *meta-commentary*, using the materials of mass culture to comment on mass culture, a satisfying symbolic counter-attack against a much more powerful cultural-economic system (the 'society of the spectacle'). Generically, such critiques take the form of the documentary, the film essay and the collage and audio-visual remix or mash-up. This suggests that montage, in the way Eisenstein conceived it, did not become *the* dominant organising principle for fiction feature films, but instead becomes a component part of a more hybrid set of formal strategies available to filmmakers in the non-fiction traditions.

## 5.3 The long shot

Political Modernism and Realism were both different responses to the limitations of standardised mass cultural forms of which, in the case of film, Hollywood was the most economically and culturally powerful force. At the same time, intense arguments over the relationship between form and politics, a kind of 'form wars', often meant that political Modernism and Realism were seen as polarised and even incompatible strategies. We should be sceptical of siding with the various protagonists in 'form wars' and instead adopt a more dialectical and totalising position. Such a position recognises political Modernism, Realism and mass cultural forms as complexly interrelated instead of compartmentalised opponents. As we map conflictual interrelationships at the aesthetic level, we can reconstitute these categories of form as symptomatic responses (each with their own strengths and weaknesses) to a larger totality, ultimately the capitalist mode of production itself.[29]

In relation to film, this wide Marxian optic can help us navigate how the long shot, as a formal component of film practice, becomes, in film theory, a polemical weapon wielded against Modernist montage as well as against mass culture cinema. The key figure here who defined the terms of the debate was the French film critic, André Bazin (1918–58), a co-founder of the journal *Cahiers du Cinéma* in 1951. In fact, as part of the 'form wars', Bazin has often been interpreted more rigidly and one-dimensionally than a close study of his work merits, although there is no doubting that, in broad outlines, Bazin's preference was for what he took to be the realism of the long shot against the shortcomings, as he saw it, of *both* classical continuity editing, Hollywood-style, and the Soviet montagists of the 1920s. In doing so, Bazin anticipated and gave a rationale for the emergence of art cinema as occupying an institutional and political space with distinct formal characteristics between mass commercial cinema and revolutionary cinema and, in the period after the Second World War, between the geo-politics of American capitalism and Soviet 'communism' (that had already degenerated into Stalinism by the time Bazin was writing in the 1940s). The long shot has been central to European art cinema's formal strategies and a distinctive marker of identity ever since.

At the formal level, Bazin wanted to avoid 'chopping the world up into little fragments'.[30] Classical Hollywood editing did this in particular ways, with particular consequences. It cut the scene according to plot motivation, itself governed by the psychology and aims of the protagonists. Match on action and eye-line match are crucial continuity editing strategies linking the edit to the causal efficacy of the individual character powering their way through the dramatic scenario, according to the American individualism which Hollywood prioritised. Thus, continuity editing (sometimes called analytical editing) provided a predictable and routine 'analysis of the reality continuum'.[31] With Soviet-style montage, the problem was different for Bazin. Here again, the editing assembled relationships and meanings a little too *a priori*, but not, as with Hollywood, according to a standardised system of mass production, but instead according to an already existing political philosophy (Marxism) rather than, as Bazin preferred, revealing 'the hidden meanings in people and things without disturbing the unity natural to them'.[32] For Bazin, these meaningful relationships should not be imposed by editing, whether of the classical continuity type or montage, but discovered within the images whose spatial-temporal integrity has been preserved by the long shot. Yet the mode of 'discovery' by the long shot still requires of course *a priori* planning and principles, as Bazin himself admitted.[33] More generally, the long shot's usefulness really depends on the problems of form and social content that a film is trying to explore. Like everything else, it has its strengths and weaknesses. In certain circumstances there are things that the long shot cannot discover no matter how hard or long you look.

The long shot was, for Bazin, the most significant development in film language and its emergence depended in part on technical developments with film stock, lenses and the accompanying technical skills, especially in cinematography and burgeoning directorial ambitions within the studio systems (the shot becomes linked to an authorial signature style, although mediated through the cinematographer). Early exponents included Jean Renoir's films in the 1930s, such as the wonderful *The Crime of Monsieur Lange* (1935), Orson Welles' *Citizen Kane* (1941), which owed much to the cinematographer Greg Toland, and William Wyler's *The Best Years of Our Lives* (1946), on which Toland also worked. But the Italian Neo-Realist movement that emerged towards the end of the Second World War and into the late 1940s, made the biggest impact on Bazin and within film culture internationally because it took the long shot out of the film studio and into the streets and other spaces of everyday life where it was mixed with other strategies, such as the use of non-professional actors in a dialogical challenge to Hollywood's star system.

The long shot is *long* in three usually interrelated ways: (1) duration (the long take); (2) distance from the photographed subject (the wide shot); and (3) depth of focus. Let us examine the implications of these elements in a little more detail. In his video essay *What Is Neo-Realism?* (2013),[34] Kogonada uses a split screen to examine two different cuts of the same film to reveal the different philosophies and politics underpinning Italian Neo-Realism and Hollywood's classical editing style. The case study for this is Vittorio De Sica's 1952 film *Terminal Station*, which was funded by Hollywood producer David O. Selznick and had (with De Sica compromising on Neo-Realist principles) two American stars, Jennifer Jones and Montgomery Clift. The compromise did not work out happily for De Sica. Selznick recut (and drastically shortened) the American release of the film, called *Indiscretion of an American Wife*. Kogonada shows how De Sica's Neo-Realist philosophy depends on a relatively longer shot duration that is less brutal in excising material that from a Hollywood 'action' perspective is regarded as redundant. With longer shot duration, the little details of life acquire visibility in the consciousness of the spectator. The overall narrative structure that a combination of long shots produces also becomes looser, less tightly bound to plot development than with classical continuity editing. Commenting on Rossellini's *Paisa* (1946), Bazin found 'an intelligible succession of events, but these do not mesh like a chain with the sprockets of a wheel'.[35] Similarly, Kogonada notes that in De Sica's *Terminal Station*, when the main characters exit the frame, the shot continues, lingering over other people in the crowded train station, whose lives and stories we never know or may be only hinted at. Selznick's version of the same film, however, cuts as soon as the star leaves the frame, because for the Hollywood producer, these other people are unimportant in terms of status and plot development. Kogonada, using montage principles ironically, reveals by comparison and juxtaposition, how De Sica's long shot develops a less individualistic, less hierarchical, more collective and more socially aware dramaturgy.

In commenting on the famous hunting scene from Robert Flaherty's early documentary *Nanook of the North* (1922), Bazin suggested that Flaherty's use of the long take while Nanook hunts a seal, allows us to appreciate 'the actual waiting period; the length of the hunt is the very substance of the image, its true object'.[36] The question of shot duration has become a deeply significant and controversial issue in recent decades. The rapid speed of both Hollywood films and indeed across television genres has, according to British filmmaker, Peter Watkins, produced an audio-visual *Monoform* structure deeply antithetical to exploring the complexity of social reality, on the one hand, and giving audiences the reflective space to *think* about what they are being presented with, on the other.[37] Watkins describes the Monoform as:

> The internal language-form (editing, narrative, etc.) used by TV and the commercial cinema ... It is the densely packed and rapidly edited barrage of images and sounds, the 'seamless' yet fragmented modular structure which we all know so well ... variations on the Monoform have certain characteristics: they are repetitive, predictable, and closed vis-à-vis their relationship to the audience.[38]

Certain strands of art cinema have in response to the accelerating speed of commercial cinema pushed their own shot duration well beyond the modest temporal extensions of the Italian Neo-Realists. Chantal Ackerman's *Jeanne Dielman, 23, quai du commerce, 1080 Bruxelles* (1975) asked the viewer to observe and experience the alienating routines of a bored housewife's daily activities. A 2-minute-plus shot of Jeanne peeling potatoes uses shot duration to create the time within which we can observe her fluctuating responses to this banal activity; she seems to be both reflecting on her situation as well as living the emptiness of her life which traditional gender roles have allotted her. This thematisation of alienation as 'empty time' is quite typical of Modernist art cinema. Watkins' own attempt to escape the tyranny of the Monoform includes his 5-hour-plus film *La Commune* (1999), which uses very long takes (e.g. 10 minutes long) for a very different effect and purpose than art cinema's thematic of alienating boredom. Here the long shot charts in time and space the complex collective dynamics of the Paris Commune of 1871, the socialist uprising and seizure of control of the capital of France, which Marx described as the working class 'storming heaven'.[39]

The long shot is also long in terms of distance between the camera and the subject photographed. In classical continuity editing, the long shot is known as the establishing shot, the master shot (which is returned to during a scene in order to re-orientate the viewer for example) or the wide shot. Typically, it is the first shot in a scene before medium and close-up shots are introduced. By contrast, where the long shot becomes the key formal principle in a film's organisation, the composition and movement of both characters and camera are arranged so that the story can develop with much of the environment of the action always visible to the eye. This is important because the long shot helps develop our capacity to read meanings into the spatial relationships between people and between people and their object world (rooms, buildings, props, nature, etc.). Thus, how the immediately perceptible environment, as displayed in the *mise-en-scène*, impacts on and interacts with character(s) is dependent on a certain distance between the camera and the subject.

Third, the long shot is long in terms of depth of focus, with foreground, middle-ground and background planes all being in focus and typically used in terms of significant action or objects all being arranged from front to back. For example, a minor film from Max Ophüls in his Hollywood period, *Caught* (1949), has an opening scene of just under 4 minutes and uses just three long shots in deep focus and one edited in close-up. The scene opens on a close-up of a catalogue which two women are evidently flicking through as they discuss the clothes and jewellery which are the objects of their desire. The women dream of affording the fur coats but know that they will need to marry rich men to achieve their dreams. The camera pulls back to reveal the two women and, over the course of the scene, the narrow, cramped apartment in which they live and where they mix their aspirations with daily humdrum activities, is explored. For example, we see the lead dreaming on her bed at one point (left foreground), the other woman doing the washing up (in the background). Ophüls brings a caustic European eye to the American dream and by using the long shot asks us to compare their dreams (including going to charm school whose brochure is the one edited in close-up) with their actual conditions and wonder whether these dreams are actually healthy or dangerous (the film's narrative suggests the latter).

The long shot is an incredibly flexible formal strategy and can be mobilised in highly diverse and quite opposing ways. Dominant cinema has integrated a version of the long shot into its repertoire by eliminating the distance element between camera and subject and stressing duration in medium close-up and deep focus to some extent. Here a mobile camera is typically like a character that is part of the scene, immersing the viewer in the flow of the action as semi-participant rather than keeping them at some distance from the action. *Atomic Blonde* (2017), featuring Charlize Theron, has an extended approximately 10-minute fight scene in a stairwell in which the highly mobile handheld camera is close to the action and gives a visceral experience of it. The scene was shot in multiple long takes that are stitched invisibly together in an apparently single super-long take. Bazin associated the preserving of the temporal and spatial integrity of action with realism and we have seen that the long shot can be said to develop our understanding of various aspects of social reality. Here, however, in *Atomic Blonde* the 'realism' is contracted down to observing and experiencing the physical exhaustion and deterioration which such continuous combat produces on the human body. Certainly this has a quotient of 'realism' but it is now dwindled down to the immediate consequences of violence, which although this can be powerful, outside of any broader social or political context, must be considered a very impoverished form of realism.

Outside of dominant cinema, the long shot often has a certain 'de-dramatisation' effect which, as we have seen, is linked to letting the social evidence 'breathe' within the story scenario rather than subordinating it to narrative drive. Bazin coupled this de-dramatisation with an appreciation in the case of Italian Neo-Realism of 'a most neutral kind of transparency',[40] as the *mise-en-scène* came from real locations, the script and plot is minimal, the actors are drawn from the milieu depicted in the fiction, and so forth. Yet Welles had already shown with *Citizen Kane* (1941) that the long shot could be a highly stylised composition in which visual structures and relations overtly invited some kind of metaphorical reading. In the 1960s, Jean-Luc Godard developed a new kind of long shot that some critics saw as a kind of repudiation of the Bazinian version and validation of the self-same strategy. Brian Henderson argued that Godard's anti-Bazinian and highly stylised long shot was a new kind of tracking shot that moved left to right and/or right to left at 90° to the scene. Rejecting composition in depth and multiple planes of action, the key action is arranged in more or less one plane (usually the middle-ground). Bazin valued composition in the depth and duration of shot because, he argued, it 'influences the interpretation of the spectacle' by giving the viewer more choice to make individual judgements as to what to make of the image, which in turn preserves the *ambiguity* of the world so depicted.[41] We can understand how this double ethical-political justification (ambiguity of the world against crass simplifications and democracy of the spectator against manipulation) has its merits, particularly in relation to the global dominance of the commercially driven Monoform (Bazin's misplaced anxieties about political montage were already moot by the time he was writing, killed off by Stalinist Socialist Realism in the early 1930s).

The long shot, however, as Bazin championed it, has been extensively critiqued following the political and structuralist turn in the late 1960s. For Brian Henderson, Godard's long shot produces a critique of the presumption of ambiguity and the democracy of individual moral choices.[42] The problem with the language of ambiguity, of individual judgement, of the infinite complexity of humanity, etc., is that while, on one level (of interpersonal relations, of life as lived every day, where the frailties and foibles of the individual character are exposed, etc.), there is an element of truth to all this, on another level, that of capitalism's structuring of our routines, its commodification of our relationships, its reduction of every value to exchange (monetary value) and surplus (profit), the language associated with humanism (the ineffable value of the individual as agent, as sensibility, as ethical-aesthetic judge) seems inadequate, complicit somehow with a system that *actually* crushes the individual while making ideological use of it and falling short of the responses needed when confronted with the 'totality' of capitalist logic. Thus, for Godard:

> composition-in-depth projects a bourgeois world infinitely deep, rich, complex, ambiguous, mysterious. Godard's flat frames collapse this world into two-dimensional actuality; thus reversion to a cinema of one plane is a demystification, an assault on the bourgeois world view and self-image.[43]

Godard's documentary *British Sounds* (1969) (made as part of the Dziga-Vertov collective) opens with an image of the British Union Jack while a female voice declares: 'In a word, the bourgeoisie creates a world in its own image. Comrades, we must destroy that image' after which a fist punches through the paper flag and we cut to an assembly line for cars and a long tracking shot left to right. Godard saw cars as something of a symbol of the contradictions of consumer capitalism. Probably his most famous use of the lateral tracking shot was in the traffic jam sequence in *Weekend* (1967), which in a humorous and absurdist manner dissects the madness and simmering violence of capitalist society in one long lateral take. But I want to illustrate Godard's anti-Bazinian tracking shot with an example from his fiction feature *Tout Va Bien* (1972), which was a reflection on the legacy of May 1968.

This tracking shot is set in a supermarket and the composition is very interestingly and deliberately arranged so as to invite a decoding of capitalism's social relationships. The shot tracks along (both left to right and right to left) behind the check-out tills so that we see the backs of the female workers inputting the prices in the tills while passing the commodities along the conveyer belts. In every aisle, customers are in the process of taking the commodities out of the shopping trolleys and putting them on the conveyor belts. As the customers and the workers perform the same movements in their allotted roles, we hear the incessant sounds of the tills punching in the prices (churning over the profits). As with Ackerman's *Jeanne Dielman*, a 'structuralist' sensibility produces a spatial analysis of entrapment while the shot duration (and soundtrack) thematise the sickening alienation and repetition of tasks that ensue. This time-space continuum is the very *substance of the image*, to paraphrase Bazin, but to very different purposes he intended, for rather than humanist 'depth', what we discover is the life-crushing monotony of capitalism or patriarchal capitalism in the case of *Jeanne Dielman*.

It is also worth pointing out that in this example there is actually significant use of depth of field. Behind the customers and the workers stretch the aisles of goods which change in type as we move laterally through the store (food goods turn into aisles of household goods, etc.). This depth of field does not produce 'ambiguity' or 'richness' but is part of the cognitive mapping of the visual field. In the aisles, the commodities belong to the supermarket. At the check-out tills the commodities begin the transition into personal objects of utility, but they must go through the exchange process first which ensures the realisation of value for the capitalist supermarket. Godard has laid out the visual-social field and given us the time to analyse it. Yet despite the 'structuralist' quality of this long shot, it is not entirely without the 'humanist' themes which philosophical/political differences and 'form wars' can blind us to. The lead character, played by Jane Fonda, wanders in and out of shot – she is not shopping but observing and composing thoughts (which we hear intermittently) for a piece of journalism critical of French society. The scene is also interrupted by student-militant types who encourage shoppers to take the commodities without paying. These compositional elements (deep focus, planes of action, discovering the meaning of the shot) and the theme of resistance, both individual and collective, suggest the long shot is being reworked but not entirely re-invented and that humanist themes of resistance and critique (which presuppose agency *against* structure) are still at work, albeit now shifted into a Marxist register.

We have already seen that deep focus, along with duration and distance, does allow the social and historical context of the action to work its way into our understanding of the meaning of events. An interesting synthesis between the art cinema deployment of the long take as a means of attending to that which exists on the margins and the more commercial cinema of genres, exciting action and star talent, can be found in *Children of Men* (2006). The film was directed by Alfonso Cuarón and shot by his long-term collaborator and cinematographer, Emmanuel Lubezki. Here the long shot works to integrate action wrapped around an individual character with a broader social and historical context that we see all around Theo (Clive Owen). The signs of poverty, social breakdown, political dictatorship, oppression of migrants, are all evident in the long takes, in the background, as the camera drifts occasionally away from Theo to pick up something that happens around him, but which, at least initially, he is indifferent to. The former romantic, now a world-weary cynic gradually drawn back into political action is a character-type that goes back famously to *Casablanca* (1942). The signs of social breakdown are all the more shocking because the action is set in London and England. The familiar-looking locations, buildings, red buses, telephone boxes, the countryside, state and public buildings, are still recognisable, but have degraded and are now transformed by a historical catastrophe. England, famed for its long uninterrupted constitutional order and 'internal peace', is now wracked by conflict, terrorism, military dictatorship and finally what looks like the beginning of a civil war, of the kind Western Europe has not seen since the 1930s. The catastrophe in the film is of course the global infertility that has threatened the human species with extinction. But this issue of biological extinction is a *metaphor* for the problem of social reproduction – the inability to socially reproduce ourselves in the context of capitalism. All the problems that we see in the film are extrapolations of our current trends, not least mass migration and the oppressive responses to it by political classes everywhere. Although the film also uses the long take for visceral immersion into scenes of action that are intensely exciting just as *Atomic Blonde* does with the stairwell fight scene, *Children of Men* also has a receptivity to our social and historical crisis that is inextricably interwoven into its use of the long shot.[44]

## 5.4 Self-reflexivity

Self-reflexivity refers to the ability of cultural works to reflect on their own conditions of production and/or reception and/or their status, perhaps as fictions, as cinematic languages or as clusters of conventions around which certain habituated meanings and expectations have accrued. The meta-commentary of montage remixes of archival work are intrinsically self-reflexive because they simultaneously comment on the original context in which the material was placed and the new context in the new work which transfigures its meanings. When Michael Moore begins *Capitalism: A Love Story* (2009) with borrowed footage from surveillance cameras in banks that have recorded armed robberies, the whole meaning and purpose of the material are transformed. In their original context, the material functions to protect the bank's money, by deterrence, by monitoring activity, by identifying robbers and by use if necessary in legal proceedings. But recontextualised in Moore's film, with the credit titles (A Dog Eat Dog Production), the soundtrack of Iggy Pop's raucous *Louie Louie II* ('The capitalists are just breakin' hearts') and the juxtaposition of numerous different robberies (including a robber on crutches), it now begins to look more like an investigation into the socio-economic system that produces this kind of footage (wealth accumulators at one pole of society, the desperate at another). This sequence is then followed by another in which extracts from an old American education film about the decline and fall of the Roman Empire (complete with dramatic re-enactments of Roman life, a voice of God narrator telling us about the Roman social, economic and judicial system and a soundtrack of 'Roman' martial trumpets) is intercut with footage from contemporary George Bush-era America, making a comparison between 'Empires' that the original educational film could not have imagined or anticipated.

Such self-reflexivity is evidently political and engaged, but in the 1970s a formalist approach to self-reflexivity was much in evidence and produced a doubly reductionist schema: first, dominant cinema was regarded as the antithesis of self-reflexivity. A popular term to describe dominant cinema of the time was 'illusionism' (it encouraged the illusion of reality) or verisimilitude (a convincing likeness of reality). Second, illusionism/verisimilitude was branded as synonymous with ideology while self-reflexivity was, in another simplistic binary, implicitly or explicitly lauded as radical, critical, politically progressive, etc., because it shattered illusionist modes of spectatorship (see Section 3.2). Dana Polan's 1978 article in *Jump Cut* sounded an early warning alarm about this trend when he warned that radical aesthetics and film theory were 'falling prey to the rise of a new ahistorical formalism'.[45] The 1953 cartoon *Duck Amuck*, he notes, is supremely self-reflexive, but that hardly makes it politically radical. In the 1980s, Robert Stam's book-length discussion of self-reflexivity deconstructed the doubly reductionist schema, ferreting out the widespread use of self-reflexivity *within* popular mass culture films from the silent period onwards and carefully discriminating between pleasurable but hardly radical uses of self-reflexivity and other more politically engaged practices.[46]

The psychological dimension of our relationship to the aesthetic experience and its compelling power is known as 'suspension of disbelief', a phrase coined by Samuel Taylor Coleridge in 1817. The very phrase seems to invite us to suspend our 'bullshit detectors', those critical faculties that prevent us from being manipulated and fooled. Yet the term refers to a rather less credulous posture than one might suppose. Suspension of disbelief involves suspending a whole range of knowledge about the real world in order to entertain (in the sense of both 'consider' and find pleasurable) the contract struck between the spectator and the spectacle. We agree not to think about certain things that might break the contract, at least not too much or insistently, on all sorts of levels. For example, logic (that *couldn't* happen, i.e. zombies, vampires, ghosts, time travel, bringing back dinosaurs, etc.) or plausibility of action (that is very *unlikely* to happen) or consistency (where did those characters go?) or the plot's dependence on chance or accident, or exaggeration (sound effects, for example, like a punch, are typically amplified in ways that are at some discrepancy with what we know from real life), and so on. Instead we agree to evaluate the story through the conventions of storytelling – so that, to take the example of plausibility of character motivation, while we think it unlikely that most people *would* go down into that dark cellar on their own, especially when the flashlight starts faltering, we suspend that disbelief and agree that this is a convention of this type of generic story (horror) just as it is a convention of the musical to express intense feelings through song or the convention of the western to resolve conflict through the gunfight.

There is nothing *inherently* problematic with that, I would contend. However, the self-enclosed illusionistic fictional world that mobilises certain *potentially* questionable cinematic pleasures (such as sexual objectification) may be well served by self-effacement strategies. Films that force the viewer to confront their own dubious pleasures are often difficult for audiences to cope with, as the initial reception to Michael Powell's *Peeping Tom* (1960) famously illustrates.[47] It may be then that, in the course of the historical development of generic and narrative conventions, audiences do suspend not only their disbelief but also their *critical* faculties regarding this or that story content and the conventions that mediate it. The compelling power of the cinematic moving image reinforces the concern. Indeed, all the way back to Plato's parable of the cave, where shadows enslaved the credulous, intellectuals and philosophers have always had an anxiety about the power of the image to seduce.[48] Even Bazin, who championed the compelling power of the *photographic* image to reproduce a likeness of what had once been placed before the lens, hints at the problem:

The objective nature of photography confers on it a quality of credibility absent from all other picture-making. In spite of any objections our critical spirit may offer, we are forced to accept as real the existence of the object reproduced, actually *re*-presented, set before us, that is to say, in time and space.[49]

This compelling power of cinema seemed to make representation and narrative itself a problem for many film theorists in the 1970s, and thus made self-reflexivity such a seductive antidote to the credibility-inducing effects of cinematic story-telling. But it is worth distinguishing between two connected but distinct concerns. First, there is the question of whether there is an ideological problem inscribed into filmic representation itself, because of its capacity to produce life-like depictions, or narrative storytelling, because of its capacity to weave patterns that imply unity, order and resolution. Raising this question on its own risks precisely falling into the trap of Formalism unless we couple it with a second question.

This is the question of the ideologies that derive from the wider social and his-torical setting in which film production/reception takes place. We will engage with the question of ideology and cinematic form in more detail in Chapter 6. Here I want to suggest that self-reflexivity *may* be a way of opening up our acceptance of the terms of the contract when those terms become entwined with questionable value systems or ideologies generated from social and historical life. I do not believe we can conclude that any formal component in the repertoire of film language has a 'politics' independent of its articulation with social and cultural values and meanings. And there is, I think, no need to demand complete and universal reflexivity of that wider culture all the way down – indeed, such a demand seems neither possible nor desirable (it would make it impossible to ever make a referentially orientated utterance). But where representations drawn from our cultural worlds become significantly politically contestable or 'thematised', as Habermas puts it, then the contract needs to be examined in a kind of auto-cri-tique of both conventions and audience expectations.

Example: *The Cabin in the Woods* (2012) is a self-reflexive commentary on the exhaustion of the conventions of the American slasher horror genre which 'force' teenagers and young adults into stereotypical roles (the jock, the scholar, the whore, the dopehead, the virgin/final girl, etc.) that reduce the ability of repre-sentation to do due justice to the complexity of teenage life. The film achieves this self-reflexive critique by combining the horror genre with that strand of science fiction genre where high tech surveillance/monitoring is used to control people and their environment, set them certain tasks, etc. (for example, *The Truman Show*). This allows the cynical white-shirted corporate management types to literally become film directors within the film as they control the set/setting of the cabin in the woods (an obvious intertextual reference to *The Evil Dead*) and in doing so this allows *The Cabin in the Woods* to comment on the conventions of the slasher genre. When the conventions are reflected on in this way, their potentially problematic (ideological) nature may be subject to interrogation. In the case of *The Cabin in the Woods*, the symbolic sacrifice of teenagers which we are familiar with from countless films, is linked to older myths, rituals and superstitions and it is suggested in a somewhat tongue-in-cheek way, this is important for the reproduction of the social (indeed world) order. The teenager, as a post-Second World War 'constructed' subjectivity, poses a problem or issue for capitalism. For they are young adults who may now start to become independent of the cultural norms of the family, on the one hand, but have yet to be completely integrated into the coercive mechanisms of the labour market, on the other. This opens up a 'space' of potential dissent which capitalism often wants to manage and neutralise (e.g. through symbolic warnings in films).

While self-reflexivity is traceable back to the Greek classics, most discussions of self-reflexivity in the modern period link it to momentous social changes, as the feudal mode of production was gradually dismantled by the economic, cultural and scientific energies of the emerging bourgeoisie. This was a long *cultural revolution*, as Fredric Jameson notes:

> The Western Enlightenment may be grasped as part of a properly bourgeois cultural revolution, in which the values and the discourses, the habits and the daily space, of the *ancien régime* were systematically dismantled so that in their place could be set the new conceptualities, habits and life forms, and value systems of a capitalist market society.[50]

One can, cautiously and with caveats, offer a sweeping historical narrative that sees self-reflexivity in the modern period beginning with the rise of the bourgeois class challenging and changing the old feudal social order and thus stimulating self-reflexive commentary on processes of artistic representation. But as the bourgeois class consolidates itself and its power, self-reflexivity becomes rather less attractive, since it potentially at least, opens up the possibility of calling into question the role of art within the new dominant social order (for example, the way it was thrust into the marketplace to become a commodity). Self-reflexivity comes in turn to be wielded increasingly *against* the bourgeois class itself, no more spectacularly than in the epoch opened up by the 1917 Russian Revolution and closed again, at least for a time, by the new world order established after 1945 (where America and the Soviet Union shared out the spoils).

Yet we also see that self-reflexivity has always been a feature of mass film culture, especially in its comedic modes, or animation. This indicates that self-reflexivity is a site of struggle, as montage has been. It is a site of different cultural politics and projects and these have to be weighed and assessed in each case. But increasingly in the 1980s onwards, we saw the very extensive appropriation and widespread distribution of self-reflexive strategies of the Modernists by mass film culture in a trend associated with postmodernism (in which, for example, the gap between Modernism and popular mass culture was overcome, but very much, it seems, on the terms of corporate commodity culture). Fredric Jameson argued, for example, that postmodern culture turned the critical tongue of parody into pastiche, the intertextual mimicry of cultural forms, but stripped of any real critical, political thrust. His example was the artworks of Andy Warhol and, in film, the reduction of historical consciousness to signifiers of the past drawn from previous films and mass media images in the 'nostalgia' film.[51]

No one can be under any illusion that the self-reflexive references to the world of Marvel and its various franchises in the *Deadpool* films, has any radical intentions or impact. Like montage, self-reflexivity is subject to mass media appropriation and neutralisation. When Deadpool turns to the audience in *Deadpool* (2016) and says: 'I know what you are thinking, whose balls did I have to fondle to get my own film?', this is not a critique of labour conditions (sexual exploitation) or an investigation of the allocation of investment decisions going on 'behind the scenes'. This is what Kamilla Elliott calls 'tie-in' intertextuality, where knowing references to other manifestations of the corporate franchise (films, toys, comics, etc.) function more as pleasurable 'capture' into a world of 'capitalist dialogics' rather more than critical Marxist dialectics.[52]

It was the German Marxist playwright Bertolt Brecht who would develop a politicised theory and practice of the Russian Formalist School's notion of 'making strange' with his theory of the *Verfremdungseffekt* (a term whose translation into English has been very contested).[53] *Verfremdungseffekt* aims to bounce audiences out of their habits of identification with characters, with the perspectives from which an action is narrated, with stock emotional responses and conventionalised perception. Self-reflexivity (making strange) is central to both Shklovsky's thought and Brecht's work, because reflecting on how the artistic or representational devices work requires de-automating our habitualised relationship to the devices. But in Brecht's case, there is politically revealing intent behind this strategy. As Sean Carney puts it: 'There is … within the *Verfremdungseffekt* an entire theory of socialization, subject-formation and the ongoing judgment of reality, tied to the ability of the human subject to be estranged from given or ideological thinking.'[54]

Estrangement is achieved in numerous ways in Brechtian theatre, such as actors stepping out of roles, direct address to the audience, interrupting the action or freezing it or mixing different styles or genres of theatre, live performance or even media (Brecht brought film into the theatrical performance). The latter strategy of combining disparate materials is exactly how *The Cabin in the Woods* works, by rubbing up two genres (science fiction and horror) against each other, so that one can be used to interrogate the other. For Brecht, revealing the artifice of representational conventions functioned (metaphorically) as a way of opening up *social* conventions, practices and institutions to critical interrogation.

As against *Deadpool*, a more politically committed self-reflexive interrogation into the economic and cultural conditions of film production can be found in the opening of Godard's *Tout Va Bien*. We are cued immediately by the credit titles, which are accompanied by a voice over calling out random scene numbers from *Tout Va Bien* with the sound of the clapperboard punctuating each declaration in that abrupt manner typical of Godard's soundtracks. This is followed by an audio dialogue between a male and female voice-over. The man, initially quite naïve states: 'I want to make a film' and this leads to a discussion concerning the requirements for making a film. You need money, says the woman: cue close-ups of Godard signing cheques for different technical functions within the film: director, *mise-en-scène*, story, cinematographer, editing, the list goes on. Godard does not spare the viewer the details of the labour process. Get on with it, you are thinking, or rather, it is that socialised desire to be excited, stimulated, entertained, to get 'lost' in the story, that is to forget about the *conditions of production* that is doing the thinking for you, and it is certainly a useful pedagogic lesson to reflect on this, although there is no need to generalise this into a principle of 'anti-pleasure' as film theorists were wont to do in the 1970s.

The voice-overs then discuss the need for stars in order to attract the finance for the film in the first place and, sure enough, French star Yves Montand and American star Jane Fonda appear on the credit titles. The female voice says you need a story to attract the stars – usually a love story. Cue little dramatic vignettes in which Fonda and Montand act out characters in love and then arguing (drama!). The female voice-over is sceptical that this is as yet an interesting scenario and demands more details. Now we start to see the assembling of context: a topographical map of France appears, then the French countryside, then a French city, then houses and inside one of the houses, Her (Fonda) and Him (Montand). So far, so 'bourgeois'.

Now the female voice-over demands more detail and the detail starts to become more 'concrete' in Marxist terms. The voice-overs identify classes: workers, farmers, the petit-bourgeoisie and the bourgeoisie. When each of these class groupings are named, we see portrait shots of groups standing still, looking at the camera, posing as classes. Then we learn that 'Him' and 'Her' will be placed in relation to these classes. And then there is a further development, as each of the classes are dynamicised. The voice-overs note that the farmers will be *farming*, the workers, *working*, and the bourgeois will be busy being *bourgeois*. With each of these verbs we now see individuals engaged in activities representing their class – with the bourgeois class being represented by the evening television news interestingly and significantly enough ('the bourgeoisie creates a world in its own image'). The male voice-over, now getting the hang of it, comments that 'under a calm surface everything is changing', invoking the surface/depth metaphor that Marxism uses to critique capitalist reification. So what we see here at the beginning of *Tout Va Bien*, is the literal assembling of the film that we are about to watch, from its economic conditions through to its cultural and political conditions, which steadily progress past the typical 'love story' and into the more Marxist territory of love plus the class struggle in post-1968 France.

## Notes

1  See Richard Sherwood, 'Documents from *Lef*', *Screen* 12(4) (1971): 25–58 and Ben Brewster, '*Novy Lef* with an Introduction', *Screen* 12(4) (1971): 59–102.
2  Sylvia Harvey, *May 68 and Film Culture* (London: BFI, 1980), p. 59.
3  Sherwood, op. cit., p. 25.
4  Nicholas Gorlov, 'Futurists and Revolution', in Christopher Pike (ed.), *The Futurists, the Formalists and the Marxist Critique* (London: Ink Links, 1979), p. 181.

5 Ibid., p. 187.
6 Leon Trotsky, *Literature and Revolution*, (ed.) William Keach (London: Haymarket Books, 2005), p. 123.
7 A.K. Voronsky, 'On Proletarian Art', in *Art as the Cognition of Life: Selected Writings, 1911–1936* (Sheffield: Mehring Books, 1998), p. 159.
8 Norman Swallow, *Eisenstein: A Documentary Portrait* (London: George Allen and Unwin, 1976), p. 32.
9 Lynne Mally, *Culture of the Future: The Proletkult Movement in Revolutionary Russia* (Berkeley, CA: University of California Press, 1990), pp. 146–7.
10 Zenovia A. Sochor, *Revolution and Culture: The Bogdanov-Lenin Controversy* (Ithaca, NY: Cornell University Press, 1988), p. 129.
11 Ibid., p. 213.
12 Swallow, *Eisenstein*, op. cit., p. 24.
13 Trotsky, *Literature and Revolution*, op. cit., p. 159.
14 Ibid., p. 161.
15 Ibid., p. 169.
16 Ibid., p. 122.
17 Boris Eykhenbaum, 'Concerning the Question of the "Formalists"', in Christopher Pike (ed.), *The Futurists, the Formalists and the Marxist Critique* (London: Ink Links, 1979), p. 51.
18 Viktor Shklovsky *Theory of Prose*, trans. Benjamin Sher (London: Dalkey Archive Press, 2009), pp. 4–6.
19 Eykhenbaum, 'Concerning the Question of the "Formalists"', op. cit., p. 59.
20 Trotsky, *Literature and Revolution*, op. cit., p. 140.
21 Eykhenbaum, 'Concerning the Question of the "Formalists"', op. cit., p. 60.
22 Tony Bennett, *Formalism and Marxism* (London: Routledge, 1979), pp. 61–74.
23 Sergei Eisenstein, 'The Dramaturgy of Film Form (The Dialectical Approach to Film Form)', in Richard Taylor (ed.), *The Eisenstein Reader* (London: BFI, 1998), p. 93.
24 Ibid., p. 96.
25 Sergei Eisenstein, 'Montage of Attractions', in Sergei Eisenstein, *The Film Sense* (London: Faber and Faber, 1970), p. 181.
26 See also Walter Benjamin's comments on the shock experience of the cinema in 'The Work of Art in the Age of Mechanical Reproduction', in Walter Benjamin, *Illuminations* (London: Pimlico Press, 1999), pp. 231–2.
27 Walter Benjamin, 'A Short History of Photography', *Screen*, 13(1) (1972): 24.
28 Eisenstein, 'The Montage of Film Attractions', *The Eisenstein Reader*, op. cit., p. 36.
29 See Fredric Jameson's, 'Reification and Utopia in Mass Culture', where he demonstrates the value of this dialectical approach in relation to Modernism and mass culture, in Fredric Jameson, *Signatures of the Visible* (London: Routledge, 1992).
30 André Bazin, 'The Evolution of the Language of Cinema', in *What Is Cinema?*, vol. 1 (Berkeley, CA: University of California Press, 1967), p. 38.
31 André Bazin, 'An Aesthetic of Reality', in *What Is Cinema?*, vol. 2 (Berkeley, CA: University of California Press, 1971), p. 28.
32 Bazin, 'The Evolution of the Language of Cinema', op. cit., p. 38.
33 Wells and Wyler's long shots 'converted the screen into a dramatic checkerboard' noted Bazin, ibid., p. 35.
34 Available at: www.bfi.org.uk/news-opinion/sight-sound-magazine/comment/video-essay-what-neorealism
35 Bazin, 'An Aesthetic of Reality', op. cit., p. 35.
36 Bazin, 'The Evolution of the Language of Cinema', op. cit., p. 27.
37 See Peter Watkins' media statement on his website, available at: http://pwatkins.mnsi.net/
38 See Peter Watkins, available at: http://pwatkins.mnsi.net/hollywood.htm
39 See Michael Wayne, 'The Tragedy of History: Peter Watkins's *La Commune*', *Third Text*, 16(1) (2002): 57–69.
40 André Bazin, 'Bicycle Thief', in *What Is Cinema?*, vol. 2 (Berkeley, CA: University of California Press, 1971), p. 57.

41 Bazin, 'The Evolution of the Language of Cinema', op. cit., p. 35.
42 Brian Henderson, 'Towards a Non-Bourgeois Camera Style', in Bill Nichols (ed.), *Movies and Methods*, vol. I (Berkeley, CA: University of California Press, 1976), p. 425.
43 Ibid., p. 436.
44 It is also worth noting that the DVD bonus material includes a documentary featuring various radical thinkers discoursing on the themes of crisis and capitalism that the film deals with. This is an unusual but very welcome integration of an explicit political project with a commercial film that cost $76 million. However, as a sign of how difficult it is to reconcile popular cinema with a sophisticated and complex political critique, the film did not recover its costs through the cinema release, recording 'only' $70 million worldwide at the box office.
45 Dana Polan, 'A Brechtian Cinema? Towards a Politics of Self-Reflexive Film', in Bill Nichols (ed.), *Movies and Methods*, vol. II (Berkeley, CA: University of California Press, 1985), p. 664.
46 See Robert Stam's *Reflexivity in Film and Literature: From Don Quixote to Jean-Luc Godard* (New York: Columbia University Press, 1985).
47 William Johnson, '*Peeping Tom*: A Second Look', *Film Quarterly*, 33(3) (1980), pp. 2–10.
48 See Mike Wayne 'The Dialectical Image: Kant, Marx and Adorno', in Ewa Mazierska and Lars Kristensen (eds), *Marx at the Movies: Revisiting History, Theory and Practice* (Basingstoke: Palgrave, 2014).
49 Andre Bazin, 'The Ontology of the Photographic Image', in *What Is Cinema?*, vol. 1 (Berkeley, CA: University of California Press, 1967), pp. 13–14.
50 Fredric Jameson, *The Political Unconscious: Narrative as a Socially Symbolic Act* (London: Routledge, 1981), p. 81.
51 Fredric Jameson, 'The Cultural Logic of Late Capitalism', in *Postmodernism or, The Cultural Logic of Late Capitalism* (Durham, NC: Duke University Press, 1992).
52 Kamilla Elliott, 'Tie-Intertextuality, or, Intertextuality as Incorporation in the Tie-in Merchandise to Disney's *Alice in Wonderland* (2010)', *Adaptation* 7(2) (2014): 191–211.
53 It has been translated, for example, as the 'alienation effect' which is potentially confusing given the Marxist use of the term 'alienation' to describe the negative effects of capitalism on our social and psychological well-being. It could be described as the alienation that liberates us from our alienation – but this all seems unnecessarily confusing. I prefer to think of *Verfremdungseffekt* as a critical, political act of de-automation (and certainly alienation does have as one of its characteristics, the sense of being turned into automatons, a loss of subjectivity, agency, etc.).
54 Sean Carney, *Brecht and Critical Theory: Dialectics and Contemporary Aesthetics* (London: Routledge, 2005), pp. 14–15.

# 6

# IDEOLOGY

## 6.1 Ideology defined

One of the recent problems with the thinking and theorising that have been done around the concept of ideology is that it has been conflated with the concept of culture. A key figure here was the French Marxist philosopher Louis Althusser, who gave an influential definition of ideology. He argued that ideology is the way we *live* (in rituals and practices), an *imaginary* relation to our real relationships. However, this imaginary relationship turns out to be synonymous with culture per se. For Althusser, our real relationships can only be discerned using scientific and theoretical discourses. As well as being somewhat elitist, this theory of ideology which collapsed ideology into culture, stretches the term so wide as to become useless as a specialised term identifying specific patterns of value linked to power relations (see Section 2.6).

To see how influential and how problematic Althusser's definition of ideology is, we can take as an example, an excellent book by Keeanga-Yamahtta Taylor, *From #BlackLivesMatter to Black Liberation* (2016), which, as the title suggests, comes out of the Black Lives Matter movement that emerged in response to the relentless killing of black people by the US police force. The fact that black lives are very expendable as far as both the police and the US political establishment is concerned, would clearly qualify as an ideology. The ideology in question is racism which 'explains' the position of blacks in America by blaming black people themselves (e.g. they are unable to take advantage of the American 'dream' and lift themselves out of poverty because of their own inadequacies, or they are 'naturally' violent and aggressive or prone to crime, or have 'problems' with authority, hence they tend to come into negative contact with the police, etc.). This ideology, as Althusser rightly stressed of all ideologies, does not just float around in the ether, it is not just 'in' people's heads. 'An ideology always exists in an apparatus and in the practice or practices of that apparatus,' writes Althusser.[1] The apparatus in question here is the police force, the broader judicial system and what has been called the 'prison-industrial' complex. In other words, this ideology is embedded in the state, and particular departments of the state, which Althusser called the Repressive State Apparatus.[2] We may also add that this ideology has an intersection with the capitalist labour market in America. When we identify such 'material apparatuses' (or, as I prefer, institutions), we start to identify social interests, power and inequality. But Althusser also insists on a definition of ideology as an individual's 'imaginary relation to the real relations in which they live'.[3] It turns out that, for Althusser, ideology is as necessary for our everyday ability to make intelligible sense of the world as culture itself. 'Human societies,' he writes, 'secrete ideology as the very element and atmosphere indispensable to their historical respiration and life.'[4] This is too wide a definition to be practically useful, as we can see when Taylor quotes two academics, Karen and Barbara Fields and their Althusserian definition of ideology:

> Ideology is best understood as the descriptive vocabulary of day-to-day existence, through which people make rough sense of the social reality that they live and create day to day. It is the language of consciousness that suits the particular way in which people deal with their fellows. It is the interpretation in thought of the social relations through which they constantly create and re-create their collective being, in all the varied forms their collective being may assume: family, clan, tribe, nation, class, party, business enterprise, church, army, club, and so on. As such ideologies are not delusions but real, as real as the social relations for which they stand ... An ideology must be constantly created and verified in social life;[5]

This is a very good description of *culture* (day-to-day existence, individual and collective relationships, institutional locations or 'apparatuses', such as church, business, etc.). But it is too general and vague to work as a definition of ideology. If every 'rough sense' of social reality is ideological (rather than cultural in the first instance), then how do we differentiate between one cultural-ideological formation (such as racism) and another (such as the language which describes oppression and exploitation)? Not all people, black or white, share the 'rough sense' (racism) that black people are to blame for their problems. Many people have a 'rough sense' that there are other better explanations for their problems. Taylor goes on to elaborate that racism works by 'rationalizing poverty and inequality in ways that absolve the state and capital of any culpability'.[6] This is exactly right but notice that *this* is a much more definite and concrete definition of ideology: not just as a rough 'making sense' activity located in institutions and practices, but a 'making sense' activity that is conducive to the reproduction of capital and state in particular historical circumstances. A more properly Marxist definition then specifies ideology as working through culture but as ideas, values, belief systems, habits and practices that defend and legitimise the interests of groups *at the expense of other groups in relationships of inequality.*

'Ideology,' writes Terry Lovell, 'may be defined as the production and dissemination of erroneous beliefs whose inadequacies are socially motivated.'[7] Examples: Sexism (male ideas about women), racism (typically, but not exclusively, white people's ideas about Black and Asian people), homophobia (straight people's ideas about gay people), nationalism (ideas about the 'superiority' of one's own nation and the inferiority of other nations, often crossed with racism), class discrimination (middle class ideas about the working class). Then there is capitalism itself which has a built-in cultural tendency to decontextualise social phenomena, individualise social phenomena and de-historicise social phenomena. We may also add that capitalism prematurely or falsely universalises capitalist culture and value systems (e.g. the only way to live).

## 6.2 Social and historical ideologies and film form

We need to briefly summarise the broader theoretical framework by which we can analyse the interaction between the social and historical cultures and ideologies that film texts draw on and the deployment of film form, particularly at the level of narrative (ways of telling stories) and genre (the conventions associated with certain types of stories). The most significant developments in this regard were produced by a trio of books by Marxist literary critics: Pierre Macherey's *A Theory of Literary Production* (1966), Terry Eagleton's *Criticism and Ideology* (1976) and Fredric Jameson's *The Political Unconscious* (1981). The hegemony of Marxist *literary* theory (compared to, say, film theory) reflects the much longer historical development of literature, the much longer and widespread development of the *study* of literature and the central political importance of literature in the educational and cultural institutions generally. With the important exception of Macherey's work, which was mediated into film studies via *Cahiers du Cinema*, Marxist *literary* thinking was not widely drawn on by film studies, although Jameson's 1984 essay on postmodernism was very influential on film studies as it was across the spectrum of cultural theory.[8] The fourth key Marxist literary thinker who should also be cited here, Raymond Williams, will be discussed in Chapter 8.

I do not have space for a systematic account of Macherey, Eagleton or Jameson's books but will draw freely on them to summarise some of the main points that need to be made concerning the question of form and the social and historical materials that (film) texts draw on. One point to bear in mind though is that all three works were much more influenced by Louis Althusser's theory of ideology than I wish to be, for the reasons already given. The practical effect of this is that, for me, ideology is much less an omnipresent effect that bathes all of social and historical life and artistic forms themselves (critics spoke of the 'ideology of form', for example). Instead ideology is an important category for Marxist critical analysis, but its presence, purchase and effectiveness are not guaranteed prior to concrete historical and social analysis. We may also expect (subject to investigation) that ideological positions, themes, voices, etc., will also be contested and challenged by other discourses. In fact, I would argue that this is actually quite common in film across the spectrum of different modes of cinematic production. This does not mean films escape all contact with ideology but that their relationship to ideology is complex and fractured, and while this was recognised by the theorists cited above, this recognition was in some contradiction with the overall theory of ideology they operated.

The key advance which Macherey helped inaugurate in Marxist cultural criticism is a shift away from thinking of the work as a 'creation' by an author and at the same time, a 'reflection' of (or failure to 'reflect') reality. Influenced by structuralism which had stressed that meaning-making was generated by the internal relationships between signs and that this was part of a language *system* (or cultural order), both simple-minded claims that the work 'derived' from the creative imagination of the individual author and (the somewhat conflicting claim) that it 'reflected' reality, were abandoned. To think of the author as a creator belongs to a 'humanist ideology', Macherey argued, whereby wider social structures are eclipsed (the decontextualisation element of capitalist ideology). In the creator model, man is '[c]ircumscribed only by the resources of his own nature, he becomes the maker of his own laws. He creates.'[9] Against this model of creation, Macherey stresses the Marxist concept of *production*. Here 'art is not man's creation, it is a product (and the producer is not a subject centred in his creation, he is an element in a situation or a system).' This production is 'a real labour of production … in *determinate conditions*'.[10]

The determinate conditions Macherey, Eagleton and Jameson concentrate on are the social and historical raw materials the texts draw on *and* the conventions or formal strategies they deploy to transform those raw materials (especially narrative and genre conventions). The text's raw materials are 'a tissue of meanings, perceptions and responses which inhere in the first place in that imaginary production of the real which is ideology,' writes Terry Eagleton in Althusserian fashion.[11] The social and historically determinate ways that a society may imagine itself, speak about itself, define itself, clearly inform the text but while some of those ways are likely to be ideological or have ideological elements about them, we are not helped by designating all those cultural raw materials as ideological, as a synonym for culture itself. Indeed, popular film culture often articulates perspectives that it makes little sense to describe as ideological.

When in *Trading Places* (1983), an example of the 1980s' business films, Eddie Murphy's character is chased around a gentleman's club by a posse of cops, having been ideologically 'misrecognised' (as Althusser might say) as a mugger by Dan Ackroyd's character (Winthorpe), this scene is hardly ideological. Instead here popular culture is acknowledging and interrogating the assumptions underpinning racist ideology and class privilege and the power of the state apparatus to reinforce both. Apprehended and put in a police car, Murphy looks directly at the camera in a self-reflexive moment – as if to say, 'this is what happens to black people in America'. Yet *Trading Places* does also have many features that we can call ideological. Some of those features derive from the ideological value systems in social and historical circulation which the film draws on. The tagline of the film is revealing in this regard: 'They're not just getting rich … they're getting even' which justifies both their aim (getting rich) and their motives (personal revenge). Clearly the aim of 'getting rich' and the superficial 'ethical' dimension given to that aim ('getting even') are highly congruent with American capitalism and helps endorse it. These ideological features also interact with a variety of formal strategies, to which we can now turn our attention.

Just as the social and historical raw materials which a text draws on (they are not really 'raw' in fact but actually already developed in various other social institutions) may be ideological or not, so the formal features of a text may work to help reinforce or patch up ideological value systems, or formal strategies may subject cultural and ideological value systems to some kind of interrogation and critique. Marxist criticism in the 1970s tended to stress the former role for formal strategies as this fitted easily enough with the amorphous definition of ideology, which here could include the 'ideology of form' itself. So here are some of the key narrative strategies that have been discussed as ideological strategies:

1. *Binary oppositions and their reconciliation.* Fredric Jameson drew on structuralist thinkers such as A.J. Griemas and the structuralist anthropologist Claude Lévi-Strauss to understand the way texts set up problems as a series of *binary oppositions* and then used characters and situations that could act as mediators between these oppositions and thus resolve them in the course of the narrative. Very typically, for example, two characters are constructed as representing different 'value systems' initially and while they start off as opposing forces, in the course of the narrative they converge and join forces or, if a man and a women, become romantically involved. In the case of *Trading Places*, Eddie Murphy's Billy Ray Valentine represents a smart, streetwise but poor black hustler while Dan Ackroyd's Louis Winthorpe III represents the white, elite, pampered and inherited privileged class. Yet, in the course of the narrative, these oppositions, which we saw generated a critique of racism and class privilege in the gentleman's club scene, are reconciled as the two characters, formerly opposed, come together and team up to triumph over the real bad guys, the Duke brothers, successful stock market brokers. Here we see how, as Jameson puts it, 'The aesthetic act is itself ideological, and the production of aesthetic or narrative form is to be seen as an ideological act in its own right, with the function of inventing imaginary or formal "solutions" to unresolvable social contradictions.'[12] This formulation of 'imaginary resolutions to unresolvable social contradictions' derived from the work of the anthropologist Lévi-Strauss and his studies of the social role of the artwork and storytelling of primitive tribal societies. In the case of *Trading Places*, social contradictions to do with inequality and racism are not 'resolvable' by the cultural text nor are they resolvable outside a major social and economic transformation that is outside the parameters of what a film like *Trading Places* can imagine or endorse. So the 'imaginary resolutions to unresolvable social contradictions' formulation certainly has a good deal of explanatory power on an awful lot of popular film culture. In the above quote, though,

Jameson is overly hasty in subsuming narrative form to ideology per se ('the aesthetic act is itself ideological') which is something I have cautioned against.

2. *Displacement.* This concept, which originates from Freudian criticism, describes how problems can be relocated from one thing which it is difficult to acknowledge or do anything about (capitalists making money in a way that impoverishes other people) onto something or someone else. If I am angry with the boss but I kick the cat when I get home as a result, that is a displacement strategy, because it is much easier to take it out on the cat than confront the boss. *Trading Places* similarly displaces the problem of capitalism onto the 'bad' Duke brothers, thus allowing the rest of the system to remain in place when the Duke brothers receive their inevitable comeuppance.

3. *Individualisation.* Here problems and solutions to problems are dealt with at the level of individual protagonists, with their broader implications or consequences bracketed off from the viewing audience. Star personas tend to reinforce this strategy as the discourses and cultural meanings around stars stress their exceptional and transcendental qualities (although this does also conflict with the contrary tendency, that they are, after all, 'just like us'). Stars make it difficult to develop 'ensemble' and more collective and dispersed kinds of narrative agency and concern, although not impossible, as Tim Robbins' star-studded social realism film, *The Cradle Will Rock* (1999) shows. Yet whether even this film overcomes the Neo-Realist objection that audiences 'see' the star rather than the characters' social and political circumstances, is another question.

4. *Redemption arcs.* Another popular strategy is the redemption narrative arc, where characters who are initially constructed as in some way ethically dubious, as Winthorpe is, for example, undergo experiences (he becomes poor, thanks to the Duke brothers), which transform them and apparently make them more decent human beings. This could be thought of as ideological because very profound socialisation processes seem to be shed rather quickly, conveniently and definitively.

5. *Focalisation.* Any story world is full of potentially different perspectives and storylines that the narration could have offered the viewer but does not. Focalisation is the *actual* path we take as viewers through the story world, the one selected from all the myriad other possibilities that would have made it another and different film.[13] We follow in the main the story of *these* characters and not others who are secondary and marginal. What makes focalisation potentially ideological is that typically we spend most of our time next to characters (following characters) who are drawn from the dominant sectors (male, white, middle class, professional, western, or at least working in and for the power-bloc, such as the police). Such proximity would be less of a problem if it was not also coupled with strong cues that encourage us to sympathise, identify and feel allegiance with these characters and their moral world-views. So the real problem is focalisation plus (a more or less uncritical) identification.[14]

It is of course possible to focalise a story through that of privileged social types, but cunningly deconstruct that privilege and our deeply in-built tendency to identify with them. Such complex strategies usually take us outside the territory of dominant cinematic modes.[15] The Cuban filmmaker Tomás Gutiérrez Alea did this in *Memories of Underdevelopment* (1968), showing how the middle-class protagonist Sergio, confronted with the historical event that was the Cuban revolution, cannot *act*; he neither leaves Cuba to join the other right-wing *émigrés* in Miami, nor supports their attempted coup in the Bay of Pigs invasion (1961). But neither can he join the revolution and escape his own elitist socialisation process (which includes a good deal of male sexism). Alea's film first cultivates identification with Sergio (he is wealthy, intelligent, but also the classic 'outsider' figure who does not apparently fit in) and we see everything from his point of view (e.g. his voice-over narration, his telescope, as he surveys Havana, etc). Then Alea deconstructs the basis of that identification by showing the limits of Sergio's inability to escape his socialisation in a moment of historical change. US and European critics, however, have often missed this second Brechtian dynamic of the *Verfremdungseffekt* and critique and instead read Sergio's ambivalence about the revolution as *the* political-ethical position which *we* the viewer should also occupy.[16] We may conclude from this that contexts of reception as well as production shape patterns of meanings available to viewers.

6. *Closure*. Another ideological strategy which has been widely discussed in popular films, is the drive towards narrative *closure*. The concept refers to the way films usually try and wrap everything up, so that all the problems which the film has explored seem resolved and all the main goals of the characters we have been invited to identify with, have been achieved. This often involves romantic coupling (the clichéd final embrace) as well as the punishment or death of antagonists who attempted to thwart the will and goals of the heroic characters. Sometimes attempts to sew everything up undermine their own plausibility since they seem to be 'rushed' or so at odds with everything that has gone before, or seem in some way to be marked self-consciously as a 'fantasy' (the end of *Trading Places* locates the five main characters on an island paradise, for example), ironic, or are simply ambiguous in one way or another, suggesting a residue of unresolved issues.

Yet while form may work in all these and other ways to patch up ideologies, narrative and generic forms may also subject the social and historical raw materials they draw on and their own attachments to ideological formations, to searching interrogation. As Terry Eagleton put it: 'The text, through its formal devices, establishes a transformative relation between itself and ideology which allows us to perceive the usually concealed contours of the ideology from which it emerges.'[17] This idea that aesthetic forms could work on and subject ideologies to *critique* was in some contradiction with the Althusserian model of ideology the theorists were working with. It is a contradiction apparent in Althusser's own brief remarks on this very subject. In relation to what Althusser calls 'real art' and 'authentic art', there is, he claims, the possibility of 'an *internal distantiation* from the very ideology' from which the works emerge.[18] Thus, in a few cases limited to works of 'art' (high art), cultural works can round on and critique the ideological matrix that the majority of cultural works succumb to. This is how Althusser rescues some *art* from his all-encompassing model of ideology.

This art/ideology relation mapped out by Macherey and Althusser entered film studies via an influential article by Jean-Luc Comolli and Paul Narboni in the pages of *Cahiers du Cinéma* and reprinted by *Screen* in 1971. On the one hand, film was, they argued, embedded in the economic system of capitalism and as a result: 'What the camera in fact registers is the vague, unformulated, untheorized, un-thought-out world of the dominant ideology.'[19] On the other hand, they mapped out seven categories ('a–g') that specified different relations between film and ideology depending on their political stances and interests and the form and content mobilised. The category which has been most discussed and most influential was category 'e'. Films in this category 'seem at first sight to belong firmly within the ideology' (note the problematic singular, homogeneous notion of one dominant ideology), but on closer inspection there is:

> [a]n internal criticism … taking place which cracks the film apart at the seams. If one reads the film obliquely, looking for symptoms; if one looks beyond its apparent formal coherence, one can see that it is riddled with cracks: it is splitting under an internal tension … The ideology thus becomes subordinate to the text. It no longer has an independent existence: it is *presented* by the film.[20]

The recasting of the text as a production of meaning by Marxist literary and film criticism shifted some of the traditional normative concerns which literary (and film) criticism has with thematic and formal unity and harmony. These critical terms are clearly not innocent, for if we understand that the society we live in is in fact full of conflict and contradictions, then searching out and praising texts for their apparently seamless integration of elements may suggest a denial of those conflicts and contradictions. As with *Cahiers* category 'e' films, Macherey, Eagleton and Jameson all stressed that criticism should be alive to the 'conflict and incompatibility of several meanings' in a text, as Eagleton put it.[21] Macherey argues that criticism must discover not the 'centre' of the work, but its 'decentred-ness'. The work relates to its historical moment not by 'reflection' but by the production of internal conflicts and contradictions. These are not the sort of imperfections traceable to poor technique or lack of grasp or control of the material, on the part of the author or producers. Rather, conflict and contradiction are the signs of the text's relationship to its historical moment. The 'incompatibility of several meanings' in a text is actually 'the strongest bond by which it is attached to reality', writes Macherey.[22] This theorisation of the value of contradiction within art works represents one of Marxism's most significant and valuable contributions to aesthetic theory, in my view.

There is, however, much more scope to expand this notion of an aesthetic-critique of ideology once we uncouple it from a model of ideology that makes culture and ideology synonymous. For example, films which encourage an identification with gangsters, outlaws, bank robbers, thieves, and so forth are cultivating, at the very least, an ambivalent relationship with the key ideological principles of private property and wealth upon which capitalism rests. A film such as *Hell or High Water* (2016) certainly stress-tests the ideology of American capitalism and the law and order apparatus that protects capitalist wealth and institutions such as banks, drawing on the long-embedded critical components of the western and heist movie genres, which have articulated powerful anti-big business and anti-law and order sentiments that have their roots in various strands of the broader popular culture. The title of the film interestingly and self-consciously evokes the sort of classic B-movies from the old Hollywood studio system where one might have found such anti-establishment films and heroes – such as the bank robber brothers Toby (Chris Pine) and Tanner (Ben Foster). On the other hand, the film is also focalised through the perspectives of the Texas Rangers, especially Marcus Hamilton (played by Jeff Bridges, who is typically and due to *The Big Lebowski* (1998), almost mythically, a point of heroic identification in his films) and Alberto Parker (played by Gil Birmingham, an actor of native American-Indian descent, which introduces further interesting cross-currents into the film's interrogative analysis of American history and ideology, with its various intertextual references to the Western genre).

At one level, the film concludes without much sense of *closure*, no romantic reconciliation between Toby and his former wife, just a working arrangement and very importantly no sense of mutual understanding or respect between Toby and Marcus Hamilton as both have suffered personal losses (both Tanner and Alberto have been killed) that have left undimmed grievances towards each other across the unbridgeable gulf of their respective positions in the social order. On the other hand, Toby has achieved his goal (he has rescued his mother's farm from foreclosure by the bank, has passed it onto his sons and the discovery of oil on the land ensures they will have more expansive life opportunities than he did). The closure at a personal level of Toby's story line in *Hell or High Water* is combined with the lack of closure in relation to what he has done and law and order as represented by Hamilton. This is an 'incompatibility' which bonds the film to the reality that personal need and social justice remain at loggerheads within capitalist society. The film manages an ending that at once satisfies traditional identification with goal-oriented characters whom we come to see as righteously motivated, while retaining a frank sense of contradiction with the wider law and order apparatus. We perhaps need an eighth category to add to the *Cahiers* list (category 'h') because this all 'feels' like a carefully worked-out, consciously articulated, and rather successful negotiation of generic conventions, commercial imperatives and ideological contradictions by the filmmakers and not really a film that is 'unconsciously' cracking apart at the seams in the sense that *Cahiers* meant with their category 'e' film.

## 6.3 Judith Williamson and the 1980s' business films

We might find films more fitting into *Cahiers'* category 'e' in a cycle of business films in the 1980s that, on the surface, seem to be about celebrating capitalism in the same way that the New Conservatism under Ronald Reagan was. In her excellent essay on the big business films of the 1980s, Judith Williamson begins with a 1988 quote from Douglas Hurd, the then Conservative Party Home Secretary in Britain.

> Those qualities of enterprise and initiative which are essential for the generation of material wealth are also needed to build a family, a neighbourhood and a nation which is able to draw on the respect, loyalty and affection of its members.[23]

By citing a British politician in the context of an essay about Hollywood cinema, Williamson is attempting to show how popular culture can be made relevant to political debates, even when the popular culture in question derives from outside the national context of reception. We will come back to the issue of articulating popular culture to political practice but for now we may also guess, when reading this quote, that there is a glaring contradiction which Hurd has unwittingly (the political unconscious of conservatism) put his finger on. For there is fairly obviously a potential difficulty in trying to reconcile 'enterprise and initiative' (making money and the generation of *capitalist* 'material wealth') with 'family', 'neighbourhood', 'nation', and attitudes such as 'respect', 'loyalty' and 'affection'. What if the building of material wealth means doing down those latter identities and values? What if to make money you end up sacrificing family, community, nation and tread all over loyalty? Base and superstructure may be in flat contradiction with each other.

Williamson immediately juxtaposes this quote from Douglas Hurd with a brief discussion of Protestantism and its long history of trying to negotiate the tensions between business enterprise and moral value. This indicates that although we are dealing with a very specific historical moment, the moment of Ronald Reagan's presidency, the period of Margaret Thatcher's three successive governments in the UK, we are also dealing with a long-standing problem which the very specific moment has exacerbated. It is useful here to refer to two kinds of contexts in which texts should be situated, which Fredric Jameson has identified. These contexts function as 'the social ground of a text' or 'semantic horizons'[24] within which we can interpret them. The first context or semantic horizon is the *immediately* political context, 'in the narrow sense of punctual event and a chronicle like sequence of happenings in time'.[25] So the rise of Thatcher and Reagan ('punctual events'), the rise and fall of movements and political trends (the decline of social democracy accelerates at a policy level in the 1980s), the shifting changes in fortunes, fashions, etc., all belong to this first narrow and immediate context or political moment.

However, we cannot simply situate a text in its immediate context (the 1980s). We must also situate it in relation to more structural and enduring socio-economic realities that stem from the mode of production itself. Here the text is situated in relation to 'the great collective and class discourses of which a text is little more than an individual *parole* or utterance'.[26] Jameson calls the 'collective and class discourses' in question, *ideologemes*, and the task of criticism is to select or name a pertinent ideologeme that intersects with the text. An ideologeme is a discourse that has 'an amphibious' quality in that it can 'manifest itself either as a pseudoidea – a conceptual or belief system, an abstract value, an opinion or prejudice' or in story or narrative form.[27] It is clear then that Williamson's juxtaposition of Hurd's discourse, Protestantism's reputation as the religion best expressing capitalist values and Hollywood films helps us identify an ideologeme that can work as both political doctrine and popular film narrative. What is that ideologeme? Well, as we have already said, it is the fantasy that business can easily be reconciled with moral values. In fact, given the very interesting fact that economic value and moral value both use the term 'value' for radically different and potentially incompatible kinds of things, we may say simply that the ideologeme in question means reconciling different definitions of *value(s)*, economic and moral, making money and doing good. This is the collective and class-conflicted debate around which Hollywood's big business films of the 1980s circle, somewhat anxiously and in a conflicted way despite their apparent celebratory quality (hence their category 'e' quality in *Cahiers*' terms). And as the contradictions and tensions around the ideologeme of value are persistent and structural, to do with the conflict at the heart of the capitalist mode of production between base and superstructure, exchange value and use value, or quite simply, making money and 'doing good', we can expect this dialogue to be conducted across a number of films. Hence, Williamson develops her argument in relation to a cluster of 1980s' films including *Trading Places, Baby Boom* (1987), *Wall Street* (1987), *The Secret of My Success* (1987), *Working Girl* (1988), *Vice Versa* (1988), *Big* (1988) and *Big Business* (1988).

In each of these films we see outsiders enter the world of business (or insiders who have become jaded, leave and then return, as in *Baby Boom*). These outsiders are coded as 'authentic' with no hypocrisy or pretence; they are morally good characters whose formation is 'outside' the system they want to join. They are also shown to be naturally good at business. Their outsider status is underpinned by their social identities. So they are children (*Big*), women/lower middle class (*Working Girl*), black/working class (*Trading Places*), working class (*Wall Street*) or they might come from the country (*Secret of My Success, Baby Boom*). The films engineer narratives which bring the outsiders *into* the world of business and/or its upper echelons (a frequently used strategy here, notes Williamson, is the 'life-swap' strategy as in *Trading Places, Vice Versa, Big*). Once the outsiders have got into the world of business and work themselves up into the executive levels where they can have an impact and be noticed, they typically encounter resistance from characters who embody all the negative characteristics of the business world (they are competitive, backstabbing, selfish, conformist, hierarchical, bureaucratic, etc.). These characters are the ones on which all the problematical aspects of capitalism will be loaded or dumped (displacement) making it easier to 'cleanse' the system when these 'bad' characters are punished or defeated. In achieving their goals, the outsider characters seem to transfer their morally wholesome qualities to the system along with their natural business acumen. What initially seems a binary opposition between moral values and economic value is reconciled by the mediations of the characters and situations the film has constructed. Williamson sums up the argument thus:

> It is central to the successful marriage of business and ethics in these films that we focus on one *individual* (or occasionally two): the good person who comes from outside the system ... and can therefore represent all the values capitalism is shown – initially – to negate. Their success within the system then seems to endow it with precisely those values.[28]

A scene in *Big* shows how this process works. Paul (John Heard) is giving a presentation to the top executives of the toy company on the new soon-to-be-released toy – a building that turns into a robot. The camera pans along the executives in suits taking notes while Paul off-screen is heard talking about market testing, focus groups, statistics, etc., the language of scientific positivism that is captured and harnessed routinely to capitalist metrics. The camera stops its pan on Josh, played by Tom Hanks, (the boy who got his wish and has turned into an adult overnight while retaining his boyhood self/subjectivity inside). Instead of taking notes dutifully, he is *playing* with the prototype of the toy and through practical engagement as a user, finding it not to his liking. At the end of his presentation, Paul asks if there are any questions – of course, there are none, everyone is suitably impressed with the graphs and the numbers, everyone except Josh, who nervously puts his hand up as if he was in a school class. Josh does not see what is fun about turning a building into a robot. Paul responds with more reports on market share and hands him some figures. We can see the binary oppositions very much at work: the language of business, markets, tests, reports, consumers, profits, all very distant from the actual use value of the toy (is it *fun?*). Josh's idea is that the robot should change into something radically different – something *organic*, a prehistoric bug with giant claws. On this idea, the whole room suddenly becomes very *animated*, and Paul finds himself slipping from centre stage as his fellow executives start excitedly discussing this idea. This is very typical of the natural/outsider figure – they are a *transformative*, energising force, renewing the other corporate types who had been, up until his intervention, acting in a very conformist, no-questions-asked manner, just assenting to what the hierarchy of the situation expected of them. By the end of the scene there feels like a much more dynamic and democratic debate going on. We shall see later that this can be discussed as the *utopian* desires which films tap into and which are complexly related to ideology. For now though, we can see how this scene exemplifies both a critique and renewal of the business world and thus works at least partially, ideologically. We can also see that while the film may not be 'cracking apart at the seams', there are certainly tensions there in trying to negotiate business and ethics.

Williamson argued that while these films were problematic, there are enough contradictory impulses going on within them to learn from, even at the level of political strategy. She argues that, in the 1980s, the left stopped talking about the working class, about manufacturing, about the moral outrages of capitalism, even though many of these films show a continuing concern with these issues (despite the ideological strategies). This indicates the way we can mine popular film culture for broader trends that can be helpful in reflecting on political strategy in a broader sense. Williamson's argument is that all these things, which Hollywood films are meditating on, show that they remain active concerns (despite the triumph of the political right) even if in a rather subterranean way.[29] Thus, political struggles for change need to be alive to these signs being emitted from popular culture and work to crystallise, expand and make politically efficacious such sentiments as the moral-political anxieties that can be found in these films (see Chapter 8). Williamson's framing of films in this way is very much an example of the broader cultural-political contextualisation which a cultural studies framework brings to the study of film.

## 6.4 Business films after the crash

The terminus of the Thatcher and Reagan settlement and the business films of the 1980s was the global capitalist crash of 2007–8 (an event from which the global capitalist economy has yet to recover at the time of writing). The financial sector, in Wall Street and the City of London, both liberated from any effective regulation in the 1980s, crashed and took a good chunk of the high street retail economy with it. The response of the political elites internationally was to bail out the banks (socialise their debt) and insist on austerity for the public sector (through cutbacks and further rounds of privatisations). Political conflict internationally intensified with revolutions and counter-revolutions in the Middle East, seismic convulsions in Southern Europe (Greece, Spain, Italy) and occupations of Wall Street and the City of London in 2011. Hollywood responded with many films engaging with the new anger and resentment against the banking system and perhaps capitalism more generally that were swirling around popular culture as a result: *Inside Job* (2010), *The Big Short* (2015), *The Wolf of Wall Street* (2013), *Wall Street: Money Never Sleeps* (2010), *Capitalism, A Love Story* (2009) and *Assault on Wall Street* (2013). The latter is an interesting film: low budget, made outside the American-Hollywood context, with low-production values and mediocre acting that compares very unfavourably with a slick product like *The Wolf of Wall Street*, the film was panned by the mainstream critics from the big news outlets. Yet it maps out the consequences of the crash for the little people much better and with more anger than many of the other fictional films listed above. The institutions of the big banks and speculators are not treated with the same ferocity in the more mainstream films and it seems likely that the funding and production context of *Assault on Wall Street* opened up a space for a significantly different tone and feel. *Assault on Wall Street* ends as the title promises, with a violent assault on bankers which mainstream critics found 'tasteless' despite the fact that violence is routinely used to 'solve' problems in mainstream Hollywood films and this is widely accepted as part of generic entertainment cinema, when it is not directed at the financial elites. Audience ratings for the film were substantially more positive, indicating perhaps a class gap between the professional critics and segments of the audience, who were perhaps closer to being on the receiving end of the crisis.

I am going to focus on one example of these post-crash films, a film called *Money Monster* (2016), starring George Clooney and Julia Roberts. The film illustrates both the extent to which a changed political context can *expand* and *deepen* the range of critical voices and perspectives that can be drawn on in a popular Hollywood film, but my analysis also shows that the semantic horizon of the class discourse is still structured within the fundamental framework of the dominant capitalist mode of production and therefore the text has certain ideological limits within which it works. A comparative analysis of the film with the strategies of the 1980s' business films of the Reagan era helps illustrate both its 'progressive' credentials and its continuing entrapment within ideological structures. In this sense, *Money Monster* might fall into what *Cahiers du Cinéma* called their category 'd' film, those with a progressive political content, but 'which do not effectively criticize the ideological system in which they are embedded because they unquestioningly adopt its language and its imagery'.[30] There has been an extensive debate around category d films, particularly in relation to the political thriller, which has attempted to reconcile progressive political content, typically about state and sometimes corporate power, within the entertainment format of the thriller (which draws on a combination of elements such as the detective story, the mystery, the murder story, the conspiracy story, etc,). John Hill has explored the problems of using the political thriller genre in relation to some of the work of Ken Loach (especially *Hidden Agenda*).[31]

*Money Monster* is not a political thriller although it does have some classic elements of it (such as the journalists as detective figures) nor is it as combatively political as a Loach or Costa-Gavras film. It was directed by the actor/director Jodie Foster and stars George Clooney who is well known for using his box office draw to get liberal films funded and distributed (Clooney was a producer of this film). The film also stars Julia Roberts and Jack O'Connell, a British actor from a working-class background. A brief plot summary then: Lee Gates (George Clooney) hosts a television show, *Money Monster* which discusses and promotes Wall Street companies and investment opportunities. His show's director, Patty Fenn (Julia Roberts) has tired of the programme and is, unbeknown to Lee, starting a new job the following week. Inevitably Patty's last show is interrupted by Kyle Budwell (Jack O'Connell), who holds Lee hostage, blaming him for losing his $60,000 inheritance from his mother when a stock option for Ibis Capital which Lee enthusiastically endorsed, lost a huge amount of money ($800 million) apparently due to a computer 'glitch'. However, Ibis Capital's head, Walt Canby (Dominic West), who was due to be on the programme becomes unavailable at the last minute. In the meantime Kyle holds Lee at gunpoint and straps an explosive device to him threatening to blow him up unless he gets answers.

The choice of locating the action on the set of a television show that uncritically celebrates Wall Street is significant in many ways. It first of all allows the film to critique the role of the media in failing to hold powerful financial institutions to account and instead act as cheerleaders for their activities. This discourse has certainly become very widely disseminated as part of a critique of the corporate or mainstream media (MSM). The growth of independent media often directly linked to anti-corporate social movements has helped popularise critical attitudes towards the dominant media (although these have also now been appropriated by the conservative Right, as in the case of Donald Trump). By bringing Kyle Budwell into this environment, the drama can be played out as live television, making it a public event and giving the action a potentially wider political implication (although the limits of that is something we will come to). The television studio setting for much of the action also helps make the film relatively cheap in Hollywood terms; its budget was $27 million and it made back over $93 million worldwide, so its 'critical' interrogation of Wall Street was, paradoxically, reasonably profitable as a return on investment.

In terms of narrative structures, we can compare *Money Monster* to the strategy of reconciling opposites that we have previously discussed. As with the 1980s' films, there is an outsider character (Kyle Budwell), who disrupts the environment of the business insiders. While the insiders, such as Lee and the show, uncritically reported the explanation for Ibis Capital's losses (the 'glitch'), Kyle brings a refreshing dose of morality and good sense back into play: he wants to know how it is 'even possible' to lose $800 million and he does not believe the 'glitch' argument for a second ('what does that even mean?'). So Budwell's intervention brings a new critical discourse into the media machine, questioning its routine recycling of Wall Street perspectives or frames, as it is known in media studies,[32] and bringing the consequences of the actions of the financiers into view. Burned by the system, Budwell tells viewers of the live show that the system is rigged. In an important critique of the displacement strategies of the political mainstream, he notes that it is not the Chinese and the Muslims that the American public needs to be worried about, but Wall Street itself. This is a good example of the kind of oppositional political discourse that can find its way into a fiction film that would be unthinkable for most US politicians to utter. The critical perspectives which the outsider brought to the business environment in the 1980s' films discussed above were nothing like as explicitly political as we see in *Money Monster* (the very title of the film suggesting the more sceptical mood which the film is tapping into, regarding capitalism). At the same time, and this is quite typical of Hollywood, such critical perspectives are put into the mouth of a character who is in some way presented as being 'suspect' (here Kyle has all the visual signifiers of the terrorist).

As is so often the case, Hollywood films are at their most critical in their earlier moments, *before* the formal strategies properly kick in and start to neutralise critique in favour of seeking what Jameson calls 'containment strategies' or 'imaginary resolutions to real social contradictions'.[33] In this case, the film sets up an initial opposition between Kyle's radical critique and Lee/Patty/*Money Monster*/Ibis

Capital/Walt Canby and slowly reconfigures it into an alliance between Kyle/Lee/Patty/the *Money Monster* team against the real villain of the situation, Walt Canby (the displacement strategy once more). It is also interesting to consider which characters are allowed the scope to grow and change in the course of a narrative, and very typically once more, it is the middle-class professionals who get to do that while the working-class character provides the trigger for their growth before ultimately dying at the end of the narrative. Indeed, the critique of the system, that Kyle brings initially, is quite rapidly replaced with a redemption arc story for Lee and Patty. Lee gets to realise that his actions have consequences (he is figured as something of a man-child in the beginning) and both Lee and Patty get to become investigative reporters as they mobilise their knowledge of the system and the resources the show has at its disposal to uncover Walt Canby's nefarious activities. The film's displacement strategy and replacement of a system-problem with the individual are cued in a scene where Ibis Capital's communications officer is discussing over the phone with Patty the possibility that there are human fingerprints all over the supposed computer 'glitch'. 'Whose fingerprints?' asks the Ibis officer at the airport where she is picking up Walt Canby, who is getting off his private jet in the background of the shot. What such unsubtle clues do is guide us away from the system to the individual manifestation of the problem. The redemption arc strategy around Lee and Patty also de-politicises the drama, making the moral growth of the characters more important than changing the system or understanding how it works. The redemption arc strategy also includes the priority the film gives to revitalising their friendship and professional working partnership (an important part of the film's ideological closure is that Patty signals that she will not, after all, leave Lee for another job).

The framework of the television show which is the means by which the action is broadcast live to a watching audience, is a very important part of the film's ideological strategies. The *public exposure* of the action has two models in media culture, which the film draws on as part of its cultural (and ideological) raw material. First, there is something of a reality television model at work in all the moments in the film where characters emote towards each other for public consumption. Much of this is done to cement the redemption arc story of Lee and Patty and their relationship. When, for example, Lee is comparing his life with Kyle's and chalking up points for each one on a *Money Monster* scorecard, what we (and with a dawning awareness, he also does) learn is that, in fact, Lee's life has been meaningless and empty, thus clearing the way for him to do moral good for once.

The other public exposure model in the film is that of public interest journalism, as Lee and Patty set about discovering what Canby has been up to and expose him live on air in the film's climax. This is a very common closure strategy for films of this sort. The presumption is that with public exposure of wrongdoing, the institutions that are there (supposedly) to protect us, will mobilise to bring justice, correct wrongs and reform where necessary. This is indeed the classic liberal assumption that media scrutiny means that powerful institutions and individuals can be held to account. But films that end satisfyingly with the exposure of the conspiracy or crime or whatever, seriously underestimate the extent to which public exposure often leads to *no effective action* whatsoever, since the political and judicial institutions are, as Marxism teaches us, part of the superstructure that rests on the base. They are not above or independent of socio-economic power and are indeed badly compromised by socio-economic power.

In *Money Monster*, Canby's exposure is actually somewhat diluted because, in this more realistic storyline, his crime does not involve such clear-cut moral wrong-doing as murdering people, but something more blurred (making money, albeit fraudulently). Thus, the extent of Kyle's ambition is to get Canby to admit that he has done something wrong. Canby initially asks (mirroring Kyle's earlier comment regarding glitches), what does 'wrong' even mean? The ideologeme that we looked at earlier in the 1980s' business films, the tension between economic value vs 'values' resolved itself by transferring the 'good' qualities of the outsider to business. In the changed political context post-crash, it is less plausible for a film to persuasively rescue capitalism so easily. At the same time, there is an implication that Canby's final public admission that he did wrong, may be enough for everyone else to recover their moral compass (although this is a bit ambiguous, with at least some people watching the action on their TV screens switching back to their everyday lives, looking very unaffected by the events). Certainly the film does not radically break out of the terms of the ideologeme of the earlier 1980s' business films. There is nothing like a hard-headed assessment of the structural predisposition of capitalist economic value to erode moral values. Instead there is vague hope that an ethical reawakening at the level of individual self-awareness can restrain capitalism (to which Marxists will always and correctly conclude that this is a pious fantasy).

The other problem with the public exposure model, as it is usually understood, is the role it casts the public in. They are relegated to exerting some tacit moral pressure on the institutions of law and order to intervene, but they themselves are not seen as political agents. Indeed, as audiences of the live broadcast, the film explicitly constructs the public as spectators and consumers who cannot act politically. When Lee and Kyle leave the station and walk down the streets of New York to meet Canby, with Lee now pretending to be held hostage by Kyle, the gathering crowd that watch them have all the hallmarks of a 'media circus', of thrill seekers enjoying the spectacle and drama (although we do hear, if we are listening carefully, a voice on the soundtrack cry 'Occupy Wall Street'). Yet the film itself cannot imagine a different kind of 'crowd' mobilised by political values rather than as atomised consumers. As Terry Eagleton remarks, ideology is often most present or effective in the silences of a text, in what it cannot show, in the structural constraints of its vision.[34] For example, crowds quickly, in Hollywood films, become mobs led by demagogues, whose use of the language of change is cynical and self-serving (as it is with Bane's 'revolution' in *The Dark Knight Rises* (2012)). The political, especially in terms of the capitalist *system* and political *agency*, remains 'unconscious' as Jameson puts it, in most popular films. The political, in the terms that Marxism understands it (collective class forces) is the 'silence' or 'not said' as

Macherey put it, around which texts typically circle but cannot explicitly acknowledge.[35] Yet we have also seen that popular films are sites of conflicting perspectives and contradictory ways of processing the social and historical material they draw on, and so are worthy of serious attention and investigation, as Williamson showed us.

## 6.5 Utopianism and ideology

Why are we such suckers for ideology? The concept of utopianism may help us answer this question. Originally utopia as a concept refers to a good place which is a 'no-place', i.e. it does not actually exist. Yet this good place, even if it does not exist, can be imagined and depicted in, say, literature, as it was by Thomas Moore in his 1516 book *Utopia*, about a fictional island that represents a perfect state (one which, incidentally, More envisaged as having no private property). The desire for a radically transformed state of affairs that would meet deeply held desires to overcome injustices, deprivations and arbitrary limitations, is one which of course capitalism both feeds and frustrates. For Marx, the capitalist mode of production is an extraordinary leap in the development of our capacities, especially our technological and cultural capacities. At the same time, as *The Communist Manifesto* makes clear, these productive forces are yoked to the social relations of capital, of profit-making and accumulation and so we have an apparently unfathomable paradox well formulated by Fredric Jameson: 'unparalleled wealth, computerized production, scientific and medical discoveries unimaginable a century ago' rubbing up against 'the disintegration of the social ... misery, poverty, unemployment, starvation, squalor, violence and death'.[36]

In this situation, the culture of capitalism is typically awash with both ideology (that must try and find ways of 'explaining' this paradox without tracking its root causes back to capitalism) and utopian desires or wish-fulfilments for a better life, which capitalism both feeds and endlessly blocks. One of the earliest Marxist thinkers to explore this dynamic between ideology and utopianism was Ernst Bloch, in his massive three-volume work, *The Principles of Hope*. Discussing Bloch's work, Douglas Kellner stresses the wide range of cultural materials which Bloch diagnosed as articulating utopian desires for a better life: daydreams, fairy tales, myths, popular culture, literature, theatre, film, religion, philosophy, technology, architecture, and so on. Utopianism in film is part of a wider and very diverse cultural scene that has utopian currents flowing through it and which are, in turn, related to the socio-economic relations of capitalism (the promotion and frustration dynamic of utopianism). Utopian desires are signs of what Bloch calls an anticipatory consciousness, which as Kellner summarises, 'perceives the unrealized emancipatory potential in the past, the latencies and tendencies of the present, and the realizable hopes of the future'.[37]

Bloch's work represents a very important validation of the political importance of hope, wish-fulfilment and fantasy. These are categories which have been appropriated by mass culture and used in problematic ways, but it is the problematic ways that need to be critiqued, not the authentic impulses for a better life. Peter Wollen cautioned against a puritanical film criticism and practice that did not value pleasure and fantasy, the backbone of entertainment: 'unless a revolution is desired (which means nothing less than coinciding with and embodying collective fantasies), it will never take place'.[38]

In his ground-breaking essay 'Constituents of a Theory of the Media', Hans Magnus Enzensberger also took to task a then popular and puritanical left-wing critique of mass commercial culture (such as the advertising industry) as cultivating 'false needs'. Enzensberger rejected this as simplistic and instead reformulates the problem of mass culture as one based on 'the falsification and exploitation of quite real and legitimate ones [needs]'.[39] It is because these needs are real that mass culture, which taps those needs more effectively than the left in many ways, is powerful and effective. 'Consumption as spectacle contains the promise that want will disappear,' notes Enzensberger. We live in a society where, on the one hand, there is scarcity and, on the other, the promise held out by the spectacle of consumerism that scarcity can be abolished by plenty. 'Consumption as spectacle is – in parody form – the anticipation of a utopian situation.'[40]

Richard Dyer's 1977 essay, 'Entertainment and Utopia' drew on Enzensberger's essay to explore how utopian sentiments underpin everyday understandings of what it is the dominant film industry offers: entertainment, escapism, pleasure. Redefining these vernacular terms within the philosophical culture of utopianism allowed Dyer to dig into the social and political roots of such notions (for example, what are we 'escaping' from in popular film and what are we escaping to?). Dyer noted that popular film does not 'present models of utopian worlds' as Thomas More and a strand of science fiction literature have done, but rather, articulates utopianism 'at the level of sensibility', offering an experience of what utopia might *feel* like.[41] It is important here to pay attention to the formal strategies by which such utopian feelings are conveyed. Focusing on the musical genre in particular, Dyer identifies five categories which help to classify the different types of utopian feelings which popular films might mobilise:

1.  *Energy*: the capacity to act vigorously which, in the musical, typically takes the form of dance numbers, but which in other genres may take the form of chase sequences or fights, where editing, for example, plays an important part in conveying the feeling of dynamicism and the athleticism of the human body (the popularity of Asian martial arts is important here).
2.  *Abundance*: the sense of plenty, of aesthetic richness, of sensuous delight and overload typically takes the form of spectacle (the parodic anticipation of a utopian situation as Enzensberger noted), of lavish sets, costumes and colour in the musical, but may take the form of impressive landscapes and sweeping camera work in other genres, such as the western, the adventure film or science fiction film (the feeling of sublime awe/wonder at nature or technological accomplishments that was much remarked upon, for example, in relation to the black futurism of Wakanda in *Black Panther* (2017)).

3.  *Intensity*: different to energy although it may well overlap in practice, this category refers to that sense which films offer of intense emotions (pleasant or unpleasant) being communicated directly between characters and between characters and audiences. Typically, in the musical, this takes the form of the song, in other films, in romantic interaction between couples, or violence between antagonists. Popular films are populated with characters who are disruptive of conventions (e.g. *Big*), habits, procedures, bureaucracy, etc. that dull how we live. Intensity makes feelings 'seem uncomplicated, direct and vivid, not "qualified" or "ambiguous" as day-to-day life makes them, and without those intimations of self-deception and pretence'.[42]

4.  *Transparency*: this refers to a quality in our relationships and interactions with people which are represented as authentic, sincere, straight, without hidden agendas or opaque motivations. Again the song in the musical is one of the key modes for this utopian feeling, but this quality is also very typically constructed around macho no-nonsense, tell-it-like-it-is male stars more generally, the ones with no time for bureaucracy or expediency.

5.  *Community*: possibly one of the most important sensibilities which the filmic experience offers, that sense of togetherness, belonging and solidarity, which can be found in the musical in the singalong chorus number or Busby Berkeley-style kaleidoscopes of dancers. Beyond the musical, images of togetherness (in the police, the army and other authoritarian institutions especially), community (small town, folksy, etc.), helping out (the rescue), combined and cooperative endeavour of all kinds, are to be found across the spectrum.

Dyer suggests that each of these utopian feelings are responses to real lacks and absences in our present society (thus giving us a real political purchase on categories like 'escapism' and 'entertainment'). So, against energy, there is exhaustion ('work as a grind, alienated labour, pressures of urban life'); against abundance, there is scarcity; against intensity, there is dreariness ('monotony, predictability, instrumentality of the daily round'); against transparency, there is manipulation ('advertising, bourgeois democracy, sex roles'); and against community, there is fragmentation and, we may add, especially in our contemporary moment, competition.[43] Much of the ideological work of film is achieved by negotiating the gaps, absences and lacks which constitute the social and historical experiences of the audience and promising satisfactions that seem to resolve those lacks within terms that do not challenge capitalism and do not adequately track the root causes of our collective sense of anxiety and disquiet *back to* capitalism. In other words, popular films tend to offer capitalist solutions to the problems of capitalism, or at the very least, solutions which capitalism can happily live with.

In his essay, 'Reification and Mass Culture', Fredric Jameson delivers a particularly lucid formulation of the twin dynamics of ideology and utopianism which mass cultural products, such as popular film, typically work through. If we just concentrate on the ideological tendency, then we end up with a criticism based on the 'empty denunciation' of popular film as manipulation. If we just concentrate on the utopian elements, then we move back towards an apparently de-politicised celebration of popular culture.

> Our proposition about the drawing power of the works of mass culture has implied that such works cannot manage anxieties about the social order unless they have first revived them and given them some rudimentary expression; we will now suggest that anxiety and hope are two faces of the same collective consciousness, so that the works of mass culture, even if their function lies in the legitimation of the existing order – or some worse one – cannot do their job without deflecting in the latter's service the deepest and most fundamental hopes and fantasies of the collectivity, to which they can therefore, no matter in how distorted a fashion, be found to have given voice.[44]

Jameson's example of this ideology-utopian dynamic is the representation of the mafia in American film and television. He describes the representation of the mafia as 'the strategic displacement of all the rage generated by the American system onto this mirror image of big business'[45] (ideology) while at the same time the image of the extended Mafia 'family' (both literal and figurative) offers a utopian fantasy of collectivity (Dyer's community category), loyalty and patriarchal authority, which American capitalism is itself dissolving.

Other writers have wanted to open up rather more space for the utopian possibilities of popular cinema than Jameson seems prepared to do. Alan O'Shea argues that: 'If only a class analysis will satisfy him [Jameson], it is not surprising he can find no source of transformative politics in popular culture; as I will argue, this is not the place to look for coherent political argument.'[46]

Accordingly, drawing on Dyer's categories for utopian *feelings* (rather than analysis of situations), O'Shea argues that popular cinema typically probes away at 'the frustrations and inhibitions in contemporary institutions and offers glimpses of transformed social relationships'.[47] Rather than looking for an already fully worked-out 'analysis' (or cognitive maps) within film, O'Shea suggests that political change comes by building on more embryonic forms of social dissatisfaction that popular films drill down into. There is certainly a danger that the Marxist critic might have unrealistic expectations of popular culture and that it will almost always disappoint as it falls short of the kind of lucid cognitive mapping which Marxist *conceptual* analysis provides. So O'Shea's critique is a valuable corrective and reminder that we should be looking for *something* else in popular film, not the unlikely confirmation of what Marxist critique already knows. That something else might be the glimmerings of popular anxiety about capitalism and the hopes and desires to overcome the life-crushing pathologies it promotes.

Yet I think the tendency towards pessimism which O'Shea detects in Jameson's encounters with popular film has less to do with unrealistic expectations about 'class analysis' than the model of ideology Jameson and other Marxists of his generation are operating with (broadly, an Althusserian one). This model of ideology leaves very little scope for popular culture to be anything else but ideology (hence the utopian elements are largely swamped by the ideological impulses). Once we uncouple ideology from culture, we can accommodate a far greater expectation that popular cinema will be a contested clash of different possibilities and meanings, depending of course, on the wider context. O'Shea's emphasis on 'feelings' reminds us of the important affective side of popular culture, the sheer thrill of its energy, directness, sense of bonding and togetherness, identification and investment in positive outcomes, etc. At the same time, we should remember that while the aesthetic is not the same as conceptual analysis, because it works through the play of sensuous forms (from the micro, such as the shot or the edit, up through to the larger aesthetic systems, such as narrative and genre), it does offer cognitive insights into the kind of world we live in. Both O'Shea and Williamson, coming from a more cultural studies background than Jameson, Macherey or Eagleton, stress the potential for drawing on popular culture as a diagnosis of the deep popular currents that *move* people and which a Marxist politics needs to be alive to in order to turn its theory into practical political action with mass support.

## Notes

1  Louis Althusser, *Ideology and Ideological State Apparatuses* (London: Verso, 2014), p. 184.
2  Ibid., p. 65.
3  Ibid., p. 183.
4  Louis Althusser, *For Marx* (London: Verso 1979), p. 232.
5  Karen and Barbara Fields, cited in Keeange-Yamahtta Taylor, *From #BlackLivesMatter to Black Liberation* (London: Haymarket, 2014), p. 24.
6  Keeange-Yamahtta Taylor, *From #BlackLivesMatter to Black Liberation* (London: Haymarket, 2014), p. 25.
7  Terry Lovell, *Pictures of Reality: Aesthetics, Politics and Pleasure* (London: BFI, 1983), p. 51.
8  See Fredric Jameson, *Postmodernism, or, the Cultural Logic of Late Capitalism* (Durham, NC: Duke University Press, 1992). As an influential critical term, postmodernism's moment has passed, in part because of some of the overinflated claims made about this 'epoch', in part because academic publishing is nothing if not fashion led and in part because some of the trends which were identified under this term and which are ongoing, have been better analysed under less aesthetically dominated terms, such as globalisation or neo-liberalism. But perhaps also, in part because the trends have become deeply embedded and no longer need a special term. Some trends have also mutated into new and even more dangerous strains, such as 'transhumanism'''. See my own discussion of Jameson's reading of postmodernism, Mike Wayne, 'Jameson, Postmodernism and the Hermeneutics of Paranoia', in Mike Wayne (ed.), *Understanding Film: Marxist Perspectives* (London: Pluto Press, 2005).
9  Pierre Macherey, *A Theory of Literary Production* (London: Routledge, 2006), p. 77.
10  Ibid., p. 77.
11  Terry Eagleton, *Criticism and Ideology* (London: Verso, 1986, p. 75).
12  Fredric Jameson, *The Political Unconscious* (London: Routledge, 2002), p. 64.
13  See Robert Stam and Ella Shohat's *Unthinking Eurocentrism: Multiculturalism and the Media* (London: Routledge, 2014), pp. 205–8.
14  Murray Smith, 'Altered States: Character and Emotional Response in Cinema', *Cinema Journal*, 33(4): (1994): 34–56.
15  Although not necessarily. A film such as *Quiz Show* (1994) offers an interesting example of a critique of its main character (Charles Van Doren from an elite background) and a complicated process of identification and dis-identification.

16 See John Mraz, '*Memories of Underdevelopment*, Bourgeois Consciousness/Revolutionary Context', in Robert A. Rosenstone (ed.), *Revisioning History: Film and the Construction of a New Past* (Princeton, NJ: Princeton University Press, 1995), pp. 102–14.

17 Eagleton, *Criticism and Ideology*, op. cit., p. 84.

18 Louis Althusser, *Lenin and Philosophy and Other Essays* (London: Monthly Review Press, 2001), p. 152.

19 Jean-Luc Comolli and Paul Narboni, 'Cinema/Ideology/Criticism', *Screen*, 12(1) (1971): 30.

20 Ibid., p. 33.

21 Terry Eagleton, 'Macherey and Marxist Literary Theory', in *Against the Grain* (London: Verso, 1986), p. 14.

22 Macherey, *A Theory of Literary Production*, op. cit., p. 89.

23 Judith Williamson ,'"Up Where You Belong": Hollywood Images of Big Business in the 1980s', in John Corner and Sylvia Harvey (eds), *Enterprise and Heritage* (London: Routledge, 1991), p. 147.

24 Jameson, *The Political Unconscious*, op. cit., pp. 60–1.

25 Ibid., p. 60.

26 Ibid., p. 61.

27 Ibid., p.73. In Chapter 1, I discussed another example of an ideologeme, the Robinsonades evident in both the Defoe story that lends its name to this image and the images of the isolated hunter or fisherman that underpins the assumptions of economists such as Smith, Ricardo and Proudhon.

28 Williamson, '"Up Where You Belong"', op. cit., p. 151.

29 Ibid., p. 156.

30 Comolli and Narboni, 'Cinema/Ideology/Criticism', op. cit., p. 32.

31 See John Hill, 'Finding a Form: Politics and Aesthetics in *Fatherland, Hidden Agenda* and *Riff-Raff*', in George McKnight (ed.), *Agent of Challenge and Defiance: The Films of Ken Loach* (London: Flick Books, 1997), or a condensed version of the argument is available in John Hill and Pamela Church Gibson (eds), *The Oxford Guide to Film Studies* (Oxford: Oxford University Press, 1998), pp. 114–16.

32 See Robert M. Entman's 'Framing: Toward Clarification of a Fractured Paradigm', *Journal of Communication* 43(4) (1993): 51–8.

33 Jameson, *The Political Unconscious*, op. cit., p. 39.

34 Eagleton, *Criticism and Ideology*, op. cit., p. 89.

35 Pierre Macherey, 'The Text Says What It Does Not Say', in Dennis Walder (ed.), *Literature in the Modern World: Critical Essays and Documents* (Oxford: Oxford University Press, 2004), pp. 252–8.

36 Fredric Jameson, 'The Politics of Utopia', *New Left Review*, 25 (2004): 35.

37 Douglas Kellner, 'Ernst Bloch, Utopia and Ideology Critique', in Jamie Owen and Tom Moylan (eds), *Not Yet: Reconsidering Ernst Bloch* (London: Verso, 1997), p. 81.

38 Peter Wollen, 'Godard and Counter Cinema: *Vent d'Est*', in Bill Nichols (ed.), *Movies and Methods*, vol. 2 (Berkeley, CA: University of California Press, 1985), p. 507.

39 Hans Magnus Enzensberger, 'Constituents of a Theory of the Media', in Reinhold Grimm (ed.), *Critical Essays* (London: Continuum, 1982), p. 60.

40 Ibid., p. 61.

41 Richard Dyer, 'Entertainment and Utopia', in Bill Nichols (ed.), *Movies and Methods*, vol. 2 (Berkeley, CA: University of California Press, 1985), p. 222.

42 Ibid., pp. 226–7.

43 Ibid., p. 228.

44 Fredric Jameson, 'Reification and Mass Culture', in Fredric Jameson, *Signatures of the Visible* (London: Routledge 1992), p. 30.

45 Ibid., pp. 32–3.

46 Alan O'Shea, 'What a Day for a Daydream: Modernity, Cinema and the Popular Imagination in the Late Twentieth Century', in Mica Nava and Alan O'Shea (eds), *Modern Times: Reflections on a Century of English Modernity* (London: Routledge, 1996), p. 240.

47 Ibid., p. 243.

# 7

# REALISM

## 7.1 Philosophy and realism

Marxism, Terry Lovell reminded readers in the early 1980s, is a realist philosophy. At that time, cultural studies and film studies had been increasingly drawn to what she called conventionalist Marxism. This Marxism came out of structuralism and Althusserian thinking and had come very close to accepting the core idealist proposition that language and other systems of representation construct reality entirely on their own terms, according to their own sign systems or conventions. If reality only exists (putty-like) according to the terms of a system of representation or a body of theory or a tradition of thought or representation, then we cannot evaluate those signifying systems by relating them in some way to the world that those systems and representations depict. Although it is very difficult for any practice to commit itself completely to a full-blown relativism and retain credibility, conventionalist assumptions have become deeply sedimented in both academic thinking and broader identity politics. The debates within Marxism around the question of realism remain an absolutely crucial intellectual resource if we are to try and think our way through this most complex and contested field. Without Marxism's philosophical resources and political commitments, we are likely to succumb to one form or another of a flourishing relativism and irrationalism that have saturated contemporary thought.

Any realist philosophy and any strand of Marxism which accords with a realist philosophy must agree, Lovell pointed out, on 'the first principle of realism: that there exists an objective and independent social world, which can be known'.[1] Here 'objective' and 'independent' mean something like a natural and social world that can be used to judge the adequacy, complexity, explanatory power or biases and blind spots of theories or cultural representations, but also social action. At the same time it is *only* through language and representation that we negotiate our understandings and actions in the world – from pragmatic everyday activity up through to the normative claims that politics makes on reality. So there is a dialectic between reality and its representation, each defines the other in a relationship of pressure and tension.

Realist claims of any sort (cinematic, scientific, theoretical or political) may well be (more or less) sufficiently adequate (better than others) to permit a substantial degree of understanding and *rational* action (that is, action that meets an immediate desired end or outcome). In philosophical thought (and capitalist political economy), rational action is typically action that meets an individually desired end. But action that has consequences that rebound negatively on the subject or actions which contradict the well-being of other subjects indicate *social* contradictions and a failure of *reasoned* action. Reasoned action is grounded in the *social* (and not just individual) well-being of all on the basis of needs. But unequal social relations of power can hold negatively consequential actions in place and reproduce them. Rational actions may well show command of the lower-level causal forces that Aristotle famously identified and which are the basis of rational action (meeting an individual desired goal). These lower-level causal forces are: material causalities *within* nature and our immediate cause-and-effect relationships *with* material nature according to our understanding of material nature's own causal forces (including the causal powers of our own bodies and the extensions we give our bodies in the form of tools). These immediate cause-and-effect powers Aristotle called efficient causes because they are designed to meet an immediate goal. Language and action that work with these combined causal forces (nature and our interaction with nature, based on our understanding of it) constitute the minimum basis of any rational action.

To make a house, for example, requires knowledge of the constituent materials the house is made of (material causes) and to interact in a cause-efficient way with them to meet a desired end (e.g. how to produce and then use the material cause of glass to act as windows). But bringing all these material and efficient causes together in a *planned way* to produce the *form* that is a house refers to the formal cause. It is the form that gives the ensemble of lower-level causes their overall shape and function (use-values). And we may broaden the concept of formal cause to include not just the formal shape of the object in the sense of the prototype (what typically constitutes a house) but the planning that gives shape to *housing* as an institution. Then there is what Aristotle called the final cause, which refers to the overall purpose of the formal cause, and here we can broaden our perspective beyond the obvious point that the form that has been made in this instance has the purpose of providing a place for people to live. For we can also think of the final cause in relation to what Marx called the mode of production: is the house primarily there as an exchange-value or as a use-value, for example?

As Habermas has argued, action and communication are integral to one another and none of these forms of rational and reasoned action (and the distinction is very important) are conceivable without language, representation and communication. The referential impulse to communication asks us to think about what the world must be like for this or that utterance or communication to be intelligible to us. Of course, 'what the world must be like' may include questionable assumptions and the internalised effects of power relations, but that is why debate, discussion, the weighing of evidence, the sifting of inconsistencies and other special decoding tools we have developed over time, such as the *symptomatic* readings discussed in the previous chapters, provide ways of *testing* the relationship between representation, language and the real. Realism as a philosophical commitment must mean a continual dialectic of comparisons between reality and its representations. Reasoned action depends on this as does a politics of realist art. Critique of representations (e.g. ideologies) is central to realism.

Film is a mediation of a mediation. That first primary mediation is what Marx called the metabolic production of life. He meant by that the 'appropriation of natural substances to human requirements' via human labour. Metabolic production is 'the necessary condition for effecting exchange of matter between man and Nature'.[2] As a mediation of that mediation, film is at once *only* intelligible by reference to the social production of life and in this sense there is an inextinguishable element of realism in all acts of communication and representation. But at the same time, as a mediation, film draws intelligible reference to the world around it into its *own* peculiar properties and characteristics. The choices and decisions made in relation to these properties and characteristics (the long shot, the edit, narrative structures, etc.) and their relation to social life constitute much of the debate around the degree and complexity of the realism on offer. We can use Aristotle's model of four causes as a way of thinking about film as a causal power and its relationship to causal powers beyond the world of the film. Figure 7.1 illustrates that film has a recording power that gives us access to material causes and efficient causes (e.g. a character opening a door) but that it reconfigures these causes according to its own aesthetic powers, such as camera framing, metaphorical suggestions, narrativisation, and so forth. This is the film's own formal (organising) cause and allows film to produce some kind of analogy with formal causes in social life. The degree of realism by which film can then locate what it depicts within a broader set of social relationships or final causes marks the distinction within Marxist theory between naturalism and realism, as we shall see.

## 7.2 Early Marxist thinking on film realism

Siegfried Kracauer's book, *Theory of Film: The Redemption of Physical Reality* was published in 1960 but his writing on film and photography went back to the 1920s, when his intellectual formation as a leftist intellectual was shaped by the history of the Weimar Republic, German idealism (especially Kant) and Marxism. By the time he produced *Theory of Film*, the radicalism of his Weimar writings was re-worked into a framework more suited to his situation as a German émigré living in America during the Cold War and the McCarthyite witch hunts of 'reds'.[3] Still, we can discern, even in this late work, the outlines of a critical and dialectical mind at work.

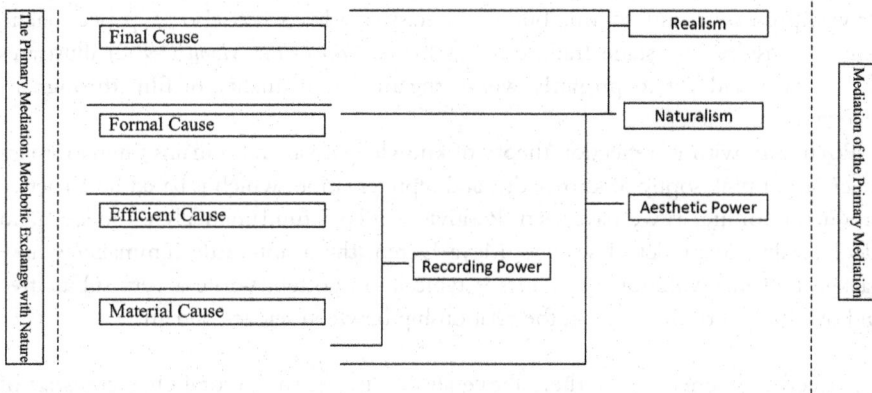

FIGURE 7.1 Aristotle's four causes as a model for aesthetic realism

Kracauer notes that film emerged at the confluence of two preceding technologies: the daguerreotype, which captured the first photographic images onto light-sensitive plates, and the various technologies of spectacle, such as the magic lantern and Phenakistiscope.

Photography was primarily associated with 'the camera's unique ability to record as well as reveal visible, or potentially visible, physical reality'.[4] Established at a time when the culture of empiricism or what Kracauer called positivism (for our purposes, essentially the same philosophical outlook) was becoming dominant, photography 'aspired to a faithful, completely impersonal rendering of reality'.[5] There was a counter-movement, that would become stronger in the twentieth century, which saw photography as an art movement. But Kracauer was critical of this 'formative' tendency because it retarded photographic penetration into extant reality and overlaid it instead with 'painterly styles and preferences' imitating traditional art forms 'not fresh reality'.[6] Kracauer was impatient with those who wanted to aestheticise reality, basically avoiding it through some pictorial or 'poetic' prettification. In the 1930s, Walter Benjamin criticised the German photographic reportage movement called New Objectivity for this aestheticisation. 'It has succeeded in turning abject poverty itself, by handling it in a modish, technically perfect way, into an object of enjoyment,' he complained.[7] 'Realism' filtered through an uncritical middle-class optic is still prone to this danger today.

It would be a mistake to conclude from Kracauer's critique of aestheticisation that he was himself a naïve empiricist/positivist, despite sometimes sounding like one. He understood that the other technological precursors to film (magic lanterns, etc.) were a legitimate and inextricable part of the medium. They tended to be more associated with fantasy, spectacle, reconstructions of scenes from literature, etc. Yet Kracauer advocated a dialectical reconciliation between these two contrasting tendencies embodied in the Lumière brothers (who focused on realist scenarios from everyday life), and Méliès, 'who gave free reign to his artistic imagination'.[8] Méliès innovated many techniques, masks, multiple exposures, superimpositions, and so on, but his fantasy worlds were also 'a paper-mache universe inspired by stage traditions'[9] as his *A Trip to the Moon* (1902) illustrates and as such had yet to properly weave the mediated quality of film through its recording capacity.

Positivism, with its reflection theory of knowledge was and remains utterly foreign to a Marxist philosophy of knowledge and representation, which is based on an active production of life, as we have seen. Positivism offers a fundamentally erroneous (and ideologically so) model of science. Maya Deren, the avant-garde filmmaker whose background in revolutionary politics is typically forgotten, wrote a very substantive and overlooked rumination on the relationship between science and art.

> Even in science – or rather, above all in science, the pivotal characteristics of man's method is a violation of natural integrity. He has dedicated himself to the effort to intervene upon it, to dissemble the ostensibly inviolate whole, to emancipate the element from the context in which it "naturally" occurs, and to manipulate it in the creation of a new contextual whole – a new, original state of matter and reality – which is specifically the product of his intervention.[10]

Deren was critical of the idea that 'realism' meant reducing to zero the role of the filmmaker on the basis that the 'scientific' stance required passive observation. Instead, as she noted, science, as the theoretical discourse of our production of life, involves 'a violation of natural integrity' because that is what social production involves. Similarly, Kracauer argued that 'Actually there is no mirror at all. Photographs do not just copy nature but metamorphose it.'[11] And film, as an extension of photography, metamorphoses reality and our relationship to reality just as our own production of social life does (hence the formulation, film as a mediation of a mediation). In one of the most famous cultural essays of the twentieth century, Walter Benjamin explored how industrial techniques of reproduction changed our relationship to reality. Freud's book *Psychopathology of Everyday Life* had shown how much unconscious meaning was packed into the Freudian slip of the tongue. Film likewise means that behaviour shown in a movie 'can be analysed much more precisely and from more points of view than those presented on paintings or on the stage'.[12] Think of how the camera can capture that look, that tic, that gesture, movement or that relationship to an object which requires decoding. As Béla Balász noted in his celebration of the close- up, a 'good film with its close-ups reveals the most hidden parts in our polyphonous life, and teaches us to see the intricate visual details of life'.[13] Kracauer once again draws the realist conclusion vis-à-vis the array of formal strategies available:

> Provided his choices are governed by his determination to record and reveal nature, he is entirely justified in selecting motif, frame, lens, filter, emulsion and grain according to his sensibilities … For nature is unlikely to give itself up to him if he does not absorb it with all his sense strained and his whole being participating in the process.[14]

As our relationship to physical reality becomes much more plastic and open to mobility in the medium of film, so too does our relationships to the evaluative dimensions inevitably linked to our relationship to the physical reality of material and efficient causes. On 'the ideological plane', says Kracauer, our belief systems are subjected to a new context that may weaken 'their claim to absoluteness' over us.[15] Once again, the critique of ideology and realism are interconnected. This is what Kracauer meant by the 'redemption' of physical reality.

## 7.3 Lumière's gardener

*The Sprinkler Sprinkled* (1895) is often credited as being the first film in the comedy genre.[16] Made by Louis Lumière, it is a one-shot film that features a man watering garden plants using a hose pipe. Along comes a boy who, unbeknown to the sprinkler, steps on the hose pipe, cutting off the flow of water. When the puzzled sprinkler examines the nozzle, the boy takes his foot off the hose and voilà! the sprinkler gets sprinkled. The man then grabs the boy and gives him a bit of a spanking.

This 'film', barely more than a minute long, anticipates a Bazinian appreciation for *mise-en-scène*. While there can be no question of film 'reflecting' reality or 'mirroring' it, for the reasons that we have already adumbrated, we should follow Kracauer's insistence that film has a capacity to be receptive to the signs and meanings woven into our social production of life. Although the recording capacity of the camera is mediated by technology, history, culture and the immediate process of production – that does not mean, as conventionalism would have it, that it is a hermetically sealed sign system uncoupled from material and social reality. We can test this proposition by asking what do we need to know about the world for *The Sprinkler Sprinkled* to be intelligible to us? The newly invented moving image captures not just 'a man' in the abstract but also a man of a certain social type. He is clearly a working man as designated by the sign system that are clothes (in fact, he is Lumière's gardener), a man working therefore on *behalf* of a wealthier man as indicated by the impressive size of the garden which the framing, the wide shot and the lens capacity allow us to see in some depth. The garden is itself a particular kind of quasi aesthetic metabolic exchange with nature, demarcated from agriculture, for example. So this little skit inevitably includes social information or signs which are both empirical (working man, wealthy owner, garden) and latently evaluative (evaluations around the relationships between workers and the wealthy) that would become more insistent in a longer film.

As film became more integrated into the large-scale commodity structures of the film business, this recording capacity of film came to be viewed with a high degree of suspicion by Marxists. Here is Adorno on the matter:

> The photographic process of film, primarily representational, places a higher intrinsic significance on the object ... than aesthetically autonomous techniques; this is the retarding aspect of film in the historical process of art. Even where film dissolves and modifies its objects as much as it can, the

disintegration is never complete. Consequently, it does not permit absolute construction: its elements, however abstract, always retain something representational; they are never purely aesthetic values. Due to this difference, society projects into film quite differently – far more directly on account of the objects – than into advanced painting or literature.[17]

There are a number of motifs here characteristic of an avant-garde suspicion of film's recording capacity: it is antithetical to aesthetic autonomy (see the early film debates, can it be an art?); it restricts construction and ties representation to what it finds in real life (in a positive version of this, as with Kracauer, this *is* its realist capacity); as a result, for Adorno, society 'projects into film' in a way that subordinates it to society's dominant modes of apprehension (film is ideology). This has been a theme of anti-realist criticism for those championing ideological critique, art, the avant-garde or fantasy genres for their apparent licence to dissolve and modify the world as it is given.[18]

A more dialectical early account of cinema was offered by Georg Lukács, the Marxist theorist whose work, primarily in relation to realist literature, will be discussed later in this chapter. In an article written in 1913 – possibly the earliest example of film theory we have – and published in the German daily paper, *Frankfurter Zeitung*, Lukács, writing before his conversion to Marxism following the 1917 Russian Revolution, remarked that film is both intensely naturalistic in its capturing of whatever is put in front of it *and* 'fantastic'. Its naturalistic ability to record what film theorists later came to call the 'pro-filmic event' (whatever is in front of the camera lens) gives film its sociological power, especially when the camera leaves the studio set and penetrates into the extant world. Yet at the same time, unlike theatre, the people and places who appear are actually *absent*, and one of the key consequences of this absence is that it allows film an enormous plasticity and latitude with its subjects and with time and space and scope for trick effects. Causality is 'neither bounded nor hindered by any content. "Everything is possible," that is the philosophy of the "cinema",' argues Lukács.[19] This gives the medium great capacities for *re-ordering* what it finds in front of the camera and, as we shall see, this 'aesthetic effect' is crucial for thinking about the realist potential of the medium. The plasticity and latitude of film mean that '[t]he *child*, which inhabits all of us is released and becomes the master of the audience's psyche'.[20]

This productively disruptive potential of film, its metamorphosing capacity, is thematised in Lumière's film exactly thus. A scenario devised for the camera is embedded into the extant (given) reality of Lumière's garden and gardener. The boy's action is introduced into this extant reality to disrupt it for the sake of dramatic excitement. The action mobilises or depends on two of Aristotle's lower-level causes: the material substance of water and its properties and our knowledge of cause-and-effect relations (the boy's foot impeding the flow of water through the pipe, the release of the blockage causing the flow to unexpectedly resume) which action and continuity editing (although not here) routinely depend on for intelligibility. The action itself (and the anticipation which cause-and-effect actions also stimulate in the audience) and the response of the gardener also mobilise a whole host of higher-level cultural evaluations around narrativisation – a scenario is established (watering), then disrupted (foot on pipe), and then concluded (child spanked), comedy and this generic form's close relationship to the prank, relations between children and worktime, between children and adults, authority, punishment and even the garden itself as an aesthetic version of our metabolic exchange with nature, in which pleasure, relaxation and play (for the wealthy) are to the fore. Even if only latently, we recognise these idea-concepts as meaningful because they refer to or imply the real social world with which they are interwoven, but it is the real social world which film, almost in its founding moment, seeks to disrupt or set in play in some way and which provides an opportunity for the audience to reflect on (the latter also requires developing modes of discussion and criticism that facilitate this). All this is there in a barely minute-long strip of early film which nevertheless represents a unique combination of socially derived signs from different practices. As the medium develops, so the question of its relationship to the real it records, especially in relation to the complexity of social dynamics and evaluations of those dynamics, becomes more pressing and more complicated to address.

## 7.4 Raymond Williams on realism

In his 1976 'Lecture on Realism', Raymond Williams sought to offer an alternative account of realism from the one being developed by *Screen* at this time (although the lecture was to be published by *Screen*). The widespread denunciation of realism at this time hinged on redefining realism as an almost universal and homogeneous classical storytelling form whose most potent ideological effect was to conceal its own storytelling mechanisms and their implications (the signifier disappears into the signified). Warning against 'the abstractions of critical classification',[21] Williams instead tried to offer a historical account of realism. Within this historical account, he insisted that realism is made up of heterogeneous formal methods that have variable effects and meanings, depending on the works as a whole in which they are used and the 'intentions' which those works display. Williams did not define what he meant by 'intentions', however. He certainly meant in part the conscious aims of key participants in the creative process. But we know that outcomes and meanings are the result of many factors, including industrial imperatives and collective cultural dynamics that cannot be reduced to authorial intentions alone, important as those also are. So when we discuss the 'intentions' of a work, we must also be discussing the outcomes which wider industrial, technological, cultural and political formations weave into the work. And, of course, as Williams also indicated in his analysis, a work may have multiple and even conflicting intentions as well as methods.

Williams' thoughts on the variability of methods and intentions were a valuable counter to the tendency, which has been very widespread in discussions of realism, to associate a method with a fixed meaning or effect or intention (we saw this in the polemics around the long shot vs montage). Rather than seeking to slot works into a pre-existing classification, we need to approach works with a more sympathetic and nuanced attention to the detail of their methods and intentions. Some two decades later, also writing in *Screen*, Alexandra Juhasz complained that 'the critique of realism and the endorsement of formalism' had led to a widespread academic indifference to vast swathes of feminist documentary practices which use realist strategies as the most politically efficacious ways of raising issues and speaking to audiences.[22] Echoing Williams, Juhasz, as an academic and filmmaker observed: 'Where many critics have seen "naïve realism", I see and make videos that utilize a variety of "realist" techniques with a variety of effects', only one of which is the dreaded psychoanalytic grip of 'identification'.[23]

Following a brief historical account of the development of realism, Williams' own lecture uses a single case study, Ken Loach's BBC TV drama *The Big Flame* (1969) to try and encourage a more nuanced understanding of formal methods and intentions. Of the latter, he identifies a number of key realist developments. Realism historically saw an *extension* of representation downwards, as it were, to include not just the aristocracy but initially the new emerging bourgeoise class.[24] Like so many realist works of the twentieth century, *The Big Flame* seeks to extend representation further to the working class, and in this particular case the Liverpool dockers undertaking strike action against the threat posed to their jobs by the development of containerisation. This intention of extension is not just to people and actions, but typically across realism, to the lives, hopes, troubles, language, dialect and relationships, that are routinely either ignored or treated stereotypically within the dominant media of the national formation. In terms of methods, this extension was often achieved by using non-professional actors, moving out of the studio to real locations, natural lighting, wide shots, long takes and dialogue that imitates everyday speech patterns (such as its meandering, digressive quality and overlapping dialogue). What we must avoid at all costs is the idea that these methods that shape the texture of the pro filmic event (as well as the audio track), alone or in combination, guarantee realism. It all, as we shall see, depends on larger compositional decisions and intentions at the level of story or narrative.

With social extension, the realist intention manifests a recurrent concern to explore how a process or event works and/or how a life is lived with particular attention to the details of the process, event or life. It might be the details of the process of building a ship, as in Paul Rotha's documentary *Shipyard* (1935); it may be the details of the life of a Bolivian immigrant working illegally in a café in Argentina and experiencing daily racism as in *Bolivia* (2001); it may be the struggle of a depressive to save her job by visiting her co-workers over the weekend to persuade them to reject their annual bonuses so that she can be kept on, as in *Two Days, One Night* (2014). In all cases, an intention manifests as a keen eye for detail (although as we shall see, that is not sufficient for realism) and for exploring the temporal process in which events unfold. In *Reifezeit* (1975), the exiled Iranian filmmaker Sohrab Shaheed Salles, then working in West Germany, begins his film with a prostitute returning home late at night. Her young son is asleep in the small cramped apartment. We watch her as she sits down in front of the mirror removing her beads, her top, her shoes, her earrings, her rings, her bracelets, and then her makeup, her false eyelashes, and so on. The action takes over three-and a half minutes to unfold as she peels off the image-layers of her trade while her son tosses and turns on the bed next to her.

Extension need not always be defined in terms of extending representation to the dominated classes and groups within society – whether in terms of class, gender, race, sexuality or whatever. Where realism extends representation *up* into the dominant classes in order to explore *their* institutions and lives, making visible the damaging consequences of their activities and privilege – then that too is a form of realist extension. This representation upwards diverges from the cele-bratory spectacle of the upper classes, as in the British television series *Downton Abbey* (although one can see how such a series could be open to a feminist reading, given the extensive agency the series gives to female characters).[25] *Downton Abbey* was written by the Conservative peer Julian Alexander Kitchener-Fellowes. But before we make too quick a judgement and read off intentions from authorial ideology alone, we may note that Fellowes also wrote the script for Robert Alt-man's *Gosford Park* (2001). A different medium, different production context, dif-ferent collaborators, different genres, different time, different audiences, etc. and a very different and far more critical and realistic version of the aristocracy at home in their country retreat.

Williams identifies a number of other features of realism, including a tendency to focus on contemporary scenarios and a 'consciously interpretive' political view-point. He notes, however, that historical scenarios are also clearly suitable for realist dramas and that they were preferred by Brecht perhaps in part because the histor-ical distance provided greater scope for the 'intention of *interpreting* an event'.[26] We shall see that this *analytical attitude* may be said to differentiate realism from its apparently close cousin, naturalism. Linked to this consciously interpretive stance is a method which Williams discerns in *The Big Flame*, which he describes as a kind of hypothesis building. The film focuses on a strike that then develops into a working occupation of the dockyards, where the workers take control of the means of production, as it were. Although there had been widespread worker occupations in France during 1968, it was not until after *The Big Flame*, in late 1970, that worker occupations began to spread as a form of resistance in Britain. In this sense, *The Big Flame* was anticipatory (as Bloch would say) and was, on the basis of experiences happening elsewhere, extrapolating from similar class struggles to construct a 'what if...' scenario in which 'a hypothesis ... is played out in rea-listic terms, but within a politically imagined possibility'.[27] Or as *The Big Flame* scriptwriter Jim Allen put it, the film is a 'political fantasy',[28] a more suggestive phrase than Williams' 'hypothesis' and one that refers back to the dialectic between reality and fantasy which Lukács discerned in his 1913 article, as well as such uto-pian categories as energy and community discussed in Section 6.5. The analytical stance and the construction of a scenario that develops latent tendencies within a social situation, bringing them to a revealing and dramatic confrontation, are, as we shall see, key features of realism as Lukács later theorised it in relation to literature.

## 7.5 Falling short: the case of naturalism

Because naturalism and realism often use similar methods in the case of film, it is important to be able to distinguish how their broader philosophical intentions can be discerned at the level of narrative composition. Within the Marxist tradition, naturalism represents an approach to social reality that falls short of realism proper. The most penetrating critique of naturalism in the Marxist tradition was developed by Georg Lukács in relation to literature. He traced the development of realism to the emergence of the historical novel in the early nineteenth century. The specifically historical novel requires the 'derivation of the individuality of characters from the historical peculiarity of their age',[29] which means exploring the relationship between the character and their environment. According to Lukács, the earlier eighteenth-century realistic social novels had not yet developed a sense of historical time and place, which Lukács associates also with an ability to explore or reveal when and how the contemporary world developed as it has. One of the great features of realism is its ability to *show process*, something which the Cuban revolutionary filmmaker, Julio Garcia Espinosa also insisted on: 'We maintain that … cinema must above all show the process which generates the problems,' he wrote.[30] Prior to the historical novel proper, Swift, Voltaire and Diderot set their satirical novels in fantasy or indeterminate places and the penetrating insights they bring are of their own society but which they cannot represent in historical terms. The later development of a historical sense understands 'history as the concrete precondition of the present'.[31]

For Lukács, our ability to see and think historically is itself historically determined.

> It was the French Revolution, the revolutionary wars and the rise and fall of Napoleon, which for the first time made history a *mass experience* and moreover on a European scale. During the decades between 1789 and 1814 each nation of Europe underwent more upheavals than they had previously experienced in centuries.[32]

The simultaneity and rapidity of change across Europe helped develop that sense of history as the product of changing circumstances and collective agency that draws all individuals into its dynamics. War as a mass experience and the mobilisation of masses of people according to secular ideologies of national liberation and identity helped people reflect on their existence as 'historically conditioned'.[33] The national situation becomes one of the great key mediating optics in the development of realism. As the nation-state develops, awareness of one's part in what Gramsci called an 'effective historical drama' or story,[34] enlarges to the national level, well beyond the smaller parochial loyalties to manor and lord in feudal times, or to the larger abstractions of a non-national kind (Christianity). Realism requires 'a real grasp of the essential and most important normative connections of life, in the destiny of individuals and society'.[35] The job of art, for Lukács, is to make those connections visible, palpable and experientially available as a narrative process.

However, after the defeat of the 1848 proletarian revolutions and the consolidation of capitalist rule, 'the mass experience of history itself … an experience shared by the widest circles of bourgeois society'[36] underwent a profound change that affected literary realism. Social and historical development altered 'the entire political and intellectual life of the middle class',[37] to wit, the leading trends are to naturalise and de-historicise bourgeois capitalist society – to regard it, whether for good or ill, as a finished product rather than a process.

Lukács' historicisation of the decline of realism into what he called naturalism can be criticised as an example of what Althusser called an 'expressive causality'.[38] In an 'expressive causality', changes in the economic-class base express themselves in other phenomena in a uniform manner throughout society, in a more materialist version of an older Romantic historiography that would talk of the 'spirit of an age'. In the case of Lukács' argument the triumph of naturalism stretches in an undifferentiated way across time, from 1848 deep into the twentieth century. Despite this problematically over-homogenised and permanent settlement as Lukács conceived it, it is true that the last half of the nineteenth century saw the development of various intellectual currents which can be read as attempts to defend and shore up capitalism, stifle critical thought, and perhaps also literary representation. There was a new type of economic analysis (neo-classical) shorn of the kind of moral-political frameworks and engagement with social and historical reality that characterised the work of Adam Smith and Marx; philosophy saw the rise of Nietzsche, a deeply anti-historical thinker, sociology emerges as the study of society founded on a split from political economy, thus losing Marx's dynamic production-orientated approach; and Darwin's scientific breakthroughs are appropriated by ideological theories championing capitalism as the expression of a timeless law of competition and survival of the fittest (including eugenic theories). Lukács finds in the work of novelists, such as Zola and Flaubert, a corresponding 'realism of minutely observed and exactly described detail',[39] evacuated of any great sense of social and historical dynamics, individuals connected in an intrinsic and necessary way to wider forces in contestation with one another, and individual destinies linked to national stories or what Fredric Jameson called allegories.[40] This literary trend he identifies as naturalism, a sort of truncated and impoverished realism.

In a famous essay, 'Narrate or Describe?', Lukács associated realism with the former and naturalism with the latter choice. According to Lukács, Zola was obsessed with meticulous detail which actually works to swamp social dynamics. There is little sense in Zola's compositional method that there is anything more or less significant about plot events. All are equally described from the perspective of a distanced observer as part of naturalism's refusal to evaluate, to reflect on the material, to make those analytical choices in its compositional structure that are a sign of probing and digging beneath the surface of reified life. This is the antithesis of the Marxist conviction that knowledge and understanding emerge not through neutral contemplation and observation, but by making *choices* and *decisions*.[41] Naturalism's wariness of engagement is reflected in the way events are linked tenuously together rather than emerging from the cumulative development of simmering social tensions and contradictions. 'An arbitrary detail, a chance similarity, a fortuitous attitude, an accidental meeting – all are supposed to provide direct expression of important social relationships.'[42] As a result of the inner social connections of reality drifting apart under a mass of disconnected details and mundane events, even when Zola identifies social problems, they are 'described as social facts, as results, as *caput mortuum* of a social process'.[43] Thus naturalism is an example of reification in the sphere of literary language. Lukács frequently turns to the metaphor of the still camera to contrast realist narration (more of which below) with description. In the case of the latter: 'The so-called action is only a thread on which the still lives are disposed in a superficial, ineffective fortuitous sequence of isolated, static pictures.'[44] Naturalism fetishizes the ordinary, the everyday, the commonplace, the trivial and, as a result, it renounces 'the representation of social contradictions in full evolution and intensification'.[45]

How can we use this distinction in relation to film culture? Naturalism and realism are difficult to distinguish at the level of *methods* because they are often associated with similar approaches, influenced by Italian Neo-Realism which has been influential internationally.[46] Many mainstream critics might write about films as 'realist' (compared to, say, more commercial cinema) when a Marxist critique would want to make sense of them as more naturalist than realist. One would, I think, want to acknowledge that even works that it makes sense to discuss as primarily naturalist can still be valuable and progressive by, for example, innovating new styles and exploring new material and themes or just speaking to realities that have been submerged in the national conversation. A film like *Rosie* (2018), about the housing crisis in Dublin, is an extremely powerful and well-observed look at its impact on one family. That said, the distinction between naturalism and realism inevitably carries with it a critical/negative charge, and demands more from an artistic or cultural milieu than it is actually delivering. In the case of *Rosie*, the film rises to the level of a 'formal cause', looking at what has gone wrong in a particular sector of society, i.e. housing. But as I indicated earlier in my discussion of Aristotle's four causal powers, to explore up to the level of the final cause would situate the question of housing within that wider frame of the mode of production. The question is whether we can develop the theoretical language, the political language and the (film) cultural language that can make intelligible those higher-level causal forces, powers or determinants that cause negative consequences for human need. Against bourgeois criticism that might be too quickly satisfied with the merest whiff of social awareness, the Marxist differentiation between naturalism and realism maintains its urgency, especially in a context in which naturalism is a current that helps differentiate art cinema from genre/commercial cinema while at the same time remaining within a worldview that sees capitalism as finished, inert and unchangeable.

Take, for example, the acclaimed film *The Selfish Giant* (2013) by Cleo Barnard. An example of British 'social realism', it seems to me to demonstrate the continuing validity of a Lukácsian critique of realism's potential collapse into naturalism, although within specific historical and political conditions. Formally, the film uses natural lighting, wide shots, mostly with depth of field, although occasionally using shallow focus, scenes shot with at least two hand-held cameras that facilitate rapid editing at times that still captures character movement fluidly without sacrificing continuity, but maintaining an 'improvisational' rough-and-ready feel. There is no extra-diegetic music to cue our emotional responses and the colour schemes are muted green, grey and black throughout. These stylistic techniques capture an environment of barbed wire, scrap metal, graffiti, rubbish, shuttered shops, desolate-looking homes and anonymous roads. Here we have a definite example of *social extension* to a layer of the working class living by scavenging and thieving. The film quickly establishes a certain mode of life for the two principal characters, a pair of teenage boys, Arbor and Swifty. With their fraught relationships to school and absence of a stable home life, they drift into thieving scrap metal, railway cables and finally electricity cables for a scrap metal yard run by Kitten, a man, who, like all the male figures from their class, is verbally and physically abusive and exploitative. All this miserablism unrelieved by any signs of humour or solidarity, except between the two boys, is counterposed by the relationship which Swifty has with horses. As with *Kes* (1969), this relationship with animals is a metaphor for the kind of honest, caring and reciprocal relationships which are to be found nowhere in the human world.

The problem is that we have no 'history as the concrete precondition of the present' (Lukács). The film begins for no particular reason at a certain moment and never offers any background to any of the characters or to any event or situation. As well as lacking historical background, personal, or any other kind, there is no interaction between this strata of working-class characters and the authorities or institutions (the council, politicians, the police, despite a brief incidental appearance, the school in any substantive way, etc.). There is no trace of the kind of consciously political analysis that Williams finds in *The Big Flame*. There is no sense of discovering the 'process that generates the problems' (Espinosa). Much of the action consists of the iteration of scenes of scavenging for scrap metal, driving a horse and cart around town, taking scraps back to the merchants and shouting at various people. This is the classic 'slice-of-life' approach that Lukács slammed. 'The more true to life the "slice of life", the more fortuitous, barren, static and single-minded compared to reality will this "reality" be.'[47] The film moves towards its climax where Swifty is unlucky enough to be electrocuted trying to scavenge live cables. But what this reveals is nothing more than the immediate causal responsibilities of Arbor and, more pertinently, Kitten. Perhaps also it reveals the respective individual traits of the characters (Arbor is the leader, Swifty, sensitive, a bit 'soft', the follower, more likely to be the victim of an accident at least in the world of cultural tropes anyway). Any broader contextualisation is missing. Although naturalism, like realism, is interested in how environment shapes lives, if environment is conceived in ways that are a-historical, de-politicised, lacking in social context and a sense of social dynamics, then we end up with Lukács' *caput mortuum* of a social process'. This seems to be a tale of 'chaotic' families and the 'excluded', two prominent motifs from the discourse of the New Labour governments between 1997–2010, which mount no serious analysis of what has gone wrong but which provides the context in which to understand the contemporary failings of British social realism, as Clive Nwonka has argued.[48]

## 7.6 Lukács against Modernism

We tend to think that naturalism and Modernism are at opposite ends of the representational spectrum, one apparently dedicated to depicting reality in a stylistically low-key manner, the other dedicated to problematising our apprehension of reality through representation. Yet in Lukács' reading, there is a brilliant series of connections posited between naturalism and Modernism. Even if we do not necessarily agree with Lukács' sweeping dismissal of Modernism (particularly problematic given the fertile interaction between Modernism and Marxism – see Section 2.3, Section 5.1 and Section 5.2), we can appreciate his tracing out of the inner relationships between naturalism and Modernism. The naturalist attention to detail, which separates characters from significant action and subsumes them within a welter of mundane details and episodes, already signals a certain faltering of the ability of narrative to orchestrate its material into cumulatively revealing dramatic situations. Modernism would intensify this loosening of narrative coherence with its emphasis on the *fragment*. Lukács generally saw this in negative terms. For him, reality was only 'fragmented' on the surface of life under capitalism, and it was the job of realist art to penetrate such surfaces and draw the significant causal forces together into a coherent story form. Hence, Lukács was critical of his fellow-Marxist Ernst Bloch for his defence of Expressionism.[49] But Lukács undoubtedly in turn underestimated the possibilities which weakening narrative drive and coherence open up for escaping the unity of time and place, for editorialising commentary, for self-reflexive commentary on the terms of our contract with cinematic language and for de-centring individual character-driven drama.

For Benjamin, Brecht's Epic Theatre is a theatre of 'interruptions' designed to frustrate uncritical cathartic investments in characters and to develop a more critical enquiring attitude towards both what is represented and how it is represented.[50] Benjamin describes Brecht's method as a drama of 'quotable gestures', an ensemble of fragments offered up to inspection. In the same way Buñuel's *The Discreet Charm of the Bourgeoisie* (1972) inspects the various social 'gestures' of the bourgeoisie (dinner parties, fornicating, socialising) as they (and the narrative) are perpetually interrupted. The episodic quality of the narrative allows for a harsh editorialising commentary on its subject (the bourgeoisie are stupid, snobbish, selfish, their lives are empty, etc.) using a mix of styles (comedy of manners, satire, farce, illogical dream scenarios, etc.). Similarly, Godard's films have an editorialising commentary or consciously interpretive stance that is 'external' to the material precisely because the story where that critique could be developed in a more classical narrative, is being broken down. In *Pierrot le Fou* (1965), at a party of the bourgeoisie, Godard puts a red filter over the scene and has the characters speak non-naturalistically in a series of disconnected statements about various commodities in the language and speech patterns of advertising, indicating the corruption of subjectivity by commercial values. Rather than character development, we have editorialising 'construction' of character by discourse and language, which is as much a legitimate subject matter as the more traditional focus of realism (e.g. the material, social environment).

Another feature of naturalism that was radically developed under Modernism is that of 'de-personalisation' and Lukács was one of the first to discern this. 'Description,' cries Lukács, 'debases characters to the level of inanimate objects.'[51] But Lukács, it seems, was unable to appreciate the ways that Modernism often developed this aspect of naturalism in ways that were either searchingly *critical* of de-personalisation as the outcome of capitalism, or it was deployed in ways that allowed stories to escape the dominance of individual agency and explore more collective, shared experiences or social structures and forces at work in the modern world. Montage, for example, a method which tends to 'de-personalise' by expanding our sense of broad connections beyond the unity of time and space, is dismissed by Lukács as a 'one-dimensional technique'.[52] The constructivist principles of montage techniques meant for Lukács an inappropriate relationship to the cultural heritage of the past. They treat it as if it were 'a heap of lifeless objects in which one can rummage around at will, picking out whatever one happens to need at the moment',[53] which was precisely what Walter Benjamin was interested in doing. Lukács was underestimating the extent to which new technologies of production and reception and new historical experiences were producing a much less settled sense of the relationship between past and present, reality and representation, than he seemed to want to hold onto, and that this was not necessarily a uniformly negative development. As we have already seen in Chapter 5, montage is necessary to rework the domination of meanings, public debate, knowledge and perceptions which the mass media have shaped, something which Lukács seems to have had no appreciation of.

In his contribution to the compilation film *11/09/01*, Ken Loach explores the relationship between the terrorist attacks on America on that date and on exactly the same day in 1973, the CIA-backed coup in Chile against the democratically elected Marxist President Salvador Allende. The films cuts from George W. Bush announcing: 'On September 11th, enemies of freedom committed an act of war against our country...' to footage of Chilean fighter jets bombing the Presidential palace of Allende in 1973. *In one cut and two shots* a vast empire of propaganda is dismantled. This is what Benjamin called an illumination, a sudden revelation courtesy of an 'interruption' (Bush's ideological speech is literally interrupted by the cut), a flash of lightning in which the hidden contours of a whole system of violence and oppression are suddenly revealed (the dialectics of history at a standstill, i.e. made visible and open to inspection).[54] But, for Lukacs' classical aesthetic preferences, montage makes connections that are too immediate and which allow 'no rise and fall, no growth from within to emerge from the true nature of the subject-matter'.[55] That clause, 'growth from within' speaks volumes of Lukacs' organicist aesthetic preferences as opposed to the more constructivist and editorialising philosophical inclinations of a Benjamin or Brecht.

Responding to Lukács' aesthetic strictures for artists, Brecht remarked: 'Literature cannot be forbidden to employ skills newly acquired by contemporary man, such as the capacity for simultaneous registration, bold abstraction, or swift combination.'[56] It is an arbitrary prioritisation of *methods*, in other words, to insist that aesthetic cognition only counts if it has evolved slowly as part of character development and action. Brecht famously argued that although Lukács accused those of experimenting with Modernism of 'formalism', it was in fact Lukács who was the formalist by insisting that the principles of realism, which he found in the early nineteenth-century realist novel, were still applicable in very changed circumstances one hundred years later, with its new social conditions, new relationships, new capacities and dangers. In many ways Brecht's riposte is in fact *almost* unanswerable.

Nevertheless, we can, I think, answer it and rescue Lukács from his own weaknesses. The answer recalls the Bolshevik defence of the classical bourgeois heritage which I discussed in Section 5.1. Life is still very multi-levelled, full of different 'temporalities' and although there are many areas of our social experiences that more Modernist or postmodernist methods may be particularly receptive to as part of an overall realist set of *intentions*, some of the formal strategies and their attendant realities that Lukács championed are still very much part of our lives, even in the twenty-first century. For example, people still grow up in families, people still have experiences of 'community' (people they know and are familiar with and have a history with, rather than just transient and impersonal relationships); people still live lives at a tempo that allows classical narrative to explore the slow germination of existing contradictions; people still have long-term relationships with people and memories, certain attachments to specific places within which significant parts of the narrative can be set, people can still differentiate between media representations or subjective traumas and the reality of everyday experiences, and so forth. For these reasons, Lukács, despite his undialectical dismissal of Modernism and his one-sided championing of certain realist strategies over others, remains relevant to our time because there are cultural and social continuities with the past.

## 7.7 Lukács, realism and film

For Lukács, realism in art overcomes the splitting between society, conceived as fixed, given and unchangeable, and individuals, conceived as isolated from each other and society, locked into their own subjectivity or individual problems, as is very often found in art cinema, or over-inflated into individualistic heroes as in commercial dominant cinema. Realism involves socialising the individual character and uncongealing environment, recovering that sense of it as made up of dynamic social forces which characters struggle to shape. So, for Lukács, realism requires *typicality* of characters and situations and *individualisation*. Typicality does *not* mean for Lukács the ordinary, the everyday, the average, the commonplace – all of which is the terrain of naturalism. 'In day-by-day existence, major contradictions are obscured in a whir of petty, disparate accidental events; they are exposed only when purified and intensified to such an extreme that their potential consequences are exposed and are readily perceived.'[57]

The typical then is not the everyday, but the key social forces, movements, trends, powers, etc., that shape existence. Typicality in characters usually means that the socio-economic class dimension of a character becomes a salient feature of their activity, their position, their relationships with others. One reason why Cleo Barnard's third feature, *Dark River* (2017) is a superior film to the more critically hailed *The Selfish Giant*, is that this socio-economic dimension to the lives of the characters is a significant feature of the story. Alice begins the story as a wage-labourer on a farm and we later learn that she has worked all over the world as a hand for hire. When she returns to her dead father's Yorkshire farm, she attempts to claim the tenancy of the farm. Her brother Joe, who has neglected the farm and works as a truck delivery driver, however, contests her right to return after fifteen years and lay claim to it. The landowner meanwhile visits and makes it clear that the farm is more profitable to him if he can sell it off to a property developer. To do that he needs a tenant willing to sell up and promises Joe a cash lump sum to do so. Joe agrees and is subsequently awarded the tenancy even though it is clear that it is Alice who would look after the land, were she to be awarded the tenancy. That, however, is irrelevant since for the landowner what matters is extracting as much value from the land as possible and that means selling to a developer rather than keeping it as a working farm. Already this brief description lays bare the key socio-economic lines of power at work within this story world. Perhaps this is why the *Financial Times* so disliked the film?[58]

Lukács also requires that this socio-economic class dimension is coupled with indivi-dualisation of characters in relation to their social dimensions and through their interac-tions with each other. Types on their own produce mouthpieces for socio-economic relations. The sort of realist literary and cinematic culture that Lukács is theorising explores the *differential* responses of individual characters to their socio-economic situa-tions, in line with the humanist tradition which celebrates the range and richness of our capacities. In *Dark River*, the characters respond differently to the trauma of the sexual abuse which Alice was subjected to by her father. Gradually and painfully, now that he is dead, she wants to reconquer and overcome that past and trauma by taking over the farm, although she must begin by living in the outhouse as the main house has too many emotional triggers for her (cue Sean Bean as her dad looming menacingly). Joe, though, who has, it seems, guiltily suppressed his knowledge of what happened, has effectively abandoned the farm and wants nature to take its course as a kind of rejection of what once happened there. However, this guilt mixes with anger at Alice's abandonment of him and this allows the landowner to drive a wedge between them. So the personal and the social are intricately woven together, contemporary economic pressures that have identified sources and agents provide the structure within which personal stories and lives are played out. The key situation at the heart of the film, the transition of the tenancy to either Alice or Joe, is definitely not an everyday, mundane event that hap-pens routinely. Rather, it is the point at which the existing social and personal conflicts converge; it is where the significant history of this family comes to a decisive turn, a decisive rupture. The situation, like the characters, is *typical* in the Lukácsian sense.

Another key concept for Lukács was *totality*, which, we have seen, is an important philosophical concept for Marxism. How might it be relevant in the context of realism? The closest approximation which this concept has to something more familiar would be that realist art creates a microcosm of the external world by compressing its key dynamics into a circumscribed fictional world. An intensive totality is 'the circumscribed and self-contained ordering of those factors which objectively are of decisive significance for the portion of life depicted'.[59] In realist films of the type we are discussing, this often manifests itself around a specific geographical location within which the typical characters live, work and converge. In *Le Crime de Monsieur Lange* (1936), the courtyard and buildings around it are where Lange lives and works as a clerk for the charming swindler, publisher and boss, Batala. It is also the location of the laundry run by Valentine. Here sex and class relations converge as the typical class relations of the boss and his financiers, the male and female working class and the 'dreamer' and creative writer Lange come together. To rub the typical characters up against each other to produce decisive typical situations, in which seeded or dormant tensions or contradictions become active in the consciousness of the protagonists, often requires an intense geographically *de-limited* location within which the characters interact, as they do in *Bolivia*, where petit-bourgeois characters bring their grievances and tensions into the café, finally boiling over into anti-immigrant racism.

The Danish film *Festen* (1999) illustrates this de-limited 'intensive' totality very well. Here the location is the country family home of Helge, a successful businessman, who has gathered family and friends to celebrate his sixtieth birthday. This example of social extension 'up' into the lives of the bourgeoisie, also includes the workers in the basement producing the food for this extravaganza and the black boyfriend of Helge's daughter, Helene, which affords an opportunity to show the deep racism of the bourgeois middle class. Once again, the situation is one in which simmering tensions and problems that have a long history within the family will come to the boil. As with *Dark River*, the theme is sexual abuse of the children by the father. The recent suicide of one of the sisters (Linda) provides the trigger for her brother Christian to revolt against Helge, the patriarch, with some help from the workers down below. All the action happens not only in one place but in a highly compressed 24 hours. Once again, there is significant individualisation as all of Helge's children respond differently to the same dilemma. The celebration, which is supposed to be an affirmation of Helge's class power and prestige, ends up exposing and destroying him publicly. *Festen*'s affinity with a Lukácsian realism is what gives the film its power, rather more than its identity as a film belonging to the rules of the Dogma manifesto drawn up by Lars von Trier and Thomas Vinterberg. However, the Dogma style did graft something new onto the country house genre which *Festen* can be located in. Using hand-held cameras (and cheap domestic camcorders at that) as stipulated by the Dogma rules, the film's form gives a nervy and neurotic undercurrent to the proceedings, while also at times looking like a grotesque family video, one that has unexpectedly shocking revelations. Had the film adopted the more conservative film language usually associated with this genre (wide shots and tripod mounted camera work to show off the stately interiors and exteriors), it would have lost much of its power. Yet the film's realist credentials rest fundamentally on its typicality of character and situation and the crisis-inducing intensive totality it constructs in time and space where a 'parallelogram of forces' converge.[60] Extrapolated from a realist narrative composition, the Dogma methods would most likely end up producing a new version of naturalism.

We have seen that Lukács contrasted naturalistic description with realist narration. We need to explore this concept of narration a little more. To understand its significance we must recall that, for Lukács, the goal of realist art is 'to penetrate the laws governing objective reality and to uncover the deeper, hidden, mediated, not immediately perceptible network of relationships that go to make up society'.[61] The work of art performs a complex artistic labour on reality in order to reconfigure it so that its 'deeper, hidden, mediated' relationships can be made visible. Lukács linked his philosophy of artistic realism to the tradition of epic poetry in which stories are told of past events that are extraordinary, filled with heroic deeds by characters who shaped the moral universe down the generations. 'The art of the epic poet,' writes Lukács, 'consists in a proper distribution of emphasis and in a just accentuation of what is essential.'[62] One way in which emphasis and accentuation can be achieved is through the temporal organisation of the storytelling. Lukács identified the fruitfulness of the *past tense* to narration as opposed to the present tense, 'slice of life' of naturalism. The past-tense mode alerts the reader/viewer to the notion that this is a story told with a purpose (to learn and understand) and it requires judicious selection of the important aspects of a life. 'Description contemporizes everything,' Lukács notes, but '[n]arration recounts the past.'[63] Given the importance of historical processes and historical understanding in Marxism, this distinction is bound to be significant.

Recounting the past can be done in many different ways. In *Festen*, it is vocalised when Christian stands up and delivers his alternative dinner party speech, where he reveals the sexual abuse his father put him through, the past, once suppressed, now returns to the awkward silence of the assembled bourgeois guests. *Dark River* uses flashbacks to explore the relationship between present and past. The final image of the film shows Alice and Joe exiting the barn they have been playing in as youngsters, going out into the farm, the landscape spread before them, as their whole lives are ahead of them, and yet this poignant image is in horrible juxtaposition to the social and personal story we have just seen which crushes their hopes and dreams.

The past tense may combine vocalisation with extended visual flashback. *Le Crime de Monsieur Lange* starts in the present. Lange and Valentine are trying to flee France. The police want Lange for the murder of Batala. Lange and Valentine stop at an inn at the border of France and Belgium, planning to cross into Belgium the next day. But Lange is recognised by the inn-keeper's son who wants to phone the police and Valentine must tell the story of what happened to the proletarian drinkers who will determine whether he should be handed in or not. The story will show that Lange kills Batala for political reasons, to protect the workers co-opera-tive which forms when Batala flees the publishing company because of his debts. When Batala returns (dressed as a priest) to re-claim his property, Lange kills him to protect the experiment in socialism. In this, the film, like *The Big Flame,* is a political fantasy. Valentine's audience are also the 'jury', who decide this is a case of proletarian justice and let Lange and her flee to Belgium. The power of the story stems from the past-tense mode of storytelling where we are constantly evaluating Lange, Batala and others as we watch. We know what has happened but not why or whether to judge it from within the existing dominant morality that is shaped by capitalist legal institutions or by another that might require that we 'uncover the deeper, hidden, mediated, not immediately perceptible network of relationships that go to make up society' (that is, the injustices of capitalist class society). Critique of the ideology of private property is central to the film's realism.

John Hess wrote very perceptively about the way *The Godfather II* (1974) and *Blood of the Condor* (1969) 'used disjunctions in time as a distancing device to help them analyse rather than simply create the filmic fantasy into which an audience is drawn unthinkingly'.[64] This idea of encouraging a critical spectatorship resistant to 'the filmic fantasy' sounds like the reference point for Hess is Brecht. But actually, the narrative composition he discusses, fits the schema for Lukácsian realism as well. It is Lukács who discusses how the past tense introduces a 'necessary distance in narration' which allows not only judicious selection of the essential but also the gradual exposition of the significance of events in the past and the present by the establishment of this mixing of tenses. It is Lukács who praises Tolstoy's epic composition in *Anna Karenina* where the author narrates the pivotal moment of the horse race twice, first, from Vronsky's perspective and then from Anna's, even playing with time, by returning to an earlier point in the narrative and exploring the growing tensions between Anna and her husband that finally reach a climax when the narrative catches up with itself, and at the race Anna's feelings for Vronsky become undeniable. Viewed as an example of a proto-modernist play with time and perspectives, we can see in Tolstoy's late nineteenth-century classical work the continuities of culture that Alexandr Voronsky warned us to be sensitive to (see Section 5.1). Similarly we can see continuities between that arch-modernist Brecht, with his Epic Theatre and the classicist Lukács who likewise links realism to epic composition. For both Brecht and Lukács, epic literature is about perspective and drawing certain moral (political) conclusions about reality which artistic com-position (and a past-tense presentation of events) have made palpable.

John Hess shows how in *The Godfather II* the past/present structure explores the way capitalism or 'business', destroys the very ideals of security, family, inheritance, comradeship and community, which it is supposed to sustain. In the present tense we see Michael Corleone's increasingly isolated trajectory, in which all his rela-tionships are hollowed out by the pursuit of the family 'business'. In the past tense, we see his father Vito, struggle to establish the Corleone family as a successful family enterprise in America and reach back home to Sicily to settle scores there as well. Yet Vito's upward trajectory already sows the seeds of violence and mistrust which will be further entrenched by the more corporate era Michael moves into after the Second World War. Hess argues that the historical perspective and the comparison and contrasts which the narrative structure facilitates destroy 'conventional linearity' and allowed Coppola 'to approach closer to a Marxist analysis of our society than any other Hollywood film I know of'.[65]

In his discussion of the Italian Neo-Realist film, *Bicycle Thieves* (1948) and the later Bolivian film *Blood of the Condor* (1969), John Hess shows how the more naturalistic linear and present-time tense of the former film gives it a more restricted critical attitude compared to the temporal composition of *Blood of the Condor*. Hess, however, acknowledges the continuities as well as the ruptures between Italian Neo-Realism and the New Latin American cinema of the 1960s. Many Latin American filmmakers studied at Rome's Centro Sperimentale film school in the 1950s and were influenced by significant aspects of Italian Neo-Realism, such as its artisanal mode of production, location shooting and working with non-professional actors. At the same time, the revolutionary conditions of Latin America in the 1960s and early 1970s were such that the influence of Italian Neo-Realism had to be transformed, it could not be uncritically accepted by the Latin Americans. This critical transformation can be discerned in the films themselves. Although Latin American films of this period may often use a Neo-Realist photographic style, their narrative structure is far more complex:

> The vast majority of Latin American films I have seen are about history or memory or both, using flashbacks, multiple time layers, historical reconstruction, historical documentary inserts and many other devices to historicize the narrative. Italian neo-realism contains none of this: its films have no memory, no history.[66]

In general terms, *Blood of the Condor* is about the racism of the white elite oligarchy, who have historically dominated Bolivia, towards the indigenous Quechua people who continue to be the victims of colonial history and contemporary imperialism. The Bolivian oligarchy were structurally interlocked with the strategic imperatives of Washington foreign policy objectives. *Blood of the Condor* had been made a year after Che Guevara was caught by the Bolivian army with CIA assistance and executed. More specifically, at the heart of the story is the proposition that the US 'aid' programme, delivered by the Peace Corps, were running maternity clinics that were sterilizing indigenous women. This was certainly a rumour that was circulating at the time. In the wider context of decades of debates about the merits of shrinking the indigenous population who were widely seen by white elites as a blight on the country's modernisation prospects, this was a reasonable fear. Equally reasonable was suspicion of North America's decades-long interventions in Latin America on the side of US business interests. While there is in fact no evidence of the Peace Corp in Bolivia practising sterilization, they did practise mass IUD-insertion projects in the indigenous communities and it is doubtful if this was done on the basis of informed consent (hence, in part, the rumours of sterilization).[67] *Blood of the Condor*, directed by Jorge Sanjinés working within the Ukamau film collective, had a significant impact in Bolivia, and as part of a growing anti-imperialist mood, the Peace Corps was expelled from the country in 1971.[68]

The realism of the film lies less in the empirical fidelity or otherwise of the Progress Corps (in the film) to the real-life action of the Peace Corps, than in the exploration of the most salient relations of power in Bolivian society. In the context of under-development that is the outcome of a long history of imperialist subordination to western capitalism, the typical characters and situations are different from a western context. Here the typical characters are the indigenous community, the US state agents inside Bolivia, the local oppressive state apparatus that assists them and the medical establishment in the city (in other words, the situation of the urban working class and capitalist class confronting each other is absent). There is less individuation, in part because within the indigenous community, this is less valued and in part one suspects because of the very low budget nature of the film. The Argentinean filmmaker Fernando Birri identified the key intentions of a realist cinema in the context of Latin America in the 1960s. What was needed he argued, was a cinema:

> which awakens consciousness; which clarifies matters: which strengthens the revolutionary consciousness of those among them who already possess this; which fires them; which disturbs, worries, shocks and weakens those who have a "bad conscience", a reactionary consciousness; which defines profiles of national, Latin American identity; which is authentic; which is anti-oligarchic and anti-bourgeois at the national level, and anti-colonial and anti-imperialist at the international level; which is pro-people and anti-anti people; which helps the passage from under-development to development, from sub-stomach to stomach, from sub-culture to culture, from sub-happiness to happiness, from sub-life to life.[69]

Note that in this call for a realist cinema, realism is intrinsically understood as a critical cinema that must actively intervene and be part of the political culture for social change. This requires an active aesthetic reconstruction that can historicise narrative, as Hess argues, rather than simply record reality as it presents itself to the camera.

*Blood of the Condor* achieves a Lukácsian-style historical narrative due to its temporal construction that is similar to *The Godfather II*. The film begins with an indigenous leader, Ignacio, in an impoverished rural community, arrested by the police along with some comrades. The police shoot the Indians en route to the station, killing all but Ignacio who is mortally wounded. Ignacio's wife Paulino takes her husband to the city to seek help from his brother Sixto, who has attempted to assimilate himself into modern Bolivian capitalism. Sixto and Paulino take Ignacio to the hospital but the doctors cannot operate without blood, which Sixto must get but which he cannot afford. Asking Paulino why Ignacio was shot, Paulino begins narrating the backstory to the events leading up to Ignacio's arrest and shooting. At this point, the narrative splits into two temporal structures. In one temporal strand, we go back in time to Ignacio becoming the community leader and then hearing more from other villages that women, like his wife Paulino, can no longer become pregnant. In the other strand we go forward with Sixto in his quest for blood that might save the wounded Ignacio. What Ignacio discovers in the first plot strand is that the local maternity centre, run by the American Progress Corps, are sterilizing the women. We have already seen in some nice touches how their conceptions of what 'modernity' looks like are completely incompatible with the Quechua people. For example, the Americans try to buy an entire basket of eggs from Paulino for their own use, but she will only give them three, despite their assurance that they will give her a 'good price' for the exchange. Paulino explains, to their incomprehension, that she cannot sell all the eggs to them because she has to take them to market where others (the Indian community) need them.

Sixto's fruitless search meanwhile in the present tense plot line culminates in him trying to get entry into a meeting where a doctor who might have the needed blood, is giving a lunch speech to an assembled body of elites, including US doctors, on the need for Bolivia to embrace western modern conceptions of progress (that is, western capitalism). The doctor's indifference to Sixto underscores what we have learned in the other timeline, that the discourses and practices of modernisation conceal and advance the interests of a capitalist and middle-class elite, both in the West and in Bolivia. In Ignacio's storyline, the Indians attack the sterilization centre and, it is implied, either kill or mutilate the three Americans. In Sixto's storyline, he returns to the hospital without the blood and discovers his brother is dead. In the final two shots of the film, Paulino and Sixto (who is now dressed in traditional Indian clothes once more rather than urban city garb) return to the community, rejecting his earlier attempts at assimilation into the dominant power bloc. The film then cuts to arms holding aloft rifles in what looks like a call to armed struggle. The power of the film lies in the way the temporal structure reveals that the impoverished rural communities cannot be helped by advancing the modernisation project of the city/the West (a form of commodity fetishism) because that only advances the racism and inequality of the city/capitalism into the 'backward' areas. The comparison and contrasts between the two narrative strands are designed to cultivate a critique of the social processes that cause the problems, rather than treat reality as a unfortunate series of events. The overt ordering of the artistic totality (what Lukács called an 'intensive totality') functions as a critique of the ordering of objective social reality (the extensive totality beyond the film) but that in turn can only happen through a critique of the ideologies of 'modernisation' which rationalise it. Yet it is worth noting that Sanjines argued that while *Blood of the Condor* successfully spoke to urban city dwellers influenced by western culture, 'It did not work – at the level of language and cultural structures – for the majority of our population who are imbued in an Andean indigenous culture: Quechua Aymara.'[70] This raises very profound questions about how film, with its deep cultural roots in urban modernity can be rethought to work for specific audiences, in this case, audiences whose cultural reference points remain largely outside the urban modern experience.

In Chapter 6, we saw that genre and popular film can certainly have contradictory relations to ideologies, and critical perspectives on the way things are can be accommodated. There can even be, metaphorically, considerable hostility towards dominant institutions within popular and genre cinema. Subterranean connections between genre cinema and realism, at both the level of styles and/or cognitive reach into social reality, often account for what is interesting in genre cinema. The social realism I have been exploring here, at its best, develops these sentiments and feelings and strategies more coherently, under less pressure to make compromises through generic expectations, narrative conventions, or the generally larger budgets we associate with dominant commercial cinema. It is the *lucid* cinema that the Cuban filmmaker Julio Garcia Espinosa called for.[71] This social realism links the concerns popular culture deals with to explicitly real-world concerns and live political issues, instead of working through the more disguised registers of, say, a comedy, a western or a horror film. Realism may be characterised by the degree of ideology critique which it performs on those worldviews which justify inequality and reinforce ignorance of what it is the powerful do and to whom. This critique includes the wider cultural frames with which we are encouraged to see the world. It may also include, self-reflexively, the cultural frames of film itself, but that, I think, is or should be a decision depending on circumstances and intentions and priorities and not an absolute universal goal in itself as neo-formalism demanded. As we have seen, to achieve cognitive reach into a reified opaque world whose realities do not yield themselves up spontaneously to the eye, realism requires aesthetic re-ordering (metamorphosing) the world that film is uniquely receptive to capturing. Although Lukács' own sporadic comments on film later in his life tend to show that he was far more comfortable with literature than the moving image medium,[72] his theory of realism is not medium-specific (or Eurocentric). It can significantly enhance our understanding of what constitutes realism in film as part of a broader Marxist humanist culture of storytelling.

## Notes

1  Terry Lovell, *Pictures of Reality: Aesthetics, Politics and Pleasure* (London: BFI, 1983), p. 23.
2  Karl Marx, *Capital*, vol. I (London: Lawrence and Wishart, 1983), p. 179.
3  See my own essay on the continuities and differences between the Weimar and American Kracauer in Mike Wayne, 'Transcoding Kant: Kracauer's Weimar Marxism and After', *Historical Materialism* 21(3) (2013): 57–85.
4  Siegfried Kracauer, *Film Theory: The Redemption of Physical Reality* (Oxford: Oxford University Press, 1997), p. 4.
5  Ibid., p. 5.
6  Ibid., p. 6.
7  Walter Benjamin, 'The Author as Producer', in *Understanding Brecht* (London: Verso, 1998), p. 95.
8  Kracauer, *Film Theory*, op. cit., p. 30.
9  Ibid., p. 33.
10  Maya Deren, *An Anagram of Ideas on Art, Form and Film* (New York: Alicat Bookshop Press, 1946) p. 12.
11  Kracauer, *Film Theory*, op. cit., p. 15.

12 Walter Benjamin, 'The Work of Art in the Age of Mechanical Reproduction', in Walter Benjamin, *Illuminations* (London: Pimlico Press, 1999), p. 229.
13 Béla Balász, 'The Close-Up', in Leo Braudy and Marshall Cohen (eds), *Film Theory and Criticism* (Oxford: Oxford University Press, 2004), p. 315.
14 Kracauer, *Film Theory*, op. cit., pp. 15–16.
15 Ibid., p. 9.
16 Ibid., p. 30.
17 Theodor Adorno, 'Transparencies on Film', *New German Critique* 24/25 (Autumn 1981–Winter 1982): 202.
18 There has been a lively debate within the Marxist literature on such modes as science fiction and fantasy and the capacity to break with what we may call empirically minded realism. The model of realism I am developing here would be compatible with such generic registers but I do not have the space to explore these debates. The emphasis here is that the social realism that I am exploring does require an aesthetic reconstruction of the world that it explores.
19 Georg Lukács, 'Thoughts on an Aesthetic for the Cinema', *Framework*, Spring (1981): 3.
20 Ibid., pp. 3–4.
21 Raymond Williams, 'A Lecture on Realism', *Screen*, 18(1) (1977), 74.
22 Alexandra Juhasz, '"They Said We Were Trying to Show Reality – All I Want to Show Is My Video": The Politics of the Realist Feminist Documentary', *Screen*, 35(2) (1994): 173.
23 Ibid., p. 174. Identification was seen as problematic because it was associated with promoting unified ego-ideals and centred subjects.
24 Williams, 'A Lecture on Realism', op. cit., p. 67.
25 See Claire Monk's qualified defence of British heritage cinema in *Heritage Film Audiences: Period Films and Contemporary Audiences in the UK* (Edinburgh: Edinburgh University Press, 2011).
26 Williams, 'A Lecture on Realism', op. cit., p. 68.
27 Ibid., p. 69.
28 John Hill, *Ken Loach: The Politics of Film and Television* (London: BFI/Palgrave, 2011), p. 87. Hill gives a fuller account of *The Big Flame* and the difficulties it had in getting broadcast approval from BBC bosses, see ibid., pp. 87–96.
29 Georg Lukács, *The Historical Novel* (London: Merlin Press, 1989), p. 19.
30 Julio Garcia Espinosa, 'For an Imperfect Cinema', in Michael T. Martin (ed.), *New Latin American Cinema: Theory, Practices and Transcontinental Articulations* (Detroit: Wayne State University Press, 1997), p. 81.
31 Lukács, *The Historical Novel*, op. cit., p. 21.
32 Ibid., p. 23.
33 Ibid., p. 24.
34 Antonio Gramsci, *Selections from the Prison Notebooks* (London: Lawrence and Wishart, 2003), p. 130.
35 Lukács, *The Historical Novel*, op. cit., p. 92.
36 Ibid., p. 172.
37 Ibid., p. 173.
38 Louis Althusser, *For Marx* (London: Verso, 1979), pp. 200–4.
39 Lukács, *The Historical Novel*, op. cit., p. 186.
40 Fredric Jameson, 'Third World Literature in the Era of Multinational Capitalism', *Social Text*, 15 (Autumn 1986): 65–88.
41 Georg Lukács, 'Narrate or Describe?', in Georg Lukács, *Writer and Critic* (London: Merlin Press, 1978), p. 131.
42 Ibid., p. 115.
43 Ibid., pp. 113–14,
44 Ibid., p. 144.
45 Georg Lukács, 'The Intellectual Physiognomy of Characterization', in Georg Lukács, *Writer and Critic* (London: Merlin Press, 1978), p. 164.

46  Laura E. Ruberto and Kristi M. Wilson, *Italian Neorealism and Global Cinema* (Detroit: Wayne State University Press, 2007).
47  Lukács, 'The Intellectual Physiognomy', op. cit., p. 180.
48  Clive James Nwonka, '"You're What's Wrong with Me": *Fishtank, The Selfish Giant* and the Language of Contemporary British Social Realism', *New Cinemas: Journal of Contemporary Film*, 12(3) (2014): 205–23.
49  Georg Lukács, 'Realism in the Balance', in Theodor Adorno, Walter Benjamin, Ernst Bloch, Bertolt Brecht and Georg Lukács, *Aesthetics and Politics* (London: Verso, 1988), pp. 28–59.
50  Walter Benjamin, *Understanding Brecht* (London: Verso, 1998), p. 18.
51  Lukács, 'Narrate or Describe?', op. cit., p. 133.
52  Lukács, 'Realism in the Balance', op. cit., p. 43.
53  Ibid., p. 54.
54  Benjamin, *Understanding Brecht*, op. cit., p. 12.
55  Lukács, 'Realism in the Balance', op. cit., pp. 43–4.
56  Bertolt Brecht, 'Against Georg Lukács', in Theodor Adorno, Walter Benjamin, Ernst Bloch, Bertolt Brecht and Georg Lukács, *Aesthetics and Politics* (London: Verso, 1988), p. 75.
57  Lukács, 'The Intellectual Physiognomy', op. cit., p. 158.
58  Nigel Andrews, 'Dark River – Lacking Life and Drama', *Financial Times*, 21 February 2018.
59  Georg Lukács, 'Art and Objective Truth', in Georg Lukács, *Writer and Critic* (London: Merlin Press, 1978), p. 38.
60  Lukács, *The Historical Novel*, op. cit., p. 107.
61  Georg Lukács, 'Art and Objective Truth', in *Writer and Critic* (London: Merlin Press, 1978), p. 38.
62  Lukács, 'Narrate or Describe?', op. cit., p. 126.
63  Ibid., p. 130.
64  John Hess, '*Godfather II*: A Deal Coppola Couldn't Refuse', in Bill Nichols (ed.), *Movies and Methods* vol. 1 (Berkeley, CA: University of California Press, 1976), p. 90.
65  Ibid.
66  John Hess, 'Neo-Realism and New Latin American Cinema: *Bicycle Thieves* and *Blood of the Condor*', in John King, Ana M. Lopez and Manuel Alvarado (eds), *Mediating Two Worlds: Cinematic Encounters in the Americas* (London: BFI, 1993), p. 115.
67  Molly Geidel, '"Sowing Death in Our Women's Wombs": Modernization and Indigenous Nationalism in the 1960s Peace Corps and Jorge Sanjines' *Yawar Mallku*', *American Quarterly*, 62(3) (2010): 764.
68  James F. Siekmeier, *The Bolivian Revolution and the United States, 1952 to the Present* (University Park, PA: Pennsylvania State University Press, 2011), pp. 141–6.
69  Fernando Birri, 'Cinema and Underdevelopment', in Michael T. Martin (ed.), *New Latin American Cinema*, vol. 1, *Theory, Practices and Transcontinental Articulations* (Detroit: Wayne State University Press, 1997), pp. 86–7.
70  Jorge Sanjines, 'Language and Popular Culture', in Coco Fusco (ed.), *Reviewing Histories: Selections from New Latin American Cinema* (New York: Hallwalls, 1987), p. 157.
71  Julio Garcia Espinosa, 'For an Imperfect Cinema', in Michael T. Martin (ed.), *New Latin American Cinema*, vol. 1, *Theory, Practices and Transcontinental Articulations* (Detroit: Wayne State University Press, 1997), p. 80.
72  Tom Levin, 'From Dialectical to Normative Specificity: Reading Lukács on Film', *New German Critique*, 40 (Winter 1987): 35–61.

# 8

# CULTURE

## 8.1 Culture defined

The democratisation of the way we think about culture, i.e. the prising away of the word 'culture' from 'inegalitarian anchorages in high-artistic connoisseurship'[1] has been a real achievement in the last few decades. It allows us to define contemporary culture broadly in anthropological terms as ways of doing and the ways in which that doing is rendered intelligible and meaningful to the participants themselves. On such an apparently simple definition a whole number of complex issues then arise. We immediately return to the problem – and we must remember that *it is a problem* – of the relationships between social being (doing, in which class is a structuring but by no means exclusive determinant) and consciousness (with 'consciousness' now unpacked into values, beliefs, attitudes, perceptions, all the ways by which what we do is rendered meaningful to us).

This doing and meaning relationship that makes culture, becomes a practical and political problem when what we do and how we understand what we do come into some substantive conflict. When, for example, what we do or what others do to us without our full understanding, damage and harm us – then the question of 'consciousness' or culture becomes incredibly important; then it is vital to recalibrate what we do or what others do that is negatively consequential for us, with an expanded or new sense of intelligibility and meaning regarding our actions and/or the actions of others.

The very fact that our forms of intelligibility may not immediately adjust to new circumstances or become suitably lucid in relation to the negative consequences of actions, indicates implicitly something about culture: to degrees, it is characterised by habit, custom, ritual, and the taken for granted. Habit is both useful and indispensable; it facilitates an economy of energy necessary for social reproduction. But it is also the case that we may keep doing something or accept that something is done to us long past the point when we ought to realise that this doing is *not* in our best interests or the interests of others whose claims to social justice need to be heard. Iterative practices cemented by deep-rooted cultural attitudes, resistant to reflexive interrogation and critical and creative thought, may block us from the changes needed. The struggle to introduce critical reflexivity into our apprehension of what we do or what is done, is a key issue for a politics of change based on social justice. Film can play a modest role in helping us with that, by, for example, staging scenarios that explore characters struggling to break with their iterative habits and adjust their consciousness to the real circumstances and experiences they are having.

What we do and how that doing becomes meaningful to us are clearly something that is shared rather than generated up by the individual alone. Culture is something shared but not shared by all: culture has boundaries and negotiating and dialoguing across those boundaries between cultures is often the stuff of everyday life. Cultures also overlap and people occupy multiple cultural worlds, navigating the differences between them. Cultures also converge under larger cultural relationships, such as national cultures with their rituals, commemorations, history and institutions that seem to embody the national. The concept of national culture is very prone to abstracting away the real hybrid nature of the distinct cultures that make it up and this has been a source of extensive critique by Cultural Studies. With regard to the national question, it is especially important to be aware that some forms of social being are not only distinct from others, part of a rich diversity of life, but in fact structurally antagonistic. Classes and their associated cultures are the paradigm instance of this. Yet there is a profusion of cultural differences at work in the world, cutting across classed cultures in very complex ways.

The British film *Philomena* (2013), for example, would be unintelligible unless you understand it in some way as about the differences between a British male, middle-class, lapsed Catholic, media professional (journalist and public relations) and an older, working-class, Catholic woman and mother originally from Ireland. One is in search of 'a story', the other is looking for her son who was taken away from her as a child by the Catholic Church. Their relationship and their relationship to their goals are shaped by their differentially classed positions in ways that are recognisably Bourdieusian (different tastes in food and culture, different kinds of knowledge, different attitudes to people, e.g. her 'sentimentalism' vs his 'dry' humour). It is a good example of how central to what we call 'drama' (which should not be conflated with fiction) cultural difference, sharing, negotiation and dialogue are. A mark of sophistication in developing a reflexive attitude to culture is not just recognising cultural difference and its negotiation but the internal contradictions of a culture, which are nevertheless often brought out *by* an encounter with at least partial difference. In the case of *Philomena*, for example, the film explores the internal contradiction between the journalist's desire to help Philomena and his desire to get 'the story', and it explores the contradiction between Philomena's faith and what the institution that is meant to embody that faith has done to her. These contradictions are activated by the conjoining of these culturally different character types around a converged, although not entirely common, goal. Since the word 'culture' is rarely just descriptive but has a long history of being closely associated with evaluative judgements, we may as well take the plunge and say that one criterion of a 'good' film is that it explores to some degree of complexity, cultural conflict and cultural contradiction as a dialogic process. *How* this is done of course would always be part of such evaluative judgements as well.

The doing and meaning relationship also poses a theoretical problem because getting the relationship between social being and culture right has been and is so extraordinarily difficult. Take, for example, the *Doing Cultural Studies* book co-authored by key figures teaching Cultural Studies at the Open University in the 1990s. The authors note that culture, especially within Marxist theory, had often been assigned secondary status behind 'hard' social science objects of enquiry, such as politics and economics. In some strands of Marxism, for example, culture was seen as 'being both dependent upon and reflective of the primary status of the material base'.[2] This, they note, has now changed across the social sciences. Today, 'culture is now regarded as being as constitutive of the social world as economic or political processes ... [and] theorists have begun to argue that because all social practices are meaningful practices, they are all fundamentally cultural'.[3]

One can see, I hope, a characteristic slippage here. In the first part of the sentence, culture, it is argued, is constitutive of the social world, something which as we saw in Chapter 1 that Marx, at his best, argued, and that Raymond Williams, for one, insisted upon. But in that second part of the sentence, something else begins to happen, and it summarises much of the trajectory of Cultural Studies to date: the cultural *absorbs and displaces* the 'social' as a distinct category. So the rigid separation of the social (once thought of as primary) and the cultural is replaced with social being collapsed *into* the cultural (just as we saw ideology has been in Chapter 6). One of the key problems with this collapsing is that the question of power becomes quite weakened. This is because the analytical distinction of culture focuses our attention on the important issue of meaning, intelligibility, values, etc. But this domain of action *is* more plural, more plastic, more flexible (i.e. has a greater room for agency) and is more able to be contested *without* organisational change or danger, than many of the phenomena we might want to more securely analyse as social (while acknowledging that the social always has a cultural dimension). The social *is* more durable and more structured than the cultural. Cultural contestation is important and *may* seed change in diffuse ways that are difficult to trace, although there is change and there is change. Social relations and social organisations are remarkably adept at resisting change, or co-opting demands for change or new trends into their own terms. For example, in the late 1990s and early 2000s, a wave of documentary films linked to the growing international anti-corporate and anti-globalisation politics were widely distributed in theatrical cinemas.[4] How much change did this contestation at a political and cultural level achieve in corporate capitalism? *Supersize Me* (2004), for example, managed to contest the symbolic power of the McDonald's brand around the world, a significant achievement for a single film (although not one operating in isolation from other events, including another high-profile film, *McLibel* that came out a year later). Yet the corporate giant managed to weather the storm and using its public relations resources turn the critique into a story of a brand willing to listen, learn, change and go 'green'.[5] Even where cultural contestation (filmic or otherwise) is directly linked to explicit and militant challenges to organisations and institutions, dominant powers can in turn generate the possibility of sanctions of some kind (economic, legal, physical) that are materially detrimental to challengers. As Terry Eagleton puts it: 'The wager of Marx ... is that at the root of meaning lies a certain *force*, but that only a symptomatic reading of culture will disclose its traces.'[6] In other words, we should not abolish the distinction between cultural and social practices even as we acknowledge and try and think through their complex relations. Marxism remains one of the crucial intellectual-political tools we have for reminding ourselves that the 'weapons of critique ... cannot replace the critique of weapons; material force must be overthrown by material force' said Marx, before adding, that 'theory', or, in this instance, culture 'too becomes a material force once it gets hold of men'.[7]

## 8.2 Raymond Williams on culture

The work of Raymond Williams provides us with a number of important concepts which, when combined, provide us with the ability to map the complex cultural dynamics within which cultural production takes place. Let us begin with three terms he discusses in *Marxism and Literature*: tradition, institutions and formations. For Williams, the term 'tradition' refers to an actively selective ordering of the past that is 'intended to connect with and ratify the present'.[8] Tradition is the word for the way the big institutions incorporate elements of the past into the dominant social order. This is an active and ongoing process of selection, inflection, recombination and, as far as possible, neutralisation of elements that may conflict with the dominant order and its interests and priorities. The institutions are not without internal dissent or contradiction. But what often provides the opportunity for something new and dissent to (re)emerge is what Williams calls *formations*. The latter have variable relationships to the durable, established and typically dominant or at least incorporated organs of the social order, the institutions and its traditions. Williams defines formations as 'conscious movements and tendencies' including artistic, philosophical, scientific but, above all, (and Williams surprisingly leaves this out) political currents.[9] But we may also say that formations may be the product of quite loosely connected events that share a theme or trend rather than a centralised organising centre. The earlier example of *Philomena* is indicative of a series of scandals and exposés of the Catholic Church in terms of sexual abuse by priests as well as by the Catholic nuns and their treatment of 'fallen women' in their institutions. Other films such as *The Magdalene Sisters* (2002), *Calvary* (2014), *Spotlight* (2015), the Polish film, *Clergy* (2018) and the French film, *By the Grace of God* (2019), are either based on real events or come out of the collapse in legitimacy which the Catholic Church has suffered in Ireland and elsewhere as a result of scandals internationally. The films in turn amplify the cases and the problems across the public sphere further increasing the impact of this new formation of exposé, scrutiny, questioning and challenge to one of the oldest and most powerful (dominant class) international institutions in the world. Such films are clearly addressing the citizen identity of audiences and position themselves within a public sphere of current contemporary news discourses.

Formations, then, are typically an example of what Williams calls *emergent* cultural and political forces. Emergence refers to 'new meanings and values, new practices, new relationships and kinds of relationships'.[10] Emergent cultures have variable relations with the dominant order and no fixed political value can be associated with the emergent. Fascism, for example, may be an emergent formation although its growth typically also rests on at least some support from institutions within the dominant order that may have need of it to 'stabilise' capitalism. Of course, capitalism is itself a deeply productive and transformative mode of production so that it is constantly generating what Williams calls *novelties*, which are new but already fully integrated into the dominant social order. But by emergence, Williams seems to mean new practices that at least on emergence have some 'alternative' or 'oppositional' political and cultural energies. By alternative, Williams refers to political and cultural forces that seek to mark out 'a different way to live and ... to be left alone with it' and this usually correlates to 'individual and small-group solutions to social crisis'.[11] Within popular culture, where value systems out of kilter with the dominant capitalist ones, are represented, it is typically at this alternative individual and/or small group level at which it is imagined. Oppositional political and cultural forces tend to want to stake out alternatives in order to transform the dominant system, to confront it rather than be left alone, to enlarge the scale of the alternative value system and embark on some mode of revolution (again this could be of a right-wing kind as well as a left-wing kind). As Williams argues, the line between the alternative and the oppositional is often quite blurred. The alternative, for example, may be forced to become oppositional due to the encroachments of the dominant culture (see Section 8.4). And the line between the oppositional and the dominant order may also be blurred because the dominant will begin the work of incorporation very early on in the life of emergent oppositional cultures.

Emergent forces speak to the new that may be, at least on emergence, offering value systems that conflict with dominant value systems, such as the way a culture of sharing in relation to the internet has come into conflict with proprietary value systems closely linked to capitalism.[12] But what of cultural materials that have a historic existence like 'traditions' but which lie outside the incorporated institutionalised traditions? Williams refers to already long-existing cultural practices that are in some relationship of tension to the dominant traditions as *residual* practices. These are persisting traces of prior historical phases, either within the capitalist mode of production or carry-overs from pre-capitalist modes of production, which have the potential to be activated in specific forms, including film texts, that contest the dominant social, political and cultural institutions. By the residual, then,

Williams differentiates these past forms from those that have been incorporated into the dominant order as tradition:

> Thus certain experiences, meanings, and values which cannot be expressed or substantially verified in terms of the dominant culture, are nevertheless lived and practised on the basis of the residue – cultural as well as social – of some previous social and cultural institution or formation.[13]

The popular cultures of the broadly feudal period include fairy tales, folklore, legendary figures, knights' tales, the occult, etc., all of which British culture, for example, is extensively stocked with. They may provide a source for both traditional (incorporated) or residual (alternative or oppositional) film production as in the numerous iterations of Robin Hood or less well known, the German-sourced sixteenth-century story of Michael Kohlhaas. This latter story was recently revived as *Age of Uprising: The Legend of Michael Kohlhaas* (2013) but an earlier German language version starring the British actor David Warner called *Michael Kohlhaas – der Rebell* (1969) was directed by Volker Schlöndorff. This film makes the point about earlier feudal story materials becoming relevant to the contemporary moment, by having the credit sequence open with then contemporary news footage of street confrontations between police and protesters from around the world before transitioning into the sixteenth-century diegetic setting of the film! Here emergent political formations recast older cultural materials and speak through them, while the dominant institutions (film production) are sufficiently internally contradictory to provide a space for that to happen.

Like the emergent, the residual's active resistance to the dominant order will be contained and prone to processes of exploitation, incorporation and reinterpretation. For example, the rural may be a site both of the residual and the traditional. As residual, rural locations and communities may articulate collective value systems, class conflict between landowners and the dispossessed or anti-consumerist values. On a spectrum that in popular western culture in particular moves *towards* the 'traditional', the rural becomes home-spun wisdom, 'authentic' and vital living, self-sufficiency or some vaguely expressed hostility to a 'modern' way of life, all the way into the more or less fully integrated traditional culture associated with the commercial heritage film. Williams also mentions another category, connected with tradition, which he calls the 'archaic' by which he means images that are 'wholly recognised as an element of the past'.[14] The archaic, we may elaborate, differs from the dominant version of tradition because the latter typically has an element of negotiating the past and the present, whereas the 'archaic' is aggressively anti-modern. In popular culture, the 'archaic' is often the site of magic and the supernatural but in our contemporary era of capitalism, industrial images are now also typically marked as archaic signifiers of the working class and/or within science fiction as traces of earlier, now transcended, modes of development within capitalism, e.g. the lower levels of the ship in *Alien* (1979) or the factory where Max works in *Elysium* (2013).

The relationship of films to these very complex set of dynamics is of course further complicated by the fact that films do not 'reflect' a given situation so much as contribute their own *production* of the contexts they come out of, as Chapter 6 and Chapter 7 have emphasised. As productions, film texts inflect the cultural resources they work with in their own ways and with their own peculiar combinations. The responsiveness of aesthetic artefacts such as films to dynamic cultural *processes* is something that Williams wanted to capture with his elusive concept 'structure of feeling' (Figure 8.1).[15] The term is an attempt to dialectically conjoin the sense of 'structures' which have definite social bases and something more intangible, possibly but not necessarily transient, but something more subjective, felt, experienced, lived but not necessarily formally acknowledged or set down in, for example, writing or doctrine, perhaps even something 'at the very edge of semantic availability'.[16] It is often a question of 'tone', style and 'attitude' produced through narrative focalisation and allegiance between spectator and character(s). Dennis Broe argues that between 1945 and 1950, Hollywood's low budget film noirs articulated the wider militancy of labour unrest in this period and an emerging middle-class alliance with the working class. Broe argues that a large body of work manifests a sympathetic focalisation and allegiance to characters who are

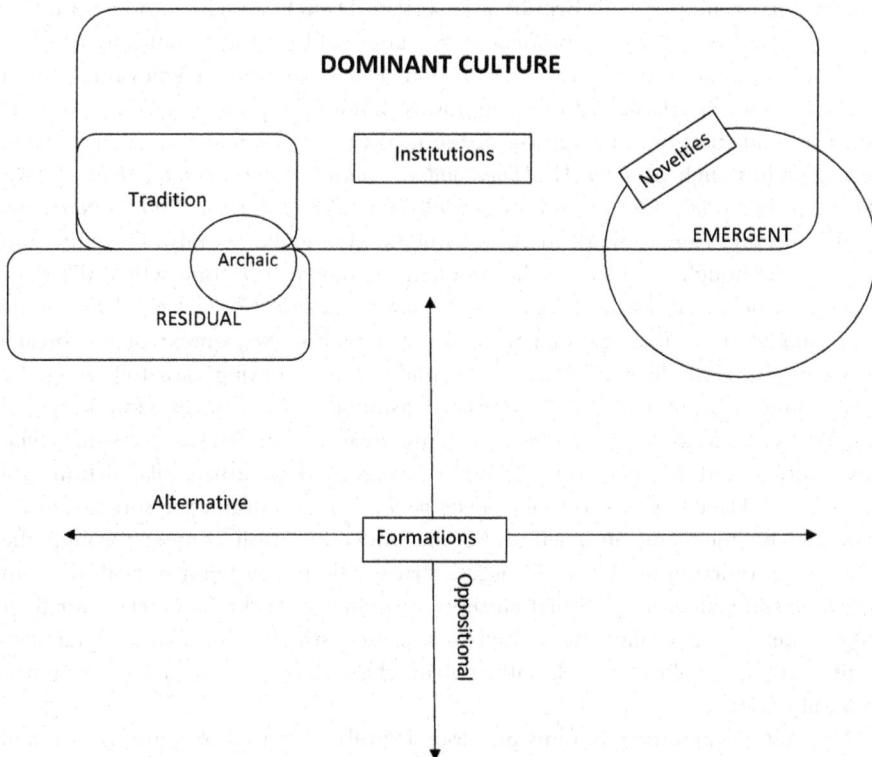

**FIGURE 8.1** Raymond Williams: mapping the structure of feeling

fugitive figures outside the law, stressing class tensions and antipathy towards state authority. But after 1950, with labour strikes in the country diminishing and Hollywood itself increasingly harassed by witch-hunts searching out 'communist' influence, more and more films shift the focalisation towards the figure of the lawman and the genre tilts towards the police procedural in which the forces of order must neutralise very unsympathetic psychotic criminals.[17] The politics of this shift are obvious.

Within the context of British film, Sue Harper has explored how the films of Alexander Korda and Gainsborough Studios in the 1930s and the 1940s often construct a kind of class alliance between the aristocracy and the plebeian/working class which licenses sexual pleasure (and an aesthetic based on fantasy and masquerades) against the sober puritan bourgeois work ethic represented by a producer such as Michael Balcon with his advocacy of a certain mode of 'realism' that affirms the bourgeois social order.[18] Korda's The Private Life of Henry VIII (1933) mobilises a mythic figure from the aristocratic past (tradition) but pulls it into alignment with the *emergent* social conflicts of its contemporary moment of production where sexual politics becomes a metaphor for all sorts of working-class utopian desires for broader social change. At the same time, the stabilising weight of tradition is also felt in the film and eventually contains the protagonists in a typically British narrative trajectory.[19]

Focusing on more recent British cinema, Paul Dave has explored how an urban pastoral style has worked to produce very varied and complex, ambivalent structures of feeling around class dynamics in which tensions and anxieties mix with a tendency towards effacement of antagonisms. Under the pressure of class polarisation and gentrification, one version of the urban pastoral emerges in such updated heritage films such as Four Weddings and a Funeral (1994), Notting Hill (1999), Bridget Jones's Diary (2001) and its sequel The Edge of Reason (2004). Narrative focalisation and camera work mark out middle-class idyllic worlds of security and affluence (although troubled by the problem of romance) beyond which the poor and the dispossessed are occasionally glimpsed or guiltily referred to.[20] The insulated middle-class urban pastoral must be seen within the context of the breakdown of the class alliance between the middle and working class following the dismantling of social democracy. Another version and vision of this same historical context can be found in the ambivalent filmic images of underclass excess in which drink, drugs and sex play out against a background of urban dilapidation and breakdown. Dave explores the film Trainspotting with its distinctive surreal/fantasy aesthetic, by mediating its relations to the wider historical context through the 1990s' phenomenon of Britart. He argues that the dominant tenor of both the film and Britart mined countercultural currents associated with the 'underclass' for their 'edgy' energy and vitality but as fuel to the reconstruction of a neo-liberal subjectivity that remakes the self rather than channelling any broader substantive political critique.[21]

The cultural industries *in* films promote a similar dynamic of appropriation and upward social mobility, a tradition of the 'performing northern working class' singing and dancing their way out of trouble, that continues with the recent film

*Wild Rose* (2018).[22] A more complex and politicised film that is a kind of riposte to *Trainspotting* can be found in *Beats* (2019), which is set in 1994 just before the emergent working-class culture of the rave scene is about to be crushed by the state (through the law and police violence). The homosocial friendship between the two teenage boys in the film stands for the wider but fragile sense of community represented by the rave scene before both the friendship and the rave culture are about to be exploded by various social pressures. The centre piece of the film is the depiction of the rave itself, a wonderful piece of cinematography and editing that evokes the utopian structure of feeling of the rave, but also including, in a bold move, a moment of montage that splices into the dancing the detonation of the Ravenscraig steelworks, shut down in 1992, and images of automated car production lines: both testifying to the wider capitalist imperatives shattering once established working-class cultures and attendant political muscle.

## 8.3 Gramsci on culture

The complex of concepts which Raymond Williams develops was his own very particular reading of the work of Antonio Gramsci. What Williams seems to have been particularly drawn to in Gramsci's thinking was its sensitivity to '[t]he relatively mixed, confused, incomplete, or inarticulate consciousness' of people in a given situation or social formation.[23] Williams constantly warned against conflating relatively formalised models of social systems, whether, say, the Marxist base-superstructure model, or theories of ideology, or bourgeois functionalist sociological models, with the actual complex and contradictory dynamics of how men and women live their social relations and conditions. Gramsci knew that while institutions give class power to those who control them and reach into the lives of what Gramsci called the 'subaltern' groups, social being matters and necessarily adapts the meaning(s) circulated by the powerful. I wrote earlier of the Catholic Church as a ruling class institution, but this now needs to be qualified by the fact that, as Gramsci noted, it 'is in reality a multiplicity of distinct and often contradictory religions' since there is a Catholicism of the peasant, the petit-bourgeoisie, the urban workers, the intellectuals and a gender-inflected Catholicism of women.[24] Thus, to use the language of media studies developed by Stuart Hall, the Catholic teaching as 'encoded' by the clergy are 'decoded' in different ways by the socially differentiated faithful.[25]

For Gramsci, the consciousness or philosophy of the classes subordinate to the dominant classes bears the marks of the power relation in the contradictory, fragmentary and 'composite' conceptions within the subaltern groups. They have not had the time, the opportunity or the resources to develop their thinking to the level of coherence and understanding or awareness of the historical lineages of their thought which the philosophers have. Nevertheless, the specialists, 'the professional and systematic philosophers' are not the only ones to practise 'philosophy' insists Gramsci.[26] The difference is not between those who are philosophers and those who are not, since 'everyone is a philosopher' because everyone articulates conceptions of the world. The difference is between the degree of coherence, reflexivity, historical knowledge and understanding which groups can muster. Popular philosophies are typically very contradictory combinations of

> Stone Age elements and principles of a more advanced science, prejudices from all past phases of history at the local level and intuitions of a future philosophy which will be that of the human race united the world over [i.e. socialism].[27]

Popular philosophies are grounded in what Gramsci calls 'common sense', a sort of 'folklore' or 'spontaneous' philosophy that revolutionary practice must engage with and help ferment into a kind of transformation that aligns better with the social interests of the subaltern classes.

It is the role specifically of intellectuals, the stratum of thinkers which every social class develops, to critically sift and cohere the consciousness of social groups to a level of coherence so that it can accomplish the strategic goals necessary to its beneficial reproduction. The dominant social groups are naturally in a better position to do this than the subaltern social groups. But the subaltern social groups can develop both their own intellectual strata (crucially important) *and* attract the support of dissident intellectuals who break away from the dominant group to align themselves with the subordinate groups, as Marx, for example, did.[28] Without independently and self-critically developing their philosophical conceptions, subaltern groups will remain subordinate not only in terms of economic and political power, but also subordinate in terms of their thinking, their deference to the powerful, their willingness to allow the dominant group to be active in shaping agendas while they are largely passive and often trusting in their 'betters', and crucially not realising that their social inclusion (such as it is) depends on them *not* asserting too powerfully their suppressed capacity for autonomous action and thought. Once the latter crosses certain boundaries, coercion and violence are the likely response from those with power. The challenge to economic power is inextricably connected with the challenge to the ability of the dominant groups to set the course of social development, make policy and frame debates in the terms that align with their interests. In short, the subaltern groups must challenge the *leadership* of the dominant social groups, and challenge their conviction that they represent the 'universal' interest. Cultural production and meaning are an important site where this battle for hearts and minds is played out. Gramsci called this struggle for leadership, which is at once both political and moral, *hegemony*. Hegemony, writes Raymond Williams:

> constitutes a sense of reality for most people in the society, a sense of absolute because experienced reality beyond which it is very difficult for most members of the society to move, in most areas of their lives. It is, that is to say, in the strongest sense a 'culture', but a culture which has also to be seen as the lived dominance and subordination of particular classes.[29]

While hegemony refers to the very powerful ways that class domination is inscribed into the imaginations and conceptions of social groups, remembering Gramsci's stress on the contradictory combinations of materials that make up popular philosophy, hegemony or leadership is always an ongoing process of struggle, an ongoing process of asymmetrical dialogue and pressure. The consent of the masses to the leadership of the dominant classes can never be assumed or taken for granted, a point Stuart Hall often emphasised.[30] Within the capitalist class system in particular, there is too much turbulence, change, crisis and conflict for hegemony to ever be a seamless process of guaranteed incorporation across the board, on every intellectual, political and cultural front simultaneously.

One of the most significant 'fronts' of struggle around which hegemony and challenges to hegemony (sometimes called counter-hegemony) are formed is around national identity. The importance of hegemony and national identity was brought brutally home to the British left in 1982 when Margaret Thatcher sent British military forces half-way round the world to reclaim the long-disputed Falkland Islands that the Argentinians had seized. The war with Argentina rescued Thatcher's chances of re-election in 1983 and allowed the Conservative government the chance to recast British national identity, recently plagued by the long-drawn-out crisis of British capitalism in its post-imperial decline, as a stridently confident world power once more. Anthony Barnett diagnosed the 'structure of feeling' that stirred itself during the Parliamentary debate on 3 April 1982 after the Argentine forces landed to take back what they called the Malvinas Islands. This structure of feeling had a very specific historical reference point, the Second World War, which indicates the importance of history and popular renditions of history. The structure of feeling which roused itself on 3 April also had a very specific symbolic figure, an imagined, mythical Winston Churchill:

> It was Churchillism that dominated the House of Commons on 3 April. All the essential symbols were there: an island people, the cruel seas, a British defeat, Anglo-Saxon democracy challenged by a dictator, and finally, the quintessentially Churchillian posture – we were down but we were not out. The parliamentarians of right, left and centre looked through the mists of time to the Falklands and imagined themselves to be the Grand Old Man. They were, after all, his political children and they too would put the 'Great' back into Britain.[31]

This was hegemonic tradition in action, framing the terms of the problem, the terms of the solution and the basis of action around a particular conception of British history and identity that came from the dominant conservative social order. Two years later, and in direct response to the surprising ease with which Thatcher had mobilised a set of cultural reflexes the left had thought were in decline, Geoff Hurd published an anthology of essays called *National Fictions*. In a relatively rare turn within film studies to a Gramscian-inspired cultural studies framework, *National Fictions* examined representations of the Second World War in British films and television made both during the war and since. What the various authors found was that the meanings of the Second World War were more contested than the conservative trope of 'Churchillism' allowed for. As Graham Dawson and Bob West argued:

> The central and founding myth of World War II is of a nation *united* though idolatry for its totemic leader, Churchill. All other mythic aspects of the war are subordinated to this one … It provides an extremely partial account, which actively *silences* a dynamic period when British politics moved to the left.[32]

The meaning of the war and indeed of Churchill was and remains a site of struggle both at the time and afterwards as the war becomes folded into subsequent evolving historical contexts, including recent iterations of the Churchill myth in two films, *Churchill* (2017) and *Darkest Hour* (2017), for which Gary Oldman won an Oscar and a BAFTA (hegemonic institutions consecrating the hegemonic myth). In his 'Notes on Hegemony' for the *National Fictions* anthology, Hurd stresses that the concept of hegemony is superior both to cruder Marxist notions that the ruling classes simply *impose* their beliefs and value systems on subordinate groups or the liberal pluralist notion that there is a free exchange of ideas and opinions uncoupled from material positions of power to propagate and act on ideas and value systems. The Second World War posed very sharply the need for the dominant classes to engage with the subaltern classes and groups to win support for the war. But they could not rely on a simple 'downward transmission of ideologies'. Instead there was across the 'front' of cultural production and communication, a *negotiation* and *struggle* around meanings, and consent had to be forged by at least in part conceding to *hearing* and *feeling* the demands and aspirations of the working classes and women, whose roles were changing dramatically under the pressure of war. Conservative appeals to 'do your duty', for example, were confronted with counter-demands for 'a greater degree of equality between the classes'[33] and the sexes. Popular film culture can be sifted and analysed for evidence of such negotiations and struggles, albeit mediated by the specific nature of film language and its conditions of production. Within British culture, the Second World War remains a singularly important but, in terms of its meaning and significance, highly mobile reference point, as such different films as *Dunkirk* (2017) and *Their Finest* (2016) (and compared to the recent Churchill biopics) indicate.

A more self-conscious and lucid understanding of film culture as a site of hegemonic and counter-hegemonic positions can be found in the work of Senegalese director Ousmane Sembène. Born in 1923, Sembène had numerous working-class jobs (carpenter, mechanic, dockworker) and was a member of the French Communist Party while working in Marseilles after the Second World War. After becoming a successful novelist, he went to train as a film director at the Gorky studios in Moscow where he likely came into contact with debates around Lukácsian realism. He then went on to make a number of films such as *Borom Sarret* (1963), *Black Girl* (1966), *Emitaï* (1971), *Xala* (1975), *Ceddo* (1977), *Camp de Thiaroye* (1988) and *Moolaadé* (2004) which established his reputation as one of Africa's most important contributors to world film culture. He remained a communist until his death in 2007. Key themes across his body of work include the recovery of popular memory as sources of critique, the critical interrogation of both Western imperialism and Arab-Islamic cultural traditions, the pan-African audience his films often speak to, and the centrality and importance of women taking an active lead in fighting for social change.[34] With his emphasis on the significance of history, culture, critique, memory, education and change, Sembène is a strikingly Gramscian filmmaker. Sembène's self-understanding of his role as a director helping audiences clarify and understand their everyday experiences is also Gramscian. This understanding is filtered through the African tradition of the griot (a figure who often appears in the films), the storyteller and raconteur, who offers parables and advice and truth telling.[35] The griot is the keeper of a community's history and legends and with their definite social role, the griot corresponds to Gramsci's thinking about the importance of the intellectuals organically connected to their classes producing moral and political values that defend their interests. Sembène himself thought of film as a form of 'night school', that is a mode of education and discussion in a popular idiom.[36] The 'night school' idea makes explicit the educational and pedagogic role of popular culture, including film, that other theorists, such as Henry Giroux, have been exploring.[37]

The complex affinities between Sembène and Gramsci have been explored by Marcia Landy in her discussion of *Camp de Thiaroye*. The story is set shortly before the end of the Second World War, where Senegalese troops recruited by the French to fight for 'freedom' in Europe are being held in a camp pending their transition back to their villages. Based on real events in Dakar, tensions between the Senegalese and their colonial French officers mounts, leading to a revolt that is brutally suppressed by French tanks. The film was banned from France for a decade, indicating the power and importance of official colonial history to French identity. Landy shows how *Camp de Thiaroye* explores the connection between colonialism and fascism, the in-built racism of colonialism, the perpetual task of treating and persuading the colonial subjects that they are inferior to the 'civilised' whites (i.e. that their subaltern status is fully justified) and, above all, the importance of recovering lessons from previous events, previous experiences and previous failures in order to break with the patterns of iteration that reproduce domination. Landy concludes:

> The film's allegory is geared to asking what, if any, are the alternatives to undergoing the same experiences again and again, and to the obstacles that obstruct the creation of a collectivity. The ending of the film returns to the beginning. Though instead of seeing the Senegalese troops disembarking on their return to African soil, another batch of recruits is headed out to Europe, thus underscoring powerfully the notion of repetition.[38]

In his final film, *Moolaadé*, this question of breaking with patterns of behaviour consecrated by tradition and religion is posed in relation to the widespread practice of female genital circumcision. Set in a small generic African village, the ritual of female circumcision practised on young girls is presided over by an alliance of female priests (the Salindana) and the patriarchal village elders. This conservative and oppressive tradition is, however, contested by another, residual culture, the moolaadé, which affords protection and sanctuary to those who ask for it. When some young girls about to be circumcised ask Collé for sanctuary, this triggers an ever-widening circle of consequences that draws in the entire village. It is interesting that the girls have heard a rumour, confirmed as true, that years earlier, Collé refused to have her own daughter cut after Collé's difficulties with childbirth due to her own circumcision. Yet this earlier act of defiance and rupture with tradition and its various justifications have been lying dormant and half-forgotten like a repressed memory within the village until the girls reactivate this earlier history by seeking Collé's help. The moolaadé that Collé invokes is linked to the giant anthill in the village which symbolically is located right next to the Islamic mosque. For legend has it that the anthill is the site of the burial of the village's first king, who was overthrown by his people when he offended the moolaadé. Even more significantly, the moolaadé is an example of African tradition that pre-dates the village's subsequent conversion to Islam. Thus two traditions, one belonging to the dominant culture that underpins female circumcision, and one that is residual and outside the dominant culture in exactly the way Williams discussed, are at play and in the subsequent battle for hearts and minds, are activated by the various participants in a struggle for moral and political supremacy. Gradually the ambivalences and questions which at least some (although not all) the women in the village have about the ritual, grow, until the reiterated behaviour (the ritual) and the whole social and sexual power relations of the village are challenged in a parable of revolt stirred once again by the moolaadé's sense of social justice. *Moolaadé* has definite formal affinities with Lukácsian realism (see Chapter 7) with its intensive totality of time and space (the village), its use of typical characters (modified according to African social relations and culture) and typical (in the Lukácsian sense) plot around nodal points of social tensions, its community/group focus and slow-burn narrative that builds cumulatively to an explosive (revolutionary) finish. As with his other films, Sembène took *Moolaadé* round Africa, showing it to audiences and having debates and discussions afterwards to thrash out the issues raised and try and cement the lessons which the film seeks to illuminate.[39]

## 8.4 Militant cultures and accumulation by dispossession

Sembène's films come out of a hybrid mode of production. In their reliance on state funding from both within Africa and France and the European Union, as well as Sembène's reputation as an auteur, the films suggest an art cinema mode of production. Yet the political intentions and characteristics of his films and the way he distributes them in Africa using the 'night school' model of screenings and discussions and debates, indicate a more Third Cinema mode of production.[40] With Sembène, then, we can now transition towards even more explicitly militant alignment and allegiance with political cultures that filmmaking, especially documentary filmmaking, has attached itself to. But to understand the pressures driving the emergence of many militant cultures, we need a concept such as David Harvey's 'accumulation by dispossession'. This points to the historic and continued necessity which capital has for theft, forced acquisition and other coercive seizures of resources in order to turn a profit. The classic liberal vision that capital makes money by investing in production which makes goods that meet needs, is only one strand of the capitalist story. Historically British capital needed to kick-start itself by both *internal* dispossession of land belonging to the peasants and the *external* power projection of empire, which seized both land and people (slaves) abroad. But Harvey argues, this accumulation by dispossession continues into the contemporary era because of the problem of over-accumulation of capital (the difficulty of finding enough sites of investment that could secure a profitable rate of return).[41] This is solved by transferring resources at less than their value over to capital, enabling capital to make a profit outside the classic investment and return on investment dynamic which liberalism imagines is the main and 'authentic' dynamic at work within capitalism. This 'transferral' happens in a whole range of ways, from imperialist war (in Iraq 2003) to privatisations of publicly owned resources, to hostile takeovers, to subordinating nation-states to the powers of the World Trade Organisation and the International Monetary Fund. The open force and lack of consent which accumulation by dispossession involves in turn generate militant resistance.[42]

Capitalism's territorial expansionism brought it into contact with pre-capitalist modes of production, often tribal in nature, where communal forms of property struck the 'moderns' as backward and uncivilised. The consequences of that history are still with us – another testimony to the incredibly tenacious quality of cultural practices and identities – in the various 'post-colonial' contexts where the descendants of those whose lands and resources were taken, continue to live. Australian cinema has been exploring this live history and its consequences for the aboriginals from as early as *Bitter Springs* (1950) to the recent *Sweet Country* (2017) with many films in between, including *Rabbitproof Fence* (2002), *Radiance* (1998), *The Chant of Jimmy Blacksmith* (1978) and John Pilger's searing documentary *Utopia* (2013).

Nor is this just the traces of a residual history whose main battles have been fought and lost in the distant past. The expansionary dynamic of capitalism both internally and externally continues to bring it into conflict with tribal and peasant modes of life much older than capitalism. Take, for example, the Japanese government's decision to build the New Tokyo International Airport in the mid-1960s on land that would displace peasant farmers who had lived there for many generations. A more resonant symbol of a global elite in perpetual transit against locally rooted labour is hard to imagine. Resistance by the farmers and leftist groups went on for over a decade, delaying the construction and although the airport was completed in 1978, attacks against it continue to this day. This long struggle was recorded by Shinsuke Ogawa and his filmmaking collective (Ogawa Pro) for over ten years as they lived and worked alongside the peasants defending their land. In *Narita: The Peasants of the*

*Second Fortress* (1971), the camera is always situated on the side of the peasants in their confrontation with the authorities and the police, in contrast to most television journalism where the camera is behind the police lines. As the conflict becomes increasingly violent, the political implications of this physical proximity with the peasants become clearer. Although the film is formally quite close to observational documentary, eschewing voice-over narration, interviews or music – although it does have some intertitles – the closeness of the camera to the protagonists, when, for example, the peasants are discussing strategy, suggests less a distant observer than a sympathetic participant. This kind of long immersion into the way of life of the people being represented on screen indicates the democratic and dialogical possibilities of ethnographic methods. The development of a democratising of the culture of film production by breaking down the boundaries between filmmakers and their subjects, by aligning with their struggles, winning their trust and confidence by breaking with the model of the dominant film industry of parachuting crews into and out of 'the field', represented a significant contribution to filmmaking by Marxist-inspired political currents in the 1960s and the 1970s.

Typically this kind of radical ethnographic filmmaking represents an example of the Gramscian move by the intellectual from the middle class forging an organic connection with the struggles of the oppressed. The conflict between an expanding capital looking for land and resources and existing (typically peasant-based) cultures that we see documented by Ogawa Pro in Japan is also currently a very live political contestation in India. The writer Arundhatti Roy, who effectively turned her back on a world of literary celebrity when her first novel *The God of Small Things* won the Booker Prize in 1997, has spent much of the last 20 or more years writing about Indian politics from 'the optic of the people'.[43] She has repeatedly challenged the hegemonic development and 'modernisation' ideologies built into such projects as large-scale dam-building programmes that are effectively handing over water resources to private multinationals and displacing millions of people in the process. Her 2010 article for the Indian newsweekly *Outlook* was a report of her time spent with Maoist-inspired revolutionaries in the jungles of central India who are fighting the state and private mining corporations trying to gain control of mineral-rich land.

This latter issue is taken up in Sanjay Kak's documentary *Red Ant Dream* (2013), in which the director is able to make contact with and spend some time among the revolutionary guerrilla fighters in central India, many of whom are women escaping from sexual violence committed by or supported by the state police. We hear the fighters talk of their experiences, their motivations and their beliefs, and what they have to say is contrasted and compared with the intermittent audio on the soundtrack of news radio broadcasts aligned with the state view on the revolutionaries as 'terrorists' and requiring a militarised response. The film contextualises the armed struggle in the jungle via leftist political movements in the Punjab. In the opening sections of *Red Ant Dream* we see marches and meetings celebrating two figures important to the local and national political history. The first is Avtar Singh Pash, a revolutionary poet aligned with the Naxalite movement of the late 1960s, who was assassinated by right-wing religious fundamentalists in 1988. The film draws on Pash's poetry to illuminate the historical continuities in the struggle. The second figure is Bhagat Singh, a young communist who was executed by the British colonialists in 1931. Both figures were killed on the same date, 23 March, a coincidence that ties them together in the popular memory that keeps their words and lives meaningful for the contemporary generation. Carrying their pictures, speaking their words, commenting on their example, these are acts of revolutionary folklore contesting official histories.[44] One of the key features of Third Cinema is its receptiveness to the importance of culture and memory (often the recovery of memory that has been otherwise erased by the dominant culture) that can work as counter-hegemonic resources.

The centrality of culture to political struggle and the affirmation of identities that are discovering their subaltern position and fighting back against it, are central to Third Cinema. It is a cinema of Politics + Culture. *El Pueblo Se Levanta* (*The People Are Rising*) (1971) comes out of the complex of left political currents that formed the American New Left in the 1960s.[45] The film focuses on the Puerto Rican working class in East Harlem and their organisation into the Young Lords party, a Puerto Rican equivalent of and inspired by the African-American revolutionaries, the Black Panther Party. The documentary film opens with a poem performed by a young Hispanic reflecting on the experience of poverty, inequality and exploitation. Throughout the film, songs, plays, educational programmes and poems are woven into political struggle and analysis. The opening section focuses on attempts by radicals to get access to the local Spanish Methodist church to repurpose it for the community. However, when the church authorities refuse this reasonable request, the Young Lords occupy the church space and establish a breakfast programme for young kids and an educational programme. As with peasant communities fighting airport expansion in *Narita: The Peasants of the Second Fortress* or the fight against the state-corporate nexus, in *Red Ant Dream*, to seize control of land, *place* becomes a site of struggle between different ways of living. When the church is reclaimed by the authorities, it is returned to its traditional social function as an anaesthetic on social conflict, whereas the Young Lords tried to refunction the space for the purposes of political consciousness-raising in a challenge to the hegemonic modes of being.

After the church occupation has been lost, the film moves from this very local and specific conflict to a broader international focalisation. For example, the Puerto Rican origins of the revolutionaries now becomes a way of exploring how the promises of opportunity made to Puerto Ricans to migrate to America gave way to the reality of joining an exploited proletariat. Footage of Puerto Rico plays over a young women discussing the poverty her parents fled and her conflicted identity as an American/Puerto Rican, with the latter identity largely submerged into the former until recently. North American imperial influence (corporate and military) on Puerto Rico, which exports goods to the Northern hegemon in another form of accumulation by dispossession, demonstrates the enlarged optic of the film which began with a dispute over a single building in New York. The film effortlessly links in feminist demands for a critique of housework, women's work and the transformation of women's role in political struggle, all once again, questions that are as cultural (about attitudes inscribed in practices) as political. The power of the film lies in its depiction of the subaltern emerging as an active subject; the people are rising and as a consequence the film itself has an inspiring story to tell and an analytical cutting edge. Alignment with the struggle of the people in the immediacy of that conflict distinguishes such documentary filmmaking from dominant traditions and, as with Ogawa Pro, required a substantial commitment of time, covering the Young Lords for a year of filming, from the occupation of the church to the death of one of their members in prison.

Digitalisation and the worldwide web have opened up new sites of contestation between corporate capital and alternative and oppositional cultures. Radical film culture has developed a myriad of different projects online in conjunction with off-line activism. The latter has also been influenced by the horizontal modes of communication and organising, without formal affiliation to party-type organs, that digital technology and platforms have facilitated. There has been an upsurge in anarchist politics as a result and its impact on filmmaking has been charted by Chris Robé using extensive interviews with participants. One of his case studies is the Canadian-based anarchist filmmaker, of Puerto Rican origins, Franklin Lopez. Lopez's digital platform, sub-Media.tv,[46] comes out of the sampling cultures of hip hop, the subversive semiotic attacks on popular culture, advertising, marketing and public relations known as culture jamming, alternative news media practices such as IndyMedia and the US-based Democracy Now! and eco-activism and anarchist direct action.[47] subMedia's longest-running project was *It's the End of the World As We Know It and I Feel Fine* featuring Lopez as The Stimulator whose 'disembodied, postmodern/sci-fi foulmouthed host ... floats over the screen in three red-bordered squares that encompass negatives of his eyes and mouth'.[48] The show was a kind of alternative news round-up programme with a focus on resistance and protest against capital and the state. Culturally, *It's the End of the World* ... mixed the earlier film culture of montage with other visual and music cultures from hip-hop, radical video, music videos, and culture jamming. After running this project for ten years, subMedia has now developed a new flagship programme called *Trouble* that moves subMedia more towards documentary film aesthetics. The tone is less humorous as The Stimulator has been retired. Thus far, the structure of the 30-minute or so episodes appears to be this: a particular theme is selected (prisons or new technologies of surveillance and control, for example) and introduced by a voice-over narrator who maps out the issues to be tackled before then leaving the argumentation to be stitched together between the voices of various interviewees. Their contributions, occasionally as 'talking heads' are typically played over a montage image track pulled from diverse sources that illustrates and reinforces the vocal exposition. subMedia use their online and their social media presence (the Facebook page has over 50K followers) to raise revenue to sustain the two-person team of Lopez and his collaborator. The revenue is raised both through donations and a subscription option for a slightly advanced access to the *Trouble* videos. In this way, subMedia have at least partially been able to address the question of precarity and long-term security that plague low-budget radical filmmaking.[49] The more in-depth analysis of an issue and serious tone of this new series accord with the idea that these videos can be used within political and community spaces as a trigger for discussion and debate offline. subMedia also provide a screening kit to facilitate this which includes additional reading and viewing material, topical questions to get a discussion started and posters to advertise the screening. The *Trouble* series, in form and mode of consumption, moves the subMedia project back towards some of the classic strands of revolutionary film culture from the past. In their manifesto statement, 'Towards a Third Cinema', Argentinean filmmakers, Fernando Solanas and Octavio Getino, argued that the film should be conceived as a 'detonator' for discussion. In doing so, the consumer-spectator becomes an actor and participant in politics and the space of the screening becomes a liberated zone combating 'solitude, noncommunication, distrust, and fear'.[50] Likewise, subMedia's *Trouble* project is motivated by a concern that while opening up certain communicative and organising possibilities, digital-based politics *may* paradoxically end up isolating people, fragmenting people, diverting people from the politics of face-to-face trust-building, dialogue and group-based offline activism.

## 8.5 The circuit of production

The *Doing Cultural Studies* book which I criticised earlier for its collapsing of the social into the cultural (Section 8.1) has been very influential across the disciplines. One reason is that it has a useful model of the 'circuit of culture' (see Figure 8.2).

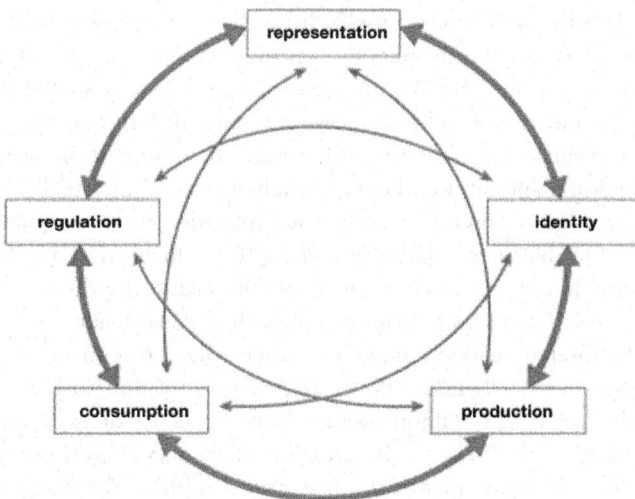

**FIGURE 8.2** The circuit of culture
Source: Paul du Gay, Stuart Hall, Linda Janes, Hugh Mackay and Keith Negus (1997) *Doing Cultural Studies: The Story of the Sony Walkman.* London: Sage/Open University.

The circuit identifies five moments or phases that shape cultural meanings. By depicting the phases as a circuit, the model avoids a more simple linear model which 'starts' with one phase (such as production) and then sees the others as deriving from that 'origin'. Instead in any real situation, the different moments, or perhaps we should really be thinking about 'determinants', will interact with each other and in doing so produce different responses to each other and thus combine differently according to different times and cross-cultural instances. The five determinants of meaning cited in the model are: representation, identity, production, consumption and regulation.[51]

The determinant of regulation refers to: '*controls on cultural activity*, ranging from formal and legal controls, such as regulations, laws, and institutionalized systems, to the informal ... controls of cultural norms and expectations ...'.[52] These are two rather different types of regulation in fact. Because one refers to the state and state power and inter-state relations, and one refers to much more pluralised and tacit modes of control in lived cultures, it might have been better to have differentiated this category into two distinct determinants, or incorporate informal norms into the moment of identity. For example, Hollywood's penetration of the Chinese film market is heavily regulated by the Chinese state through restrictions on the number of films that can be imported, when those films can be distributed and where, how much of the box office will go back to the Hollywood studios as well as censorship restrictions on content.[53] Yet the concerns and motivations driving these controls have a complex relationship to and may not reflect the informal cultural norms of ordinary people in their day-to-day life, given that many Chinese people are fully aware that the Chinese state is a very problematic and undemocratic apparatus.

The moment or determinant of representation would refer, when applied to film, primarily to the film product itself, although it would also include marketing and promotional material surrounding the film. Representation of people and places and the issues they are dealing with quickly takes us to the heart of the politics of a film and all the complex tools for textual analysis that film studies have developed to evaluate those politics. Generally, the more those representations align with the dominant culture, the more likely it is to be a profitable commodity, which, as we saw in Chapter 4, is the prime motivation for the capitalist mode of production. A film like *In the Valley of Elah* (2007), which offers a critical account of the US Army and its involvement in Iraq, cuts against the dominant culture of patriotism in the US and it is perhaps not surprising that it made only $6.7 million in the US. In foreign markets, however, where there is a stronger appetite for critical perspectives on US imperialism, especially in relation to the war on Iraq, the film took nearly $23 million at the theatrical box office. If representation directs our attention to the text, the question of identity directs our attention to the wider cultural contexts of identity that may determine the reach, profitability and responses to the film texts. National identity and contestations around it are one such arena, although national identity is often also policed by the regulatory powers of the state and not just by tacit norms. Sembène's *Xala* had 12 cuts forced on it by the Senegalese censors before it could show in Dakar while *Ceddo* was banned outright for many years in the same country. The dominant national identity tends to be closely aligned to the dominant classes although it is not uncontested. Ken Loach's films have often made significant interventions in debates around national identity, national self-image, national history, and so forth, in such films as *Land and Freedom* (1995) and *The Wind that Shakes the Barley* (2006), both films about aborted revolutions in Spain and Ireland respectively, that stirred up debates about the past and the present in those countries especially. Equally, his 'smaller', less epic stories contest dominant conceptions of national identity. *I Daniel Blake* (2016) and *Sorry We Missed You* (2019) tackle poverty and precarity in contemporary Britain, stripping away the layers of media and state propaganda about 'the nation' and its prosperity.

The moment of consumption can be measured in terms of box office but can also be decoded using qualitative methodological tools to explore patterns of reception. Access to audience responses to films beyond professional film reviewers has been facilitated by digital online review sites and social media platforms and although methodological problems of representativeness remain, the integration of some kind of reference to reception is now much less of a logistical challenge for researchers than it once was. A Marxist contribution to audience studies would, Janet Staiger has argued, explore how 'contexts of social formations and con-structed identities of the self in relation to historical conditions explain the inter-pretation strategies and affective responses of readers'. Drawing on Marxist textual analysis, Staiger notes that because 'the historical context's discursive formation is contradictory and heterogeneous, *no* reading is unified'.[54] In her account of the way gay men and straight and lesbian women responded to the deep cultural myths of *The Silence of the Lambs* (1991), she explores the interaction between the film's own representational strategies and the wider public discourses that both the film and the audiences are drawing on.

*The Battle of Algiers* (1966), Gillo Pontecorvo's account of the Algerian armed struggle for independence from French colonial rule, has been watched by very dif-ferent kinds of audiences, presumably identifying with very different protagonists which the narrative focalisation strategies give access to, and drawing different con-clusions. British army officers in Northern Ireland showed the film to their troops, to help them understand counter-insurgency tactics, while IRA cells watched the same film to understand how insurgent armed resistance can be effective.[55] Similarly, the American Black Panthers screened the film because it was relevant to their own struggle against the racist US state. Yet following the invasion of Iraq in 2003, the Pentagon arranged a screening of *The Battle of Algiers* in order to understand guerrilla warfare from the perspective of imperialist power.[56] The circulation of *The Battle of Algiers* into different social, historical and national contexts is extraordinary. Writing after the 2005 terrorist attacks in London by radical Islamists, *Guardian* journalist Ian Jack recalled the first time he saw *The Battle of Algiers* in the early 1970s and an argu-ment he had with a friend afterwards. Recalling the brutally honest scene where Algerian nationalist women plant bombs that blow up French colonialists, Jack had said to his friend something to the effect that 'terrorism was a terrible thing'.

My friend wasn't so shocked. What he saw in the film was the difficult route to victory in a liberation struggle ... He pointed out rightly, that the French had air bombed Algerian villages ... My problem may have been – may still be – a want of empathetic imagination. I could see myself as a European in a café, my son eating an ice-cream, but less easily as a Berber villager cowering under the sound of French jets.[57]

That argument between Jack and his friend in the early 1970s was clearly informed by the wider discursive interpretations of the then contemporary events, a dialogic clash whose relevance Jack revives in the context of British involvement in and occupation of Iraq in 2003 and the London terrorist attacks. Jack re-watched the film twice again on DVD and this leads to a measure of critical self-reflection with regard to 'empathy'. Yet even where middle-class empathy is widened to include those outside the range of identities and identifications they are typically used to, there is a characteristic difficulty (as with Jack's article) in drawing the *political* conclusions of that new evidence of and feeling for lives far more brutalised than their own. Jack writes of Berber villagers and French jets but not of the Iraqis and US and British atrocities. Jack is not a film critic but his ambivalences are quite typical of the film criticism surrounding art cinema, which likes to raise the problems it finds to a less politically fraught, more a-historical humanist level (the human condition), in which the specificities of phenomena such as western imperialism or capitalism and the political-moral demands these phenomena make on us, are weakened.

Finally, there is the moment or determinant of production itself, which, as I argued in Section 3.3, must be understood as mediated by other determinants, such as the repertoire of formal choices that one would classify under the moment of representation, but equally, as here, by the other determinants in the circuit of culture just discussed. As with each of the other determinants in the circuit of production, not only is there complex interaction between the determinants but there is complex heterogeneity going on within each of the areas identified. Film production, as I argued in Chapter 4, even in the case of a single film, can be a hybrid of *modes* of production. But we must also understand that modes of production are nested within the dominant capitalist mode of production, both at the level of the film industry and at the level of the social formation itself. Integrating the circuit of culture back into a more explicitly Marxist framework (such as the base-superstructure model) ensures that the question of class power (both as economic imperatives and social stratifications) returns to the surface of our attentions, where it should properly be. Otherwise there is always the danger that the proper attention to complexity slides into a liberal pluralist framework where questions of class power and inequality begin to disappear from view. Marxist film theory and Marxist-inspired film practices provide us with the resources to keep that optic close to hand.

# Notes

1 Richard Johnson, 'What Is Cultural Studies Anyway?', *Social Text* 16 (Winter 1986–87): 42.
2 Paul du Gay, Stuart Hall, Linda Janes, Hugh Mackay and Keith Negus, *Doing Cultural Studies: The Story of the Sony Walkman* (London: Sage/Open University, 1997), p. 2.
3 Ibid.
4 Mike Wayne, 'Documentary as Critical and Creative Research', in Thomas Austin (ed.), *Rethinking Documentary: New Perspectives, New Practices* (Milton Keynes: Open University Press, 2008).
5 Mark Sheehan, '*Supersize Me:* A Comparative Analysis of Responses to Crisis by McDonald's America and McDonald's Australia', in Chris Galloway and Kwansah-Aidoo (eds), *Public Relations Issues and Crisis Management: Asia, Australia and New Zealand* (Boston: Cengage Learning, 2005).
6 Terry Eagleton, *The Idea of Culture* (Oxford: Blackwell, 2000), p. 107.
7 Karl Marx, 'Introduction to the Critique of Hegel's Philosophy of Law', in Erich Fromm (ed.), *Marx's Concept of Man* (London: Continuum, 2004), p. 170.
8 Raymond Williams, *Marxism and Literature* (Oxford: Oxford University Press, 1988), p. 116.
9 Ibid., p. 119.
10 Ibid., p. 123.
11 Raymond Williams, 'Base and Superstructure in Marxist Cultural Theory', *New Left Review I* 82 (Nov./Dec. 1973): 11.
12 See Yochai Benkler's *The Wealth of Networks: How Social Production Transforms Markets and Freedom* (New Haven, CT: Yale University Press, 2006), for an example of an alternative framing of emergent practices.
13 Williams, *Marxism and Literature*, op. cit., p. 122.
14 Ibid., p. 122.
15 Ibid., pp. 128–35.
16 Ibid., p. 134.
17 Dennis Broe, *Film Noir, American Workers, and Postwar Hollywood* (Gainesville, FL: University Press of Florida, 2009).
18 See Sue Harper, *Picturing the Past: The Rise and Fall of the British Costume Film* (London: BFI, 1994).
19 See Mike Wayne, 'Constellating Walter Benjamin and British Cinema: A Case Study of *The Private Life of Henry VIII*', *Quarterly Review of Film and Video* 19(3) (2002): 249–60.
20 Paul Dave, *Visions of England: Class and Culture in Contemporary Cinema* (Oxford: Berg, 2006), pp. 1–24, 45–55.
21 Ibid., pp. 83–99.
22 See Mike Wayne, 'The Performing Northern Working Class in British Cinema: Cultural Representation and its Political Economy', *Quarterly Review of Film and Video* 23(4) (2006): 287–97.
23 Williams, *Marxism and Literature,* op. cit., p. 109.
24 Antonio Gramsci, *Selections from the Prison Notebooks*, (eds) Quintin Hoare and Geoffrey Nowell-Smith (London: Lawrence and Wishart, 2003), p. 420.
25 Stuart Hall, 'Encoding/Decoding', in Stuart Hall, *Culture, Media, Language: Working Papers in Cultural Studies* (London: Hutchinson, 1980).
26 Gramsci, *Selections from the Prison Notebooks*, op. cit., p. 323.
27 Ibid., p. 324.
28 See Deirdre O'Neill and Mike Wayne, 'On Intellectuals', in Deirdre O'Neill and Michael Wayne (eds), *Considering Class: Theory, Culture and the Media in the 21st Century* (Leiden: Brill, 2018).
29 Williams, *Marxism and Literature*, op. cit., p. 110.
30 Stuart Hall, 'Gramsci's Relevance for the Study of Race and Ethnicity', *Journal of Communication Inquiry* 10 (1986): 14.
31 Anthony Barnett, 'Iron Britannia', *New Left Review I* 134 (July/Aug. 1982): 34.

32 Graham Dawson and Bob West, '"Our Finest Hour?" The Popular Memory of World War II and the Struggle over National Identity', in Geoffrey Hurd (ed.), *National Fictions: World War Two in British Films and Television* (London: BFI, 1984), p. 11.

33 Geoff Hurd, 'Notes on Hegemony, the War and Cinema', in Geoffrey Hurd (ed.), *National Fictions: World War Two in British Films and Television* (London: BFI, 1984), p. 18.

34 Mbye Cham, 'Official History, Popular Memory: Reconfiguration of the African Past in the Films of Ousmane Sembène', *Contributions in Black Studies: A Journal of African and Afro-American Studies* 11(4) (2008): 21–2.

35 Françoise Pfaff, 'The Uniqueness of Ousmane Sembène's Cinema', *Contributions in Black Studies: A Journal of African and Afro-American Studies,* 11(3) (1993): 13–14.

36 Jared Rapfogel and Richard Porton, 'The Power of Female Solidarity: An Interview with Ousmane Sembène', *Cinéaste* Winter (2004): 201.

37 See, for example, Henry Giroux and Grace Pollock, *The Mouse That Roared: Disney and the End of Innocence* (Lanham, MD: Rowman and Littlefield, 2010).

38 Marcia Landy, 'Gramsci, Sembène and the Politics of Culture', in Mike Wayne (ed.), *Understanding Film: Marxist Perspectives* (London: Pluto Press, 2005), pp. 82–3.

39 Rapfogel and Porton, 'The Power of Female Solidarity', op. cit.

40 Mike Wayne, 'The Dialectics of Third Cinema', in Yannis Tzioumakis and Claire Molloy (eds), *The Routledge Companion to Cinema and Politics* (London: Routledge, 2016).

41 David Harvey, *The New Imperialism* (Oxford: Oxford University Press, 2005), pp. 180–1.

42 David Harvey, *The Enigma of Capital and the Crises of Capitalism* (London: Profile Books, 2011), pp. 48–9.

43 The phrase is from Argentinean filmmaker, Fernando Birri, 'Cinema and Underdevelopment', in Michael T. Martin (ed.), *New Latin American Cinema* (Detroit: Wayne State University Press, 1997), p. 94.

44 Teshome H. Gabriel, 'Third Cinema as Guardian of Popular Memory: Towards a Third Aesthetics', in Jim Pines and Paul Willemen (eds), *Questions of Third Cinema* (London: BFI, 1989), p. 54.

45 Michael Renov, 'Newsreel: Old and New: Towards an Historical Profile', *Film Quarterly* 41(1) (1987): 25.

46 subMedia.tv can be found at: https://sub.media

47 Chris Robé, *Breaking the Spell: A History of Anarchist Filmmakers, Videotape Guerrillas and Digital Ninjas* (Oakland, CA: PM Press, 2017), pp. 352–81.

48 Ibid., p. 373.

49 Ibid., pp. 337–40.

50 Fernando Solanas and Octavio Getino, 'Towards a Third Cinema', in Michael T. Martin (ed.), *New Latin American Cinema* (Detroit: Wayne State University Press, 1997), p. 55.

51 du Gay et al., *Doing Cultural Studies*, op. cit., p. 3.

52 Patricia A. Curtin and T. K. Gaither, *International Public Relations: Negotiating Culture, Identity and Power* (London: Sage, 2007), p. 38.

53 Xu Song, 'Hollywood Movies and China: Analysis of Hollywood Globalization and Relationship Management in China's Cinema Market', *Global Media and China* 3(3) (2018): 180–1.

54 Janet Staiger, 'Taboos and Totems: Cultural Meanings of *The Silence of the Lambs*', in Jim Collins, Hilary Radner and Ava Preacher Collins (eds), *Film Theory Goes to the Movies* (London: Routledge, 1993): 143.

55 Veronica Horwell, 'Mother of All Battles', *The Guardian*, (Screen), 20 June 1997, p. 9.

56 Michael T. Kaufman, 'What Does the Pentagon See in "Battle of Algiers"?', *The New York Times*, 7 September 2003. Available at: www.nytimes.com/2003/09/07/weekinreview/the-world-film-studies-what-does-the-pentagon-see-in-battle-of-algiers.html

57 Ian Jack, 'Back to the Future', *The Guardian*, 30 July 2005. Available at: www.theguardian.com/film/2005/jul/30/features

# FURTHER READING

## Chapter 1

Stuart Hall, 'The Problem of Ideology: Marxism Without Guarantee', in Stuart Hall, *Critical Dialogues in Cultural Studies*, London: Routledge, 1996.

Karl Marx and Friedrich Engels, *The Communist Manifesto*, Harmondsworth: Penguin, 1985.

Michael Ryan and Douglas Kellner, *Camera Politica: The Politics and Ideology of Contemporary Hollywood Film*, Bloomington, IN: Indiana University Press, 1988.

Mike Wayne, *Marx's Das Kapital for Beginners*, London: For Beginners, 2012.

## Chapter 2

Louis Althusser, 'Ideology and Ideological State Apparatuses', in *Lenin and Philosophy and Other Essays*, London: Monthly Review Press, 1971.

Roland Barthes, *Mythologies*, Basingstoke: Macmillan, 2013.

Steve Ross, *Working Class Hollywood: Silent Film and the Shaping of Class in America*, Princeton, NJ: Princeton University Press, 1998.

## Chapter 3

Nicholas Garnham, 'Contribution to a Political Economy of Mass-Communication', *Media, Culture and Society*, 1, 1979.

Stuart Hall, 'Cultural Studies: Two Paradigms', *Media, Culture and Society*, 2, 1980.

David E. James and Rick Berg (eds), *The Hidden Foundation, Cinema and the Question of Class*, Minneapolis, MN: University of Minnesota Press, 1996.

Julia Lesage, '*S/Z* and *Rules of the Game*', *Jump Cut*, 12–13, 1977. Available at: www.ejump cut.org/archive/jc55.2013/LesageRulesOfGame/index.html

Colin MacCabe, 'Realism and the Cinema: Notes on Some Brechtian Theses', *Screen*, 15(2) 1974.

Vincent Mosco, *The Political Economy of Communication*, London: Sage, 2009.

Graeme Turner, *British Cultural Studies: An Introduction*, London: Routledge, 2003.

## Chapter 4

Julianne Burton, 'Film Artisans and Film Industries in Latin America', in Michael T. Martin (ed.), *New Latin American Cinema, Theory, Practices and Transcontinental Articulations*, Detroit: Wayne State University Press, 1997.

Jennifer Holt and Alisa Perren, *Media Industries: History, Theory, and Method*, Chichester: Wiley-Blackwell, 2009.

Paul McDonald and Janet Wasko (eds), *The Contemporary Hollywood Film Industry*, Oxford: Blackwell, 2008.

Mike Wayne, 'Post-Fordism, Monopoly Capitalism and Hollywood's Media-Industrial Complex', *International Journal of Cultural Studies*, 6(1), 2003.

## Chapter 5

André Bazin, *What Is Cinema?* vol. 1, Berkeley, CA: University of California Press, 2005.

Tony Bennett, *Formalism and Marxism*, London: Routledge, 1979.

Sylvia Harvey, *May 68 and Film Culture*, London: BFI, 1980.

Dana Polan, 'A Brechtian Cinema? Towards a Politics of Self-Reflexive Film', in Bill Nichols (ed.), *Movies and Methods*, vol. 2, Berkeley, CA: University of California Press, 1985.

Richard Taylor (ed.), *The Eisenstein Reader*, London: BFI, 1998.

A.K. Voronsky, *Art as the Cognition of Life: Selected Writings, 1911–1936*, Sheffield: Mehring Books, 1998.

Peter Watkins, http://pwatkins.mnsi.net/

## Chapter 6

Richard Dyer, 'Entertainment and Utopia', in Bill Nichols (ed.), *Movies and Methods*, vol. 2, Berkeley, CA: University of California Press, 1985.

Terry Eagleton, *Criticism and Ideology*, London: Verso, 1986.

Fredric Jameson, 'Reification and Utopia in Mass Culture', in *Signatures of the Visible*, London: Routledge, 1992a.

Fredric Jameson, 'Class and Allegory in Contemporary Mass Culture', in *Signatures of the Visible*, London: Routledge, 1992b.

Fredric Jameson, *The Political Unconscious*, London: Routledge, 2002.

Terry Lovell, *Pictures of Reality: Aesthetics, Politics and Pleasure*, London: BFI, 1983.

Judith Williamson, *Deadline at Dawn: Film Writings 1980–90*, London: Marion Boyars, 1992.

## Chapter 7

Theodor Adorno, Walter Benjamin, Ernst Bloch, Bertolt Brecht, and Georg Lukács, *Aesthetics and Politics*, London: Verso, 1988.

Siegfried Kracauer, *Film Theory: The Redemption of Physical Reality*, Oxford: Oxford University Press, 1997.

Georg Lukács, *Writer and Critic*, London: Merlin Press, 1978.

Raymond Williams, 'A Lecture on Realism', *Screen*, 18(1) 1977.

## Chapter 8

Frantz Fanon, *The Wretched of the Earth*, Harmondsworth: Penguin, 2001.

Antonio Gramsci, *Selections from Prison Notebooks*, (eds) Quintin Hoare and Geoffrey Nowell Smith, London: Lawrence and Wishart, 2003.

Stuart Hall, 'Gramsci's Relevance for the Study of Race and Ethnicity', *Journal of Communication Inquiry*, 10, 1986.

Marcia Landy, *Film, Politics and Gramsci*, Minneapolis, MN: University of Minnesota Press, 1994.

Raymond Williams, *Marxism and Literature*, Oxford: Oxford University Press, 1988.

# INDEX

# FILM INDEX